Adventures in the ROTOR WIND

From the Office to the Jungle

Elke Kummer

Copyright © 2017 by Elke Kummer

Adventures in the Rotor Wind
From the Office to the Jungle
by Elke Kummer

Printed in the United States of America.

ISBN 9781498497299

All rights reserved solely by the author. The author guarantees all contents are original and do not infringe upon the legal rights of any other person or work. No part of this book may be reproduced in any form without the permission of the author. The views expressed in this book are not necessarily those of the publisher.

Scripture quotations taken from the New King James Version (NKJV). Copyright © 1982 by Thomas Nelson, Inc. Used by permission. All rights reserved.

Editing: Iola Goulton, *Christian Editing Services*
           Pam Lagomarsino, *Above the Pages Editorial Services*

Photo of the author by Maïlys Baerg

All other photos taken from Elke Kummer's private archive

www.xulonpress.com

Contents

Introduction ix
Preface xiii
My Helicopter Ride to the Stone Age 15
Where in the World is Papua? 18
The Adventure Begins 23
Chocolate, Cheese and Toilet Paper 26
The Headlong Dive into My New life 33
The Dedication 47
A Turbulent Day 53
Thank God, it's Sunday! 57
Shopping, My New Skill 60
Game On 64
No Wrenching, No Flying—Mechanics Matter 70
Wanted: Women, Land, and Pigs 76
My Bumpy Journey as new "Jungle Cook" 80
No Ordinary Desk Job 86
Shopping, Wamena-Style 92
Beauty, Hardship, and Miracles 94
How to Lubricate a Cog in the Machine 99
Celebrating a Life Well-Lived 102
Balm and Poison 104
Point X-Ray 107
A Fiery Welcome 112
What's Worse than a Toothache? 113
The Big Serpent Turns in the Ground 118
Carjacked 121

Wrenches, Pencils, and Arrows........................... 125
Our Own Wheels—and Other Things that Kept us Rolling 127
Money Makes the Blades Go Round 131
Building Permits, Papuan-Style 133
Unsettling Advice 135
Fluffy Feathers and Flying Rocks......................... 138
A Somersault of Events................................. 143
So Familiar, Yet So Strange 147
Going Home! Or Are We?............................... 152
The Aftermath of a Tragedy 159
Home Sweet—Sour—Home............................. 162
Cloudy With a Chance of Flying Cars 165
Lake Habbema—Almost 171
A Field Day for the Greenhorn 175
Guardian Angels on Overtime 182
Burning Both Ends of the Candle......................... 184
Off With a Bang 187
Redefining Christmas 189
Beauty and Tragedy 194
A Concrete Alibi 200
She Came, Saw, and Conquered 202
Progress!... 207
Taking the Unseen Challenge 213
Friends, Fun, and Fuel 217
The Cool, Spacious Fruit of our Labor 223
A Momentous Event 228
The Ton of Bricks 232
The Flight That Wouldn't End 238
Rich and Poor 241
Point of No Return 245
Dirt Roads, Rats, and the *JESUS* Film 249
An Unexpected Threat.................................. 254
The Lord Gives, and the Lord Takes Away................. 257
Trouble, Joy, Sadness, and Kindness at Tiom............... 260
Welcome to the Jungle 265
Search and Rescue 285
Flying the Extra Mile 293

Contents

Flowers, Faith, and Thankfulness 295
The Desire of the Heart. 297
You Can't Escape Your Fate 300
Emotional Roller-Coaster 303
Breakdown in the Jungle. 306
Eastern Exposure 310
Grounded 314
Empty Shelves 321
A Visitor from Home. 324
Differences 331
The Beginning of a Wonderful Friendship 335
Shock Waves. 340
As Iron Sharpens Iron 344
A Matter of Perspective. 348
Single Heroes 355
What's in a Name? 358
High and Dry 360
Along Came Lady 366
The Flying Housewife. 368
Rats! 371
Strange Encounters. 374
At the Neighbors. 378
Worn and Broke 382
Closing a Chapter 384
The Race Against Time. 386

Glossary 389
Recommendations for Further Reading 393

Introduction

This book is a true story. Most names are original, but I changed a few names for privacy reasons. Current names of mission organizations have been left out for confidentiality reasons as well.

Representative dialogue is used on most occasions when the exact words were not recorded. Dialogues have been recounted from the gist of conversations I or others remembered. Emails, letters, photos, newsletters, friends' stories, and pilot logbook entries have helped me to recollect events. Many more occurrences impacted our lives, but for various reasons cannot be published in a book.

Elke Kummer

A big Thank You …

… to everyone who lived these stories with me,
who assisted me in writing this book,
who supported us all these years financially and in prayer,
to Helimission for sending us,
and most of all to God!

Preface

Germany, mid-1990s

I flipped through a science and nature magazine at the little library I ran in my small hometown in Germany. The article featured indigenous people in Irian Jaya (now called Papua), Indonesia. A photo showed tribal men wearing nothing but a hollow gourd, partially covering their private parts. I was shocked.

I'd never want to go where people walk around like that!

God has such a sense of humor. A few years later, the sight of a Papuan man in his traditional attire would be as normal to me as seeing someone wearing a baseball cap.

Town hall and church of Grebenstein, Germany

My Helicopter Ride to the Stone Age

November 2001

As I looked through the helicopter windshield, I marveled at the rugged, untamed Papuan landscape below. Towering gray rocks stuck out of steep, forest-covered mountainsides. Waterfalls rushed down the slopes into raging white-water rivers. Here and there I saw a cluster of tiny huts and gardens and sometimes even steel-roofed buildings next to a grass runway. We had long left the last road behind us, which connected some mountain villages to the town of Wamena where I lived.

We were heading to an isolated pioneer mission station in the middle of a jungle-covered mountain range. Although the people had lived there for countless generations like their ancestors, they had only been discovered a few years earlier. I was about to meet some of the last people on earth who still lived in Stone Age conditions! While I looked at the exotic vegetation, patches of sand, and brown ponds gliding by below me, my feelings fluctuated between excitement and apprehension.

Andy's voice in my headset interrupted my thoughts: "Would you like to take the controls for a while?"

My heart raced. I had never had the courage to ask if I could fly a helicopter. During my childhood in Germany, my father had sometimes taken our family along on flights in the light aircraft of a flying club, but he had never allowed me to take the controls (unlike my brother). Now my time had come!

Andy explained a few basic things about helicopter flying and the cyclic and collective control sticks, and then I took the controls. I was amazed at how sensitive they were.

"When I learned to fly my instructor told me: 'You pull up the stick, and the houses get smaller, you press down on the stick, and the houses get bigger,'" Andy said.

I guessed the same applied to trees, as there were no houses in sight for miles around.

When we got to a cloudy area a few minutes later, Andy took over the controls again. I was disappointed that my first try to steer a helicopter had come to such a quick end, but I couldn't wait to write to my brother about it.

Life is fair in the long run!

Back home I had loved to look at the beautiful German landscapes with the neat small towns, forests, and patterns of differently colored fields. However, the many roads, train lines, and other infrastructure marred the landscapes. Every square inch of the forest was managed. What a difference compared to the majestic and untamed beauty of New Guinea—the second largest island on earth situated just south of the equator on the Pacific Ring of Fire!

After about an hour and a half of flying, we came to an area where the mountains were completely forest-covered and looked uninhabited. At a closer look, I noticed smoke rising from a tiny hillside patch. It turned out to be a garden and a few huts. Part of the reason the Moi people living here hadn't been discovered earlier was they didn't live in villages but in tiny hamlets scattered all over the area.

Then I noticed metal roofs in the middle of a clearing on the hillside. People had built three wooden houses around a small, flat, empty patch at a short distance from each other. We landed on that cleared spot, which turned out to be the Moi mission station helipad. The three resident missionary families welcomed us.

A few young tribesmen looked on from a distance. They were carrying bows and arrows and were wearing nothing but long hollow gourds covering sections of their private parts. They were virtually still living in Stone Age conditions.

A few minutes ago, I had looked at another world from a bird's-eye view. Now, I had been dropped in it for real.

As I watched the helicopter take off and disappear behind the forest-covered mountains, a strange feeling crept up inside me: "Left behind."

Young Moi men

Where in the World is Papua?

Germany, February 15, 2000

It was two days after our first wedding anniversary, and I had just kissed my husband, Hans, good-bye at the train platform. I wiped a tear from my eye as I walked back to the carpark, praying for a safe trip for Hans to Papua, Indonesia. Two years earlier, I would have had trouble finding the place on a map, but now it was about to become part of my life.

I thought back to when I first heard about Papua when it was still called Irian Jaya. The area had only been renamed "Papua" a few weeks earlier, in January 2000. In the summer of 1998 when Hans and I had just become engaged, we attended a Helimission meeting. Reverend Ernst Tanner, the founder and director of Helimission, had given a report about the work of the Swiss organization in different parts of the world. Some of his words were still going around in my mind: "Irian Jaya, on the western half of New Guinea, is a spiritually dark place full of witchcraft."

Not very inviting!

I had hoped Helimission wouldn't send us there. Until that day, I hadn't even heard that the island of New Guinea was split in half and divided between Papua New Guinea in the East, and Irian Jaya (now called Papua, a province of Indonesia), in the West. (For more information see "Irian Jaya" in the glossary at the end of this book.)

"We've started operations there to help with relief efforts during a famine caused by a catastrophic drought brought on by El Niño weather last year," Ernst had continued his report. He was a charismatic man in his early seventies with a distinctive nose and billowy gray hair. "Army helicopters from Australia and other countries are there to deliver food aid to the remote mountain villages, but because they are too big, their rotor wind blows the peoples' grass-thatched huts away."

What a thought: You go somewhere to help people and destroy what little they have in the process!

"That's why Helimission was asked to join the effort with our lighter helicopters to do the food distribution in the small villages. Our team is operating from a town called Wamena, which sits on a high plateau in the central highlands. During the relief work, we found out missionaries would like to use our helicopters for their pioneering work in the long run. Even though missionaries moved to the Wamena area over forty years ago, there are still several unreached tribes in Irian Jaya. These tribes can only be reached by helicopter, so we're planning on operating there long-term."

Helimission often used their helicopter fleet for relief work after natural disasters and to help people in isolated areas in need of medical treatment. However, the heartbeat of the organization was to assist pioneer missionaries in taking the gospel to unreached people groups in remote, isolated areas.

Political map of the Republic of Indonesia as of January 2000

Political map of New Guinea as of January 2000

Hans had just completed the training and received his license as a helicopter mechanic. We had planned to go to Madagascar in May 2000 for a three-month interim phase and then on to Bible college in the USA. These plans had been thrown for a loop when a team member in Papua had been evacuated to the USA for medical reasons. Helimission Papua now desperately needed more staff to run operations. Since we hadn't planned on leaving Germany before May, Hans was going to Papua by himself for five weeks while I stayed behind in my hometown of Grebenstein to finish my work contract at the town council. Hans was going to work on an important helicopter inspection with Brian, the Helimission base manager in Papua.

The thought of going on a short-term trip and Bible school first with short visits back home had been consoling. Now our assignment had changed to going to Papua long-term, and it was urgent. There was no easing into my new life. It would be straight from the office to the jungle! There had always been a huge difference between my sheltered, steady life growing up in Germany, and the adventure stories I loved to read and watch on TV. I had been especially captivated by stories of missionaries like Hudson Taylor, which I had heard in the Christian kid's group. Now my long-awaited adventure of trusting God with my life, finances, and health was approaching fast—unnervingly fast.

"Hi, *Mausi*, I made it to Wamena!" (Mausi: pronounced Mouzy, a German term of endearment) Hans told me over the phone three days later.

"I'm so glad! How are you? Did you have a pleasant trip?"

"Not exactly. The first part was fine, but starting in Singapore, the food got rather strange." Asian food had never made it to the table at the traditional Swiss mountain farm where Hans had grown up.

"But the worst was the flight from Jakarta to Papua. First, the plane wouldn't gain altitude after take-off, and after a while, I heard an engine re-start—twice."

Besides problems with the engine, there had been two hard landings. Hans' head had slammed into the seat in front of him, and luggage had fallen from the Boeing 737's overhead compartments onto unlucky passengers.

"I might not be able to come home as planned. The airplane is down for maintenance and repairs now, and there isn't another one. Oh, and the boat that sails between Papua and Java has burned down—with the parts for the Helimission motorbike, by the way."

"Oh, dear!"

That was not the kind of report I had hoped to receive from the place I was to call home for the next three years!

"When I called headquarters to tell them I might not make my flight home, the lady at the office suggested I take another plane," Hans continued. "She couldn't imagine there is none! I tried to paint a more thorough picture of the situation here, so I told her what had happened to me at work."

"What was that?"

"I was standing on top of a helicopter parked on the grass working on the rotor system, while a naked Papuan man was sitting and singing at the bottom of the ladder."

I laughed at the thought of that phone conversation! Hans was rather shy and introverted by nature but had a good sense of humor. He had grown up in a conservative home and church and adopted the Swiss work ethic and reliability. Ever since his time working in a cross-cultural team in Albania for Helimission, he had enjoyed working with people from different countries.

Hans was staying with Brian and Luana and their children, Briana and Philip, this time. Briana was just turning sixteen, and Philip was thirteen years old. Hans had already worked with the family in Albania on his first Helimission assignment, and they had become good friends.

I still wasn't convinced I'd like the "dark place full of witchcraft," but I couldn't wait to meet Brian, Luana, and their kids. I was so glad we'd be working with nice people already experienced on the mission field—unlike myself.

"You don't need to worry about hot, humid climate, Mausi," Hans told me. "It's quite bad on the coast, but the weather here in Wamena is perfect all year. We're at sixteen hundred meters above sea level, and it's not too hot during the day and is cool at night." (Altitude of the Wamena airport: 5,085 feet/1,550 meters above sea level)

What a relief!

"It rains most nights, but not too often during the day."

Another relief came when Hans told me Brian had taken him to a mission house where we would house-sit for our first few months. There was a shower with hot water and a sit-down toilet.

"No 'squat-pot,' phew!"

I had only used standard toilets for sitting on and never come across an Asian squat toilet. While these toilet/shower combinations were a great multi-purpose solution for a small, simple bathroom, I doubted I could successfully use one—especially if I was sick.

The Adventure Begins

May 7, 2000

Click!
Finally, we strapped ourselves into the seats of the Lufthansa Boeing 747 that was to take us from Frankfurt, Germany to Singapore and Jakarta—the first part of the trip into our new life. All we needed to do for the next twelve hours was to sit, wait, and then eat when the flight attendants served a meal—what a change! Last minute activities and strong emotions had filled our last few days. I was exhausted.

After Hans had returned from Papua, we packed and stored our belongings. We canceled all contracts and insurances that were now obsolete. We had sent off five boxes with our belongings, including tools, books, and household items. It had been emotional for me to take leave from my workplace of ten years at the town hall and our small church fellowship. Hans and I had met there when he came to Germany to train as a helicopter mechanic.

It had been even harder to say good-bye to our families. My eyes filled with tears when I thought of my dear grandmother, who had made one of her fantastic cheesecakes for our last meal together before our departure. Our afternoon coffee together had been a daily routine for the two of us for so many years. Would I ever see her again on this side of heaven? It would only be a few more weeks until my brother's wife would deliver her first baby boy. It about ripped my heart out, that I shouldn't see him until he'd be three years old.

The idea of following Jesus' command to go into all the world had been exhilarating, and I was still excited, but the reality of leaving everyone and everything behind who had been dear to me had hit me hard in the last few days.

I tried to get comfortable in my seat and go to sleep. No success. So many thoughts went through my head: *What will my life be like when I get out on the other end?*

So far, I had never been away from home for more than four and a half weeks. My cross-cultural experiences were limited to trips on Russian sailing ships and mostly European holidays where I hadn't even scratched the surface of the cultures.

After a stopover at the magnificent Singapore airport with its carpeted floors, lush tropical plants, and a multitude of colorful shops, we flew to Indonesia. It was dusk when we arrived at the capital, Jakarta. We went through customs, exchanged some money, claimed our four suitcases, and headed for the exit.

"Welcome to Indonesia!"

Lita, a young lady from the Indonesian Helimission office, greeted us. The air outside was warm, humid, and polluted and we heard the call to prayer from a mosque. Lita, the first Indonesian I had met, spoke English quite well, was talkative, and friendly. A great start. She took us to the hotel where we'd wait for our flight to Papua.

While I looked out the car windows, scenes of the German television news flashed through my head: "Jakarta ..." We had heard the city had about eleven million inhabitants. There were skyscrapers and slums, and every size house imaginable in between these two extremes. Billboards, kiosks, and food stalls with power lines running along and over them lined the roads. Everything looked exactly like it had on TV. The dense traffic was a far cry from the well-regulated traffic in Germany. The driving style of the motorbike and scooter riders was unbelievable. Their daring maneuvers looked more like "hara-kiri," than getting from A to B, but somehow there seemed to be order in this chaos.

This traffic is only the first of many things which are different from what I'm used to!

Our German passport photos we had taken for the visa process didn't have the right background color, so Lita had ordered a photographer to the hotel to take new photos.

I guess if the prophet doesn't come to the mountain, the mountain has to come to the prophet.

The photographer and his assistant brought all the equipment, including a red sheet for the correct background color. We put on our nicest clothes and soon everything was taken care of.

After stretching out on the beds for a while and taking a shower, we left for the airport long before dawn. I had been apprehensive about the flight to Papua, after hearing Hans' story of his first flight in that direction, but I wouldn't have had to worry. The flight out of Jakarta was beautiful. In broad daylight, most of the city was not an overly pretty sight with all the smog, but at night it was stunning. The streets had interesting patterns, and there was a sea of lights as far as I could see.

We ascended next to a huge cumulonimbus cloud which was occasionally lit up from within by flashes of lightning. Next, the rising sun gave the scene a golden glow before fully illuminating the magnificent blue ocean, dotted with tiny islands, atolls, and coral reefs which looked like opals in their vibrant shades of green, blue, and turquoise. The tropical cloud formations were spectacular.

Now I see how Indonesia can consist of seventeen thousand islands, some of them are tiny!

Hans had been right with his description of the food: it needed getting used to—but it was tasty. I quickly grew to like *Sambal*, a hot sauce made of petite chili peppers served with nearly every savory Indonesian meal.

Chocolate, Cheese, and Toilet Paper

"Ladies and gawntlemen, we'll shortly arrive at Jayapura-Sentani. Please fasten your seatbelts …"

We were on our third and last leg of the island-hopping flight to Papua. We grudgingly put our seats into an upright position, rubbed our red eyes, and opened the window shades. Our eyes hurt from the bright light, but we were instantly rewarded by the stunning view. Approaching the Sentani airport was spectacular! The runway ended just short of Lake Sentani. Mount Cyclops, covered in a dark, green, lush tropical rainforest, towered above the town and the lake. The immense, winding lake was framed by light green hills. Many tin-roofed houses lining the sides of the lake were built on stilts on top of the water. People paddled their canoes back and forth to their houses built on tiny islands, which dotted the lake.

Since I knew virtually nothing about Papuan history, I was unaware this place had a turbulent past. Sentani used to be one of General MacArthur's bases in World War II during the New Guinea Campaign. Countless American and Japanese airplane wrecks were strewn across the island, some hidden under the surface of the lake.

We disembarked the airplane after our second mostly sleepless night. A wave of hot, humid air hit us. We were grateful to receive all four of our suitcases in the cramped arrival terminal.

"You must be Hans and Elke," a tall man with a baseball cap greeted us in American English. "I'm Ralph. Brian asked me to pick you guys up. His flight from Wamena is delayed."

Ralph, an American mission pilot, took us to his house on the mission compound near the airport. His lovely wife, Valerie, was pouring melted chocolate into tiny molds. What a relief: there was chocolate in Papua! (As trivial as this may sound, one of my biggest worries had been that I might not be able to buy chocolate, cheese, or toilet paper—not necessarily in that order. I was glad to hear all the above were available—at least on the coast—most times). We enjoyed a cold drink and cookies while trying to cool down under the ceiling fan.

Brian eventually arrived from Wamena. Hans had told me so much about him from their time in Albania, and I had read about him in Helimission newsletters. Finally, I met him in person! Brian was slim and of medium height. He wore glasses and a baseball cap over his curly, light brown hair. We checked into a hotel, and Brian filled us in on what had happened in Wamena since Hans' departure, about four weeks prior. Unfortunately, it wasn't all good news. While Brian was concerned and slightly brooding that day, he would turn out to be charming, funny, and entertaining with a winning smile, but with a professional, competent, no-nonsense approach to aviation and mission work.

During dinner, Brian gave us advice about life in Papua as a couple.

"The people here don't walk around holding hands with their spouses. I wish we could do that and demonstrate a loving relationship, but it would be offensive. We also need to be conscious about how we dress, not showing too much skin or wearing tight clothing." The list went on.

Countless opportunities to offend the people. We better learn quickly!

Brian prayed with us before we settled in for the night—my first night in Papua!

"Fried rice for breakfast?" I looked at Hans and then back to the breakfast buffet. Apparently, toast and jam wasn't the choice breakfast for Asian people, but it was available upon request. As I had expected when I set out to move to a foreign country and culture, we had a steep learning curve ahead of us. Rice was part of almost every Indonesian meal. There were different varieties, prepared in various forms.

Jan, our twenty-four-year-old Indonesian co-worker, picked us up. He had found a battered old van with a driver, who would take us to the police station and the immigration department in Jayapura, the provincial capital. Jan had been in a foul mood when we had briefly met him the previous day. I was relieved to now find him to be a friendly, self-confident and handsome guy with a good sense of humor. We'd not only work, but also live together with him for the first few months.

Already at this early hour, the humid heat was hard to bear. While riding through the town, I noticed the people on the streets were partly indigenous Papuans and partly Indonesians from different islands. Even during our first stop, I realized that when interacting with Papuan people, we could scrap the few bits we had read about the Indonesian culture. Indonesia was made up of numerous ethnic groups and their individual cultures. Most of them were Austronesian, with light brown skin and dark, mostly straight hair. The Melanesian people originating from New Guinea were dark-skinned and frizzy-haired. Their cultures vastly differed from those of the transmigrant people from other parts of the extensive Indonesian archipelago.

We'll have to get used to sticking out like sore thumbs.

I was about one head taller than the average Indonesian woman, and my hair was long, blond, and straight. My fair skin turned red in the sun and back to white, but never tanned. Hans was about an inch taller than me, tanned marginally better, but also had ash-blond hair, which he kept very short.

We drove on to Jayapura. The road was narrow and wound along the lakeshore.

"Whoa! Did you see how the guy passed us just before the bend?" I exclaimed.

"They do that all the time," Jan explained. "That's why you often see cars in the lake and other accidents."

"Oh!"

It seemed that praying was as important as filling up the fuel tank for getting from Sentani to the coastal capital city of Jayapura. I tried not to think of the dangers too much and instead focused on the beautiful views of the Sentani Lake and the general area. A lot of the houses we saw looked very simple and poor, but there was lush, green vegetation everywhere. Along the lake, there were small wooden houses with tin roofs built on stilts on the water.

"I can't believe how close to the road people built their homes!" I gasped. "Look, there's even someone sitting on the edge of the street!"

This scenario was worlds away from the safety-conscious mindset found in Germany.

Jayapura was a busy port town, partly built on the slopes around a bay. The flat town center was full of shops, banks, and offices. After having some photocopies made of our paperwork, Jan took us to the immigration office where we sat down in the waiting area. It had gotten even hotter, and sweat ran down our backs—partly because we were tense. We didn't know what to expect or how to behave. All we knew was these people had the power to send us straight back to where we came from.

I had read in a book how a missionary family had lost their visas and been sent home because the husband had mixed up two Indonesian words. I was so glad we had Jan with us who seemed to know how things ran here and also had an invaluable relationship with the personnel. We sat upright and smiled at everybody walking by. The uniformed employees ignored us when they walked past. Once in a while, one of them greeted Jan; they would exchange small talk, smile at us, and disappear in their cubicles.

After what seemed like an eternity, the employees processed our paperwork, and we were free to go. Jan had a few more errands to run before we could have lunch. We were hungry, thirsty, tired and sweating in this infernal heat. Hans had a headache. Having worked with Helimission for over a year, Jan knew how to make westerners happy.

"Oh, Jan, you certainly made our day," I said when we walked out the air-conditioned bakery/restaurant, satisfied with the taste of pizza still lingering on our tongues. We drove back to Sentani. Unlike Jan, Hans and I weren't heartbroken when we heard we couldn't get an afternoon flight to Wamena. We were so sleep-deprived, jet-lagged, and exhausted from the trip halfway around the globe and then on to Jayapura that we slept all afternoon.

At 5:20 a.m. the next morning, we managed to wake up the receptionist and checked out of the hotel. We were ready for the sixth and final flight of the journey to our new home. Jan picked us up with a car and driver again. The place he was taking us to looked suspicious in the faint dawn light. It turned out to be the airline facilities that did most cargo flights between Sentani and the interior town of Wamena where we would live. Wamena was the biggest town in the world totally reliant on air transport because there were no usable roads or navigable rivers to connect it to the outside world.

Most office and storage buildings were still dark. We sat on a bench outside and were instantly attacked by mosquitoes potentially ridden with malaria. Slapping these at least helped us stay awake. Things began to stir inside and eventually an airline employee appeared at a counter window. Jan talked to the man and came back frowning.

"The first flight which I booked for us is only taking fuel drums, but no passengers."

A bit later, we were informed the second flight would be delayed because the Fokker 27 had a technical problem and couldn't be repaired before parts would be flown in. That was too much for Jan to take, who had been eager to get back to work in Wamena—even on the previous day. I stayed behind with our luggage while Hans and Jan tried to find another way for us to get to Wamena.

People started crowding in. A heavyset Papuan lady with a mop of curly hair sat down next to me.

"Ke Wamena?" She asked, and I nodded. I pushed our huge luggage pile together as close as possible to make room. Since I couldn't say more than "Good day" and "Thank you" in Indonesian, I couldn't explain we were moving from one continent to another which would have put the amount of luggage into perspective. The lady's luggage, like several other people's, only consisted of a few cardboard boxes. A mentally-challenged man with broken and betel nut-stained teeth got closer and closer. I had seen several people chew betel nut. This local narcotic was chewed with other ingredients, turned blood red, and was spat out. *Yuck!*

Where are you, boys?

I kept looking in the direction where I expected Hans and Jan to return. After what seemed like an eternity, a car came speeding up to me, and Hans called out from the inside: "Hurry, our plane is already starting the engines!"

We grabbed our suitcases and bags and off we went.

"What's going on?"

"Jan got us seats on a flight of another cargo airline."

We sped to the other end of the airport and straight onto the tarmac, stopping next to a huge plane. One of its two propellers was already spinning.

"I can't believe I'm getting a ride in a Transall!" I said when I found out what our ride would be. "An ex-military classmate in my admin training constantly talked about them, but so far I've only seen them on TV."

Next, I spotted a Russian Kamov helicopter, which I recognized from a photo Hans used to have on the wall.

"Man, we get to see a lot of interesting aircraft in this part of the world!"

When I boarded the Transall, I was reminded more of Russian ships I had sailed on than of any other airplane I had been in. It wasn't a comfortable passenger plane with tidy wall panels, but rather a reliable workhorse, built for cargo and troop transport. There were foldout canvas seats along the walls of which only a few had complete seat belt sets. The cargo in the middle consisted of large white, woven plastic sacks, which smelled like tents, and also boxes of food supplies. After take-off, I got up and looked through the few small, dirty windows trying to get a glimpse of the beautiful green, hilly landscape.

When I sat down again, I felt something on my foot. Rice flowed out from a hole in one of the white bags. I closed the hole with my hand and called the loadmaster. He thanked me, got something to close the hole with, and then invited me to sit in the cockpit. He didn't have to say that twice! I imagined my brother turning green with envy when he'd find out about this. I sat down right behind the pilot, co-pilot, and navigator. The loadmaster offered me water and a snack. He spoke English well, and we talked about Indonesia, airplanes, etc. (Hans still claims the reason for the invitation was the long-blond-hair-factor rather than the loss of rice).

To my disappointment, clouds obscured most of the landscape. We flew over vast expanses of lush, green rainforest, occasionally interrupted by rivers, lakes, and swamps. In the following months, I would fly this route many times and each time more and more of the beauty of Papua would be revealed to me. In some areas the land was flat, and in others rock formations made it look like the back of a gigantic dinosaur with pointy, green scales. There were swampy areas with small lakes reflecting the sunlight. A large palm oil plantation looked like a large patchy sore in the landscape, otherwise untouched by humans.

One river was enormous. With its many extensions, the Memberamo River covered a wide area, meandering through the vast green expanses as far as the eye could see. After flying over the Memberamo, we entered an impressive mountain range. During clearer weather on later flights, I would see spectacular views. Sheer gray and white rock jutted out of the dark green forest-covered mountain sides. Waterfalls turned into white-water rivers rushing through narrow gorges. White limestone sinkholes dotted the hills. In between, there were tiny villages, consisting of thatched round huts—some looking like clusters of mushrooms—on the mountain slopes. A few metal roofs reflected the sunlight.

The Headlong Dive into My New life

Wamena as seen from a helicopter cockpit

May 11, 2000

When I got off the airplane, I thanked the crew twice with a hearty handshake. The clouds were disappearing, and the sun was shining from a bright, blue sky. Although it was warm, the air felt fresh after the sweltering, humid coastal heat. The mountains around the valley looked magnificent. For six years I had hoped to go into missions. Finally, I had arrived!

We walked to the Helimission office at the airport. Brian and Philip were gone with a helicopter, but Luana and Briana came to meet us.

"Welcome! You finally made it!"

How I had looked forward to meeting them! Mother and daughter were slim and beautiful with blue eyes and shoulder-length light brown hair. I would come to know Luana as intelligent, competent, hardworking, and tough enough to deal with the daily challenges, as well as caring in a matter-of-fact, practical way. Sixteen-year-old Briana would turn out to be friendly, funny, and inclusive of others, as well as intelligent and sensitive. She was beautiful inside and out.

We loaded the luggage into the battered Helimission off-road car, and the two drove us to our new home. For the first few months, we would be able to rent this simple but fully furnished and equipped missionary house which had a sit-down toilet and hot shower. The house was made of black vertical boards and a low metal roof. It had louver windows, consisting of several parallel glass panes, which opened and closed like venetian blinds.

"Meet Ibu Marice," Luana said as we entered. "Hans probably told you that the house helper of the missionaries who normally live here will work for you while you're staying here. By the way, Ibu means mother in Indonesian and is the way you address a married woman. Men are called Bapak or short: Pak."

The wonderful smell of fresh baked bread and cake filled the air. Ibu Marice, a good-looking, short, plump lady of the Western Dani Tribe, greeted us. Her expression and soft brown eyes were friendly, and her hair was braided along her head in neat rows. It was a strange thought for me to have a house helper. In Germany, I only knew of rich, elderly, or disabled people having domestic help. In this situation, I didn't have a choice anyway because Ibu Marice was employed at the house. This way I could just pay her salary and enjoy having her help while getting used to the whole concept. I was glad she knew how things worked—especially the washing machine and the wood-burning oven. The beautiful bread and banana cake attested to her ability to use the latter. What a pleasant welcome. As we got to know her better, we found how blessed we were to have Ibu Marice. She was such a sweetheart, trustworthy, godly, and diligent.

"This is for you." Luana, who was very organized, handed me a small notebook in which she had written the name of our house helper and several important phone numbers, including one for the local butcher.

"I'm sorry I have to do this to you, but we have to go to the butcher down the road. He sometimes doesn't kill a cow for a few weeks, and he killed one this morning."

I piled our luggage in the bedroom and off we went to the butcher, while Hans went straight to the office.

"If we're lucky, we might still get the fillet. All the beef cuts cost the same and usually the meat is pretty tough."

There was no time to lose. And besides, we had to arrive at the scene before the flies did. We drove along our street to a little house on a corner with a shed next to it. Between the house and the shed there it was: half a cow lying on some dirty mats. The chopped off head was leaning against the wall with the horns, and we looked into the—now useless—esophagus and windpipe.

Karina would fall over backward if she saw this! The father of my sister-in-law was a butcher. Karina had also learned the trade and worked at their hygienic-minded shop for a while. Oh well, Luana was quite experienced from several years on the mission field, and she was a nurse, so I trusted she knew what she was doing. Luana introduced me to the butcher, a transmigrant from South Sulawesi. With a huge knife, he cut off an enormous piece of meat and put it onto an old-fashioned weighing scale hanging from a rafter.

All the while Luana was giving me valuable advice on what to pay attention to and what to ignore—like the souvenir vendors who were trying to sell us their merchandise for outrageous prices.

While we were waiting for the meat to be cut up, Luana took me to the souvenir shop next door. I was amazed to see what was on display; there were *nokens* (the traditional net bags of the Papuan women), stone axes, and necklaces and bracelets made of cowry shells—the traditional currency of the highland tribes before money was introduced. Woven trivets and baskets looked decorative and useful. Next to elaborate feather headdresses and fossils, there were carved mummies (imitations of a real mummy kept in a village outside Wamena). And here they were: the *kotekas*, long hollow gourds the men used as their only piece of clothing which I had been so shocked about in the magazine back home. It hadn't taken long for me to see the first man walking down the street "dressed" in one of them. The women, however, dressed in regular clothes. I hadn't seen a single one dressed only in a traditional grass or bark fiber skirt yet.

When we returned to the butcher, his friendly, plump wife came out and invited us into their cozy home. She offered us freshly baked cookies. I peeked over to Luana, and when she nodded, I knew it was fine to eat them. When the lady offered us water to drink, Luana politely declined. The water had probably not been boiled and might have given our sensitive stomachs some problems.

I had only been in Wamena for about an hour, but my mind was already going into information overload mode. Most of what I had seen so far, was entirely different from what I was used to, so I tried to remember everything for future reference. Luana, who had lived here for two years, was a fountain of knowledge, and I was so glad for every piece of advice she gave me.

We loaded the black plastic bags containing large beef chunks into the car and drove on through the streets. Luana pointed out where I could buy all kinds of things. Occasionally, a pig or goat crossed the street. The town smelled of dust and smoke. Most roads were sealed in the middle but didn't have sidewalks. Pedestrians walked on strips of dirt, gravel, and grass between the road and the open concrete drainage ditches. The streets were lined with small houses and kiosks made of wood or bricks and metal roofing.

The bigger shops looked like oversized concrete garages with crude shelves inside. They were filled with food and household goods, candles, matches, toothpaste, soap, tea, instant coffee, powdered milk, string, etc. Even in the hardware stores, some food items were sold as well as toys and bicycles. Curiously, most shops lining the main shopping street, sold the same things.

We went into the main grocery shop and stocked up on toilet paper (had I mentioned how relieved I was that we were able to buy that here?), shampoo, cookies, chocolate, and a whole box of *Super Mie*, instant noodles with seasoning. (A few days later, I had my first bowl of Super Mie, but because I didn't know what *Cabe* meant on one of the included tiny packages, it wasn't a pleasant experience. Cabe pronounced "cha-bay," is a small, extremely hot chili pepper. Most Indonesians love spicy food, and I learned not to take big bites before testing how spicy a dish was).

The Headlong Dive into My New life

After shopping, we went to Brian and Luana's house. A traditional Papuan fence surrounded the property, and a beautiful Bougainvillea bush adorned the front porch. Briana gave me the tour of the house and beautiful garden, showed me the two dogs, a cat, and several rabbits. During the short time they had lived there, the family had transformed this shell of a house and empty plot of land. Bananas, pineapples, berries, vegetables, and flowers were growing all around. Pretty river pebbles kept the path from turning muddy on rainy days. Later, we drove back to the airport to pick up Brian, Philip, and Hans for a tasty lunch of soup and grilled cheese sandwiches.

Hans had a special history with Philip. Not only had the boy sometimes assisted Hans with car maintenance in Albania and they had played together in their spare time, but they had also shared a traumatic event. Just hours before civil unrest destroyed the Helimission base in Albania in 1997, Hans and Philip had fled the country in a heavy truck and on a ferry under dramatic, dangerous circumstances—including a severe storm at sea. Luana and Briana had made it out on the last civilian flight out of the country, and Brian had managed to flee last in the nick of time. After a traumatic ordeal at the Durres port, he and other foreigners had been rescued by the Italian navy. Philip had grown up a lot since then and was now a bright and handsome teenager, with his mother's blue eyes, his father's curly hair, and a winning smile.

"Sorry, you're still not getting a break and a chance to unpack," Luana told me after lunch. "This opportunity is just too good to pass up. A family is selling their belongings before going back to the USA.

We drove to the expat housing compound where the family lived. I hadn't shipped a lot of household goods, so this would be useful since we'd have to move from the fully-equipped house soon. A Papuan guard opened the sliding gate for us, and we entered the compound enclosed by a concrete wall with broken glass on top to deter thieves. The houses were built around an open field with soccer goals. All the houses seemed identical and were set on the compound in symmetrical order with flower beds in the front. The whole scene was a stark contrast to the rather untidy rest of the town. I was welcomed warmly and looked at hundreds of items for sale.

When I got to bed that night, after finding the sheets in one of the four suitcases, my head was aching and spinning.

What a day!

Apart from arriving at my new home for the coming years, I had met my new colleagues and friends and learned about shopping in Wamena. At the missionary sale, I had purchased several household items, language books and tapes, and I turned down two dogs. The decision about the washing machine was still out, although one newly-learned principle was always to buy what I would need when it was available because it might not be there when I returned again.

One thing had become clear: social isolation wouldn't be an issue for me. Many missionaries struggled with that, especially during the language study phase when they weren't able to communicate clearly with the local people. While so far I only knew two phrases in Indonesian—the official language spoken in Papua next to two hundred fifty tribal languages—I had met westerners who spoke English and made me feel welcome.

I shuddered when I thought of an older Papuan man I had seen while I was observing street life from the car. He had been running along the street in the cold at dusk with his arms crossed to keep himself warm. The raindrops had pelted his naked skin, since the only clothing he wore was the traditional gourd, leaving ninety-nine percent of his body uncovered. My first impulse had been to ask Luana to stop so that I could give him my jacket, but I had only borrowed it myself. And besides, there were so many people in the streets without the clothes I thought were necessary to survive and stay healthy. Later, I found out many of these people were not too poor to buy clothes, but rather wanted to preserve their traditions and hold on to the way their people had lived for ages.

Eventually, I fell asleep.

The following morning, we got up at five a.m., had some breakfast, and Jan and Hans went to work. I enjoyed the first quiet hours in our house and started unpacking and setting up.

How good that I was able to buy all these nice things at the sale. Who knows when the boxes with our stuff will arrive?

Besides our clothes and some essentials, I had brought a few lightweight special items along in our suitcases. While putting photos in frames and hanging a beautiful silk scarf on the wall, which a friend had decorated for me, I remembered the words of Hans' missionary aunt. "Take along some things that will brighten up the walls of your place and make you feel at home, but you won't be heartbroken over if you lose them."

Wise words. The place started to look homely already.

"Hi, Elke, how was your first night?" Luana asked me on the phone.

"It was fine, thanks, just a bit cool and lots of noises in the wooden house. We couldn't figure out what the strange sound was coming from our wardrobe." I tried to mimic the sound.

"Oh, that's just the *cicaks*, the little house geckos. They are a bit annoying because they leave their droppings everywhere, but they keep insects like cockroaches under control."

She asked if I could help her set up the house for a small concert. Briana had taught some of the missionary kids to play the piano and tonight they would perform for their parents, friends, and teachers.

"Wow, there's lots going on here. I've only been here for a day now, and there's a sale and a concert."

"Yes, you'll find there's little entertainment in Wamena in the evenings, so we try to make our own, by inviting each other for meals and putting on little concerts. Tom, a single pilot, has a video projector and tries to come by good movies to show every other Saturday night."

(The nightlife in Wamena changed drastically over the following years—to a negative effect, I'm afraid).

Luana picked me up, and we set up for the evening. We had lunch with the men in the *pondok*, the Papuan-style gazebo with a traditional thatched roof.

"All right. Are you ready for your orientation on the helis?" Hans asked after the meal.

Was I ever! Since I had been a child and my father had told me about helicopters, I had run to the window when one flew over the house. I still couldn't believe helicopters would be a part of my life now—*and* doing such great work!

At the airport, I met Alex, the other team member involved in Helimission operations in Wamena besides Brian, Jan, and Hans. Alex was a bright and gifted young Papuan man, who assisted with many of the hands-on tasks around the helicopters and was a great asset to the team. I was looking forward to learning some Indonesian so that I could communicate with him too. Meanwhile, the limited English he knew was of great help.

Hans gave me an introduction to the basic safety rules around the helicopter, explained how the major components worked, how to fuel, and how to unhook the doors, so the whole side of the passenger compartment could be opened to put in stretchers for medical evacuations (medevacs). This was so exciting! (I would soon find out, that things done around a running helicopter, with the ear-bashing noise and forceful rotor wind, were much more exciting yet!) I loved how much the whole family could be involved in the work of Helimission. We wives were counted on as team members, and even Briana and Philip were often able to help with various tasks.

Next, I had my first thorough look around the pilots' and maintenance offices, which had been set up in a small wooden building with a low metal roof. The two rooms were stuffed full of aviation charts, accounting books, and maintenance manuals. Hans had taken over the maintenance office and was setting it up. The room used to be a small kitchen/diner. Apart from a photocopy machine, it held a refrigerator, sink, and kitchen counter, which had become the (rather tall) desk. Hans had vacuumed the office and put all the folders and manuals into shelves. I went about cleaning up the kitchen corner and took notes of the things I wanted to bring from home to set up the kitchen.

I thanked God for Luana, who had offered to feed us for two weeks. It would take me a while to figure out how to use the woodstove, and the two electric hotplates were slow. Now I seriously needed to learn to cook with the ingredients available in Wamena. Luana had gone through her pantry and given me a packet of everything I'd need, but wasn't available in Wamena and also some frozen meat to start with. Without her help and generosity, we'd probably have wasted away quickly.

Ibu Marice was another godsend. In the mornings, she would clean the house and bake bread or wash laundry if necessary. I had never used a twin tub washing machine before. In Germany, all I had to do was open the automatic washer, put in the laundry and detergent, turn on the machine, and then take the freshly-washed

The Headlong Dive into My New life

laundry out again after an hour or two. This one now required several steps, and I surely didn't want to break someone else's washing machine, since we were only house-sitting. Thankfully, I could leave our laundry in Ibu Marice's capable hands and wander off to work at the office.

On Saturday, our third day in Wamena, we started working at the office again at seven o'clock in the morning. There was a knock on the door and a very tall, brown-haired, clean-shaven man in blue pants, a pilots' shirt, and sturdy boots entered. He was around fifty years of age.

"Good morning!" he said in a tone more cheerful than I could muster at this hour and introduced himself as Tom. Hans had told me about him before. He had been impressed. This ex-military pilot had been flying mission airplanes in Papua for several years and was appreciated everywhere for his calm, humble attitude and love for the Papuan people. On the weekends, he would sometimes go off by plane to show the *JESUS* film in different villages. His wife, Rosa, was away at the moment, and I would get to know the whole family later on. Rosa was a teacher at the school for missionary kids (MK's). In contrast to Tom, Rosa was rather short and gray-haired. She was very energetic, with a fiery Mexican background. The couple was a prime example of the expression "opposites attract." I'd come to appreciate Rosa's keen sense of social justice and dedication to helping underprivileged children get a quality education. The couple had three mostly grown-up children, at boarding school on the coast and in college. The whole family was well-known and loved.

Hans and Brian got the Internet connection to work, while I was still busy cleaning up the office kitchen and making coffee with much improvisation because the plumbing didn't work yet. While I was organizing the kitchen, Brian came in.

"Elke, would you like to go along on a medevac flight in an airplane with Tom? He just asked if anybody wanted to come."

This was the other Tom, a single pilot in his early thirties who held the movie nights on Saturdays. He had brown hair, a trimmed beard, and was compact and energetic.

I swallowed and took a deep breath. "Wow, sounds like a great opportunity, but is it a serious case?"

"Hey, Tom, is it a messy one?" Brian yelled out the louver window.

"I don't know myself yet. Apparently, the man has fallen off a tree," Tom replied from the outside. He had to do another flight first, so I still had an hour to get up my courage and make up my mind. I figured it would be a good way of getting to know a scenario like that without having to help much myself yet, so I decided to go. It would be a short flight. If I felt queasy, I could stay on board and wouldn't cause trouble if I fainted.

After Tom had returned, he let me get into the co-pilot's seat of the Cessna 206. Tom explained to me how to buckle up and open the door in case of an emergency. We took off against the wind, before turning the other direction and heading down the Baliem Valley. The weather was clear, and I was surprised to see how small Wamena was. Two days ago, when I had arrived on the Transall, I hadn't been able to see much because of the clouds. Wamena seemed to be enormous and confusing from the ground, especially since I wasn't used to the grid pattern in which it was laid out. Every street corner looked the same to me, and Luana had shown me helpful ways to find my way by remembering landmarks, signs, etc. or by counting the streets to find the right one.

The view of the landscape was breathtaking, and I was so glad I had gotten up the courage to go. Now I saw the wide and winding Baliem River for the first time.

"Do you see that symmetrically-shaped rock down there?" Tom pointed to the spot. "That's Pyramid Rock. Close by there is a village called Pyramid. It was one of the first mission stations in this area and has an airstrip."

Then he turned the plane into a gap between the mountains, entering a valley. To me, it seemed like the wing was about to scrape the mountainside. When I looked out the side window of the banked plane, I looked straight into a giant, gaping, round hole in the rocks, which had trees growing inside it. I later found out there were many similar sinkholes in the limestone mountains where caves running through most of them had collapsed. There were even caves with rivers flowing through them. What a fascinating island this was!

To line up with the Wolo runway and reach the correct altitude, Tom had to turn inside the narrow side valley. I held my breath.

Is he aware we're heading straight for a mountain?
I looked over, and his face didn't show the least bit of concern. I figured he knew what he was doing since this was his everyday work—and his eyes were open. The plane came around, and we touched down on the grass airstrip.

The pilots flying around these mountains have to be well-trained and need nerves of steel!
Soon I would learn that Wolo wasn't the hardest place to land by far.

I exited the airplane and looked around the first Papuan village I'd ever seen from the ground. On both sides of the airstrip, the whole population of Wolo seemed to have gathered.

Such a beautiful place and not a hotel in sight!
Tom and the villagers loaded the injured man into the plane on a stretcher. To my relief, I couldn't see any open wounds because someone had bandaged him with rags and cloth strips. The family paid the airfare and off we went again.

"You should feel sorry for the guy; he'll feel every little bump," Tom said to me over the intercom. I did.

A few minutes later, we landed in Wamena, and the man was taken to the hospital. I had survived my first medevac flight without fainting. A good start.

I was glad for the opportunity to help Luana prepare lunch. I felt slightly useful and learned a lot. When I was younger, I hadn't been enthusiastic about my grandmother's attempts to teach me to cook. Now cooking became essential and frequently having guests over for meals was part of life.

After lunch, Briana took me on a short bicycle ride out of town. We passed bicycle rickshaws, battered old cars, and lots of pedestrians. Some ladies carried large loads in their net bags, strung over their heads and hanging down their backs, as well as a toddler on their shoulders. We rode past sweet potato gardens and fenced little hamlets with grass-thatched wooden huts. Many of the wood fences or low stone walls were lined with pretty, dark red plants. Also from this angle, the Baliem Valley was beautiful and again, I marveled at the stark contrast between the completely flat valley and the steep mountains all around, which presented themselves in different shades of green and sheer gray rock. The afternoon winds had set in and taken away the midday heat.

"I can certainly feel the altitude now," I said to Briana, panting on an uphill stretch. I was glad somebody had told me physical training was helpful preparation for living in the tropics. I had then joined a cardiovascular exercise group and wondered how much more I'd be panting if I hadn't. The air at five thousand feet (sixteen hundred meters) above sea level was thinner than at my hometown, which was located close to sea level.

I can't believe that last Saturday I was still in Germany!

Next, we went to a little market where fruit, vegetables, and other things were offered on dirty mats and bags on the ground. The vendors were exclusively Papuan. Some ladies sat on the dirt in the open, others on concrete under long rows of tin roofs on pillars. Some men were selling firewood and others were gambling in the back of the market. Briana carried a Papuan net bag over her head and down her back like the local women. I wasn't about to try that yet. I pictured myself being strangled if it would slide down my straight hair to the front, or the vegetables getting smashed on the ground after dropping down my back. And besides, I didn't think I could carry that much weight on my head anyway. We bought some pineapples and other fruit and vegetables and headed home to cook dinner with Luana.

It had taken nearly a week, but now it got us: "Montezuma's revenge." Hans and I both got diarrhea. Since the toilet was inside the bathroom, we were lucky to have Jan as a housemate; he took very quick showers!

We declined Brian and Luana's invitation to stay after dinner. All we needed now was rest after this eventful week and still battling jet lag.

Jan was a huge help, and we were glad he was living with us, especially since we didn't speak any Indonesian yet and our only means of communication with Ibu Marice were hand signs and desperate facial expressions. Jan would become like a brother to us. He had a good sense of humor, was a bit proud, but zealous and dedicated to building up the work and base of Helimission in Papua. His grandfather had come from the Maluku Islands to bring the gospel to this island. Jan carried on the family tradition of mission work in the third generation.

"We usually cook our vegetables before we eat them," Jan was reported saying when he had first eaten salad. By now he had grown to like salad. To my relief, Jan liked and tolerated western food well, unlike many other Indonesians we would meet. They could eat potatoes or pasta all day if they had to and then feel hungry soon after because they hadn't eaten any rice yet.

We'd learn a lot of things from Jan—sometimes unintentionally. When he'd go to bed with a thick jacket, or he picked herbs in the garden, we knew he was in for his monthly bout of malaria. From his complaints, we'd find out which malaria treatments caused nasty side effects and which ones did not, the cycles of burning up with a fever, and then shivering and chattering teeth. We'd also learn about herbal remedies and prophylaxes like a bitter tea made with papaya leaves. This all encouraged us to be diligent about applying mosquito repellant and mostly staying in at night when we were on the coast. (Later, Jan took strong liver cleansing medicine and came down with malaria less frequently). Thankfully, Wamena was malaria free because the Anopheles mosquitoes, which carried the disease, couldn't stand the cold nights. Some medicines used for malaria prevention had become ineffective due to resistance. Avoiding mosquito bites was the most effective malaria prevention of all.

Our first Sunday came, and we were glad for a day of rest. We looked like ghosts, were sick and tired, and slept most of the day. Luana and Philip came to bring us some bottled drinking water because we hadn't identified the cause of our stomach problems and water was always the first suspect. Since Luana was a nurse, she was a wealth of medical knowledge, which she often shared with us.

"You have been careful and used filtered water to brush your teeth, right?"

"Of course! Look, Luana, this is the medicine we brought from Germany for diarrhea."

"Oooh, I wouldn't take that if I were you."

"Why not? The pharmacist recommended it."

"Well, this is fine in some areas, but here where there are dangerous bacteria and parasites, it can cost lives."

"How so?" I was perplexed.

"They stop the bowel movements, which expel the harmful bugs. If this process is stopped, it gets dangerous. That's why it is better to take charcoal pills, which absorb toxins. Charcoal pills also help with poisoning and have few side effects—apart from coloring the stools black."

That was a small price to pay.

Another effective way to prevent or cure certain stomach ailments was a small shot of high percentage alcohol. This, however, was not acceptable to everyone and in every place. (We were surprised how opinions about alcohol could divide Christians everywhere, especially in the USA, while at the same time, the use of guns seemed widely accepted there; whereas, this would have been a huge issue in Germany where the sensible consumption of alcohol was widely accepted).

The Dedication

May 15, 2000

"Mausi, you should have seen that!" Hans reported on Monday night.

I had been too sick to sit in a helicopter for the twenty-five-minute flight to the Bible dedication at Ninia, so I had stayed at home. Although I was so disappointed to miss the event, the rest had done me good.

"About three thousand Papuan people came to Ninia from all over the mountains. Most of them on foot and in their traditional attire: grass skirts for the women and kotekas for the men."

By now I had started to get used to the kotekas, the men's clothing here—if that was possible.

"The people were dressed up in all kinds of feathers and furs and had painted their faces and bodies. Apparently, some had walked for days. When we approached Ninia, we saw large groups of people running over the mountain trails."

"Wow! I wish I could have come."

"And you should have seen the way they celebrated: painted warriors were running back and forth on the airstrip with their spears, bows, and arrows, hooting and hollering their battle cries. Looked pretty weird. What a different way to celebrate!"

(The next time I went to Europe and saw the yodeling "mountain tribes" of the Alps of our home countries, I thought this would seem strange to the Papuans as well).

The southern Yali Bible was the first completed Bible translation on the western half of New Guinea and had taken decades to complete. What a victory! Many missionaries who had worked here in the pioneer days had come back for the historic event, and it was a great reunion of many old friends of various skin colors and cultures.

"All along I wished Stan Dale and Phil Masters could have seen this," Hans mused.

We had heard about how these two missionaries had been martyred by tribesmen in 1968 during their quest to reach people of this area. This day was the ultimate proof their sacrifice hadn't been in vain.

On the second day, I felt well enough to go along, but I think I didn't eat anything all day, just to make sure. I was so excited to go on my first ever helicopter ride in Papua!

I had thought the views in and around the Baliem Valley were breathtaking, but I was blown away by what unfolded before my eyes now. We took off and followed the Baliem to where it left the Grand Valley on its way to the southern lowlands toward the so-called South Gap. From the altitude of five thousand feet where its brown waters calmly meandered through the wide, flat plateau, the river began its descent to the lowlands. After we had left the wide-open valley, the mountains closed in on either side, and we could see them towering above us while the waters of the Baliem turned into a raging white torrent in the gorge underneath us. The steep mountainsides were covered in green forest, adorned by rushing waterfalls and alternated by walls of sheer gray rock. Here and there a landslide marred a bank. Sweet potato gardens and clusters of little thatched huts attested to people living in this wild and rugged area.

How can anybody live here?

We followed the Baliem River for a few minutes and then turned into a side valley. After about twenty-five minutes of flying, we reached Ninia and landed on a flat spot on a mountain flank.

"How in the world did that airplane get up there on the hillside?" I asked after looking around.

"You might not have noticed, but this is the airstrip in front of us," Hans teased. "It has quite a slope and up there is the turnaround and parking area for the airplanes."

"Oh!"

Apparently, the Wolo airstrip I had seen on Saturday was a "piece of cake" compared to this one. The steep mountainside on the top end and a cliff on the bottom limited the length of the airstrip at Ninia. It started with a nine percent slope. In the middle, there was a stretch with five percent, and the last bit had an unbelievable nineteen percent slope. This airstrip was a challenge for the pilots. Ninia also had a wind-curfew, which meant airplanes could land there only until nine o'clock every morning before the winds picked up and made the landing too dangerous. Many of the highland airstrips had similar problems. Sometimes the helicopter had to go instead of an airplane if there was an emergency call from one of these airstrips after the wind-curfew. Due to the comparatively small surface of the rotor blades, a helicopter is much less affected by turbulence than an airplane wing. A helicopter can also fly the approach from a different direction if there is a crosswind at the airstrip. In bad weather and poor visibility, a helicopter can fly slowly, stop, turn, and even land to wait for the weather to clear.

Pilots had to take the strong winds and drafts into account when they approached Ninia, even before the curfew. A wind sock at the end of the runway indicated wind direction. In certain conditions, the pilots had to head for the cliff and then got lifted onto the airstrip by an updraft. Most pilots had stories of passengers freaking out during the approach. A visiting female airline pilot was reported as saying: "Either you guys are insane or you are heroes."

One thing was clear: the pilots needed strong nerves, comprehensive training, and a lot of experience to do this kind of flying. (Several years and accidents later, the Ninia airstrip had major work done, to make it safer).

It felt as if I had entered a different world. So far, since arriving in Papua less than a week ago, I had spent most of my time in towns with other foreigners, whose language I spoke. Now I was on the turf of the indigenous Papuans. We walked across the airstrip and went into one of the old mission houses to put down our belongings. We walked past a vast number of Papuan people sitting on the ground. The smell was overpowering. It came from hundreds of bodies smelling of smoke, sweat, and pig fat, which they greased their bodies with to stay warmer during the cold highland nights. The sun had now climbed over the mountains, and its rays were taking away the morning chill.

"Yesterday, there was a more traditional celebration, but today it's more formal with church and government representatives and lots of speeches," Luana explained. "That's why there are so many people in suits."

The contrasts were as stark as could be: some people were almost naked, dressed in their traditional attire, some wore suits and ties, and everybody else wore clothes in between these two extremes. While there was obviously no dress code, I had still wanted to wear something appropriate, so I had asked Luana for a suggestion. Usually, I wore jeans and a T-shirt, but for this occasion, I had put on a white short-sleeve blouse and flowy navy colored summer pants with a pattern.

Hans wasn't wearing his usual mechanic's overalls, but khaki pants, a long sleeve shirt, and a cap to protect him from the sun. He also wore a whistle around his neck so he would be heard over the helicopter noise in case he needed to get someone's attention.

"Look, Mausi," Hans called out to me. "People come running over the trails again like yesterday!"

"Wow, and they're all carrying stuff in net bags. They're not even wearing shoes!"

The net bags contained contributions for the grand feast. Smoke was rising from all around the grounds where rocks were heated for the numerous cooking pits where the pork, sweet potatoes, vegetables, and greens were going to be steamed. I walked around and was mesmerized by all the sights, sounds, and smells. I took photos of the people, the airplanes taking off and landing, the village, and the celebration.

"Thud-thud-thud-thud-thud!" Here came the helicopter full of dignitaries and other guests, so Hans had to make sure the landing spot was clear of people. The curfew had set in, and Brian was shuttling in passengers from the nearest usable airstrip.

I couldn't understand anything spoken in Indonesian or Yali on the large stage set up for the celebration. So, I tried to stick around the expats who were mainly speaking English.

"The Yalis have eyes like cats," I overheard a man saying to some people around him. "Last night I was walking with them on the

The Dedication

trail, and all I could make out was the white shirt on the guy right in front of me!"

The man talking was Wesley Dale from Australia. He had tried to get into Ninia by plane the previous day, but they had arrived over the airstrip just after the wind-curfew. Instead of going back to Wamena, he had chosen to be dropped off at the nearby Holuwon airstrip. Without any means of communication, he hadn't heard the helicopter would be shuttling people to Ninia from the surrounding villages. Wesley and several Yali men had walked twelve grueling hours to Ninia—while the helicopter would have needed only a few minutes. The men came across the spot where Wesley's father, Stan, had been attacked by warriors for the first time.

"I thought of how my father had to walk most of that same path after being wounded," Wesley said. Even one of the Yali men walking with Wesley had found the path too tough and decided to overnight about half way.

Only later, I would read the story of Stan Dale in *Lords of the Earth* by Don Richardson. The book described the hard work, grueling hikes, and extreme sacrifices that had been necessary to reach the Yali people with the Gospel. Wesley's father, Stan, along with Bruno de Leeuw, and many Dani and Yali people, had built the airstrip and mission station at Ninia. Later, Stan and his companion, Phil Masters, had paid the ultimate price for reaching the Yali, when warriors in the Seng valley killed and cannibalized them. Amazingly, Wesley had nonetheless gone back to Papua as a missionary and Bible translator himself. Perhaps it was best I didn't know all the history. Otherwise, the day would have been even more overwhelming for me than it already was!

Brian had shuttled several loads of the guests back to the Holuwon airstrip in the afternoon, and the clouds were closing in.

"So, you're hoping to make it out tonight," a lady asked when I picked up our bags to fly home. The thought of possibly having to spend the night hadn't even crossed my mind. For most people here, it seemed to be normal that the weather was the deciding factor in staying or leaving—not people's schedules and plans.

With dark clouds hanging overhead, it was going to be a rather scary flight, but I trusted Brian who had flown here for two years. He knew what he was doing so I decided to relax and enjoy. To him, this was nothing out of the ordinary. We had to fly under the low clouds above the river in a narrow gorge. To me, it seemed as if the rotor blades were about to hit the rock wall or trees on either side of the helicopter. Underneath us was the white-water river, above us the fog, and on both sides, we were sandwiched by rocky cliffs, tropical plants, and trees. It was better for my nerves that I sat in the back and didn't see the whole spectacle. After Brian had negotiated the narrow gorge for a while, it felt like a relief when the terrain opened up. We soon arrived at Holuwon, which was situated on an open-sloped plateau. Jan helped refuel the helicopter from a drum, and off we went, home to Wamena.

What a day!

In the weeks following the Bible dedication, Brian flew hundreds of the newly-printed southern Yali Bibles to villages of that particular tribe. In our home countries, most people had Bibles in their homes but didn't care to read them. Conversely, in many areas where people didn't have God's Word in their language, the hunger for it was great. It warmed my heart when we later saw video footage of young Yali people reading from those Bibles with beaming faces. However, it was daunting to think how much work still lay ahead. Bible translations were in process in different parts of Papua, and several New Testaments had been completed. But only in one tribe out of two hundred fifty on this side of the island, the people could now read the entire Bible in their heart language. What would it be like to not have the stories of creation, Moses, Joseph, Abraham, David, and the Psalms? But it was a start.

Bible translation work was jointly done by expat missionaries and dedicated tribespeople. Besides translators and language helpers, translation consultants were needed. Most of these projects were supported through the prayers and gifts of people all around the world. Today, many translation projects are fully in the hands of Papuan teams.

On that day in May 2000, in Ninia, we didn't have the slightest idea yet of all the processes involved in Bible translation, but we felt it had been a milestone in the church history of Papua.

A Turbulent Day

May 18, 2000

After the historic event at Ninia, we were back to the more mundane things of life—for two days. Now, the next excitement came our way. It was hard to believe we had only arrived in Wamena one week ago.

"Everybody get your Sunday best out again," Luana said. "The vice president is coming, and we're supposed to stand by with the helicopter in case she needs to go somewhere."

The vice president of the Republic of Indonesia, Megawati Sukarnoputri, was the daughter of the country's first president, Sukarno. I had seen her on TV in Germany but hadn't dreamt of ever meeting her.

"Do we often do flights like this?" I asked Luana.

"Rarely. Mostly it's mission flights or medevacs, but this is an excellent opportunity to show some gratitude to the government for granting the visas, work permits, and so on."

That made sense. The average three percent of flights done for the government included surveys after landslides or other disasters and consecutive food aid.

A member of the security team came to give us a briefing. We were given Indonesian government name tags, so we were allowed to get close to the vice president as operators of the helicopter. I was nervous. For the life of me, I couldn't memorize the name of the vice president, so Jan wrote down her popular name for me: "Ibu Mega." That was better.

"Wow! Jan, you've already met the governor of Papua at Ninia, and now you are about to meet the vice president of Indonesia," Luana teased.

"Oh well, they are just humans like me," Jan replied, but the fact he had a big grin on his face and was whistling songs gave away that he was more excited than he let on.

Friday came, and it got serious: Vice President Ibu Megawati Sukarnoputri arrived in Wamena. All cameras were in position, everybody was dressed up with their name tags on, and was ready for action. The airplane was too far away to get quality photos or footage, and by now we had heard that Ibu Mega was not going to fly with our helicopter, but we were supposed to stand by in case there would be problems so we could evacuate her. She only wanted to visit a few places in Wamena: two schools, the hospital, and the orphanage.

Jan and Hans were sent to the hospital with the helicopter battery cart, and Philip, Briana, and I went along to wait for some photo opportunities. The men waited next to the helipad with the battery cart, while the youngsters and I walked over to the office building suspecting the entourage would go there first.

"Hurry, get over here!" Briana, who was ahead of me, yelled.

I turned around and jumped behind a car for cover. A crowd of half-naked Papuan men armed with sticks ran past me into the office building. Brian had previously followed the government convoy and landed the helicopter in front of the hospital. He ran up the turbine, ready to take off if things would get any tenser. A bit later, the group of angry Papuans disappeared in the direction we expected the vice president's convoy to appear from. Brian took off and flew a few rounds overhead while we wondered what would happen next. All of a sudden, the crowd came running back and assembled next to a wall. One man started talking; then we heard the crowd applauding, and as suddenly as they had come, they disappeared.

"Looks like they didn't have any business with the vice president, but with the Bupati!" Briana found out. I didn't know the first thing about politics in Papua and was still confused. Later, I learned the Bupati was the regent of this Jayawijaya area.

The vice president arrived with her entourage, and all the spectators ran toward her. Briana and I had our cameras in position and tried to anticipate where she'd appear next after visiting some buildings. Eventually, we managed to get a reasonable shot over the heads of people who were pushing, shoving, and stretching out their hands, before she disappeared into another building.

In the midst of all the hustle and bustle, I heard some words from behind me that seemed to come from another world: "Guten Morgen, Elke!"

I turned around, and there was Gerhard, a German agricultural development worker I had met a few days earlier along with his family. He was bidding me a good morning in German. Amongst Americans, Indonesians, a vice president, soldiers, police officers, and hordes of Papuan people in all stages of being dressed (or not), I hadn't expected to hear my mother tongue. Soon, all the excitement was over, and the government entourage drove off in a car. Next, I saw two Papuans walking past wearing jerseys of German soccer clubs.

No way! I better get used to all kinds of conflicting information, and I will have to expect the unexpected at every corner.

Brian flew back to the airport, and we all got into the car to go there as well. Since the gate leading to the office and hangar was locked, we had to find a way around via the airport, which was blocked by crowds of people with spears, bows, and arrows. I wouldn't have dared to go anywhere near them, but Hans inched the car forward right into the crowd while Briana and Philip shouted, "Permisi!" (Excuse me!) out the windows. We were totally immersed in the crowd, and it got eerily dark when bodies touched the car all around. Eventually, we made it through to the office, and I breathed a sigh of relief.

Several of the prohibited Papuan Morning Star flags of the independence movement were flying in the wind at the airport. A man in a black suit was standing on the back of a truck talking to the people with a megaphone. We learned he was a well-known and respected pastor who tried to appease the people. Ibu Megawati left with her entourage; the excitement was over, and everybody went back to work. I wondered if life would go on like this. It felt like after a life of paddling on a tranquil lake with the occasional wind gust during the first part of my life; I had now joined a white-water rafting adventure.

Demonstrations and small riots were a part of life in Wamena at the time, and we would have to get used to it. Ever since the western half of New Guinea had become part of Indonesia in the nineteen-sixties, many Papuans were opposed to it. They rather wanted Papua to be an independent state, like Papua New Guinea on the Eastern half of the island. Apart from demonstrations of the population, sporadically there were armed clashes between a group of Papuan freedom fighters and Indonesian authorities.

The government-sponsored transmigration program brought people from overpopulated areas of Indonesia by the shipload each week. These new transmigrants brought their cultures and religions and needed land to live off. Many Papuans felt this influx of outsiders threatened their way of life and that their traditional land rights were disrespected.

Thank God, it's Sunday!

May 21, 2000

I stiffly sat behind Hans on the scooter, while he carefully steered it over the narrow boards, running the length of the large steel bridge over the Wamena River or *Kali Oue* as the locals called it. Several of the boards, which were supposed to cover the bridge at a right angle, were missing and I saw water rushing underneath. This ride wasn't as relaxing as it was meant to be.

 Monday through Saturday, the men worked from the early morning until well after dark, but on Sundays, everybody took time off unless there was an emergency. We had enjoyed sleeping in after our turbulent first full week in Papua. Now Hans and I were exploring the area around Wamena on Luana's scooter. The Kali Oue flowed straight out of the mountains and into the Baliem River a few hundred meters downstream from the bridge. The Oue's riverbed consisted of beautiful pebbles of all sizes, which were dug out, put onto dump trucks, and used in the construction of buildings and roads as well as for decoration in gardens and lining paths. In several places in town, I had seen people sitting on piles of these rocks, splitting them with hammers to make gravel. The Kali Oue also powered the hydroelectric power plant that produced most of the electricity for the town, which rarely experienced a power outage (at the time).

 We rode on toward the end of the wide-open valley, past sweet potato fields, square fishponds, and people walking, riding bicycles or motorcycles, or driving in cars.

"Hi, Hans and Elke, I'm so glad you came," a lady I had met at the missionary sale welcomed us to the get-together before the expat Sunday afternoon service at the small international school. "Help yourselves to tea or coffee and some snacks."

We mingled with people we had already met throughout the week and got to know others we hadn't seen yet. The majority of the attendees were either American or Dutch. After finishing our drinks, we made our way inside for the church service and sat down in a big circle in the largest classroom. Every Sunday, someone else was responsible for the service, the music, and children's church and sometimes there were guest speakers. We sang hymns and contemporary songs, which were mostly new to me. We shared prayer requests, prayed for each other, and listened to a sermon on tape.

"Why don't you all take turns preaching?" we asked afterward.

"Oh, don't ask a pilot to preach," was the reply.

What a shame. We would have loved to hear about people's experiences with the Lord from their everyday lives, and most attendees had even been to Bible school.

When it was our turn to run the service a while later, Hans mustered all his courage and spoke himself. He hadn't been to Bible school, and his English wasn't perfect, but he had a Bible and plenty of stories to share from his life. Many times, he had experienced God's help, provision, protection, and intervention. Several of our new friends thanked him afterward, and some were encouraged to speak themselves as well when it was their turn next. Others appreciated theological exegesis from tapes more. I started to look forward to these times of fellowship, learning English hymns and praise songs, and hearing about peoples' lives and ministries when we shared prayer requests. I loved the way people prayed for one another.

"Sorry, Mausi, I can't come along to the service," Hans would later say on a Sunday. "I need to sleep."

One look at him said more than a thousand words. His tired eyes and slumped posture told of a stressful week with long hours and minimal sleep. All he could do on some Sundays was sleep, eat, read the Bible, and pray. Working on helicopters was a matter of life and death since a small mistake could lead to a crash. Rest was of utmost importance. While our relationship with the Lord was the most important factor for our resilience and effectiveness on the mission field, not everybody had the same way of maintaining it. Hans was an introvert and didn't like music much. While he loved powerful sermons, large groups drained him of energy and when combined with music, put him over the edge. Singing certainly wasn't his "love language" with the Lord.

Later, we became convinced that without making Sunday a dedicated day of rest (except for emergencies), we wouldn't have endured the first year in Papua. But then again: God himself took a day of rest after creating the world; how much more did we need to rest after six days of work?

Shopping, My New Skill

May 22, 2000

"Wow! A real passenger plane with seatbelts for everybody," I commented when we boarded the plane to the coast on Monday. Luana was taking me along to the coast for purchasing supplies and other business.

Shopping hadn't been a favorite pastime of mine, but I didn't mind it and had occasionally enjoyed browsing through gift or clothes shops. Now, I found myself dreaming at night that I was going shopping in the city, looking at pretty scented candles, pictures, and china and buying my favorite coffee in Germany. This reminded me of stories I had read from people who went on long ocean voyages and started dreaming of long walks in the countryside or food they craved and couldn't get.

We were able to buy all the food we needed to survive and much more in Wamena. However, many things that made life easier, like foils and wraps, or made food more enjoyable, like sauces, dairy products, and nice pasta, were not locally available.

Luana had been feeding us frequently, and the next visitors were about to arrive, so it was necessary to stock up on supplies again.

When we left the Sentani airport, there were plenty of taxi drivers who wanted our business—for outrageous prices.

"Let's see if we can get a fair deal for the whole day to go to Jayapura," Luana said and approached a driver. When people saw our white skin, they often assumed we were rich and automatically

Shopping, My New Skill

increased the prices. This man also wouldn't come down on the price, so Luana started walking. The driver came after us, and we had a deal.

"I bet you he has tuberculosis," Luana whispered to me when the driver kept coughing and spat out the door when we stopped. "We better keep the windows open."

In those days, most cars in Papua didn't have air-conditioning anyway, so it was just as well.

My shirt stuck to my back in the scorching heat and humidity, while we stocked up in different shops in Abepura and Jayapura. We packed our groceries in cardboard boxes, loaded them in the taxi, and went back to Sentani.

Next, we visited Sue, an Irish nurse from Wamena, who was also taking care of business here on the coast and had come down with malaria. I would find that Sue was a true gem among the missionaries in Papua. I could only describe her as a savvy, friendly, and resolute version of Mother Teresa (although not by appearance) and a wealth of wisdom and experience. She would become a wonderful friend to us. With her decades of experience, she wasn't easily shaken, and it was wonderful to meet somebody who had such a close, loving relationship with the Papuan people. She lived and worked with them, and they loved and respected her. As a midwife, she had helped countless babies into this world, and she was also a Bible translator.

After a spicy Indonesian restaurant dinner, we had one more store to visit. This one was the shabbiest I had seen, but sold several items we wanted to buy. I felt uncomfortable in the dusty shack full of dust, spider webs, cockroaches, and mosquitoes.

"Good job!" Luana said when I slapped a mosquito on the back of my hand. She was treating too many people for malaria and kept reminding us that not getting bitten was the best malaria prevention. We finally found all we needed and walked back to the guesthouse in the dark through some side streets. We carefully repacked our supplies, making sure everything fit tightly and the cardboard boxes wouldn't break.

"We need to tape them around the edges and under the bottom so that nothing can fall out, and no little hands can slip in," Luana advised. Now, two weeks after my first trip to Wamena, during which

I had wondered if people didn't own suitcases, I was the one traveling with cardboard boxes. Amazing how quickly things could change!

In the morning, we went to the cargo plane company and found out we were in luck and could get onto the flight, unlike our first attempt. The cargo was loaded, strapped down, and passenger seats were put in and locked in place. Luana and I buckled up in our seats behind the cargo. This time, we each had matching seat belt sets. The plane accelerated for take-off. Suddenly, it started shaking violently and veered off to one side. To our relief, the pilots managed to abort the take-off, and the plane came to a halt before running out of runway space. With our hearts pounding, we looked out the window to see if a tire had blown up.

"I guess we'll have to look for another plane to Wamena," I said to Luana. To my utter amazement, the plane taxied back to the end of the runway, accelerated again, and we took off without a problem.

If that was the take-off, what will the landing be like? Lord, please help us!

The next surprise of the day was a perfectly fine and smooth landing. Luana walked up to the pilot and asked what had been the problem.

"Apparently, the front wheel shimmy damper steering is worn and caused the violent shaking," Luana informed me.

"I think, I'll call them 'adventure airline,'" I said to Hans later, rolling my eyes. "Four times booking, one time flying!"

Over time we had to acknowledge, however, that the earsplitting, noisy F-27 Fokker planes were relatively reliable, after all, with several flights daily to Wamena. (And at least, none of the many people walking on the runway would miss them coming).

I shook my head when I thought of the drastic turn my life had taken in the last few weeks. The adventure books and movies I had loved from my childhood on, had been a far cry from my stable and sheltered life in Germany. I had never experienced financial problems. The garbage was divided into five categories, and we knew months in advance when to put out the bins for which collection. Foreigners sometimes made fun of us Germans obeying a stop sign

Shopping, My New Skill

at three in the morning. Maybe it was this overly-regulated lifestyle that had made me long for adventure.

It was the same in matters of faith. Good health care, insurance, and an all but fail-safe welfare system seemed to make faith in God's provision less meaningful than in other parts of the world. In the Christian children's group, I had been particularly fascinated by stories of missionaries like Hudson Taylor, who had followed God's call to work as a missionary in inland China. Over and over, Hudson Taylor had experienced God's provision, sometimes after his faith and trust had been severely tested.

Apparently, the adventure stories from my childhood had impacted me more than I had initially thought. Later on, in my vacations from work, I had swapped my desk, file folders, and the familiar surroundings of my orderly hometown for the masts and rough ropes of Russian square-rigged tall ships on the open sea and ocean wind. After a few weeks, it had been back to the nine-to-five job and separating my garbage. However, I had started taking Russian Bibles along for the crew of the sailing ships. The organization I had obtained the Bibles from had then sent me their newsletters with more adventure stories (from this day and age). That's when I had told the Lord I'd be willing to go to the mission field myself—if at all possible, with a husband.

Things hadn't exactly gone smoothly from then on, but now here I was: more adventure than I could wish for—even on a shopping trip—and total reliance on God for our financial needs as well. Like many missionaries, we weren't receiving a salary from our organization but were supported by friends, family members, and other believers who donated money so we could work overseas. We never knew how much money would come in each month. It wasn't easy to come to terms with this new financial situation. I never doubted God would give us all we needed, but which things did we truly need and which ones were just nice to have and might be considered extravagant by some? Ultimately, most people supporting missionaries give a tithing to the Lord but entrust it to them to be used wisely. While everybody should be responsible with the money they have, this became a lot more real when we had to accept "the widow's mite!"

Game On

End of May 2000

Ernst Tanner, the director of Helimission, arrived with his wife, Hedi, and son, Simon. They had just visited Nepal to investigate possible options for Helimission to start operating there and Ernst had been awarded the title of Dr.h.c. (honoris causa–honorary degree) by the International University of Kathmandu. After our visitors had settled in, we all walked around the outlines of the planned hangar building, which had been marked with stakes on the field. The construction would be carried out by an experienced expat contractor and a team of tradesmen. However, somebody in our organization had to oversee the process. Lack of personnel made for quick promotions: Hans had initially thought he'd help Brian with maintenance. Instead, Brian had appointed him as Chief of Maintenance, and now our leadership asked him to oversee the hangar building project too!

"... and Elke can do the bookkeeping and pay the bills and salaries together with Jan," Ernst said—and my jaw dropped.

I hadn't even thought about that side of things yet. Luana had already introduced me to the bookkeeping of normal operations, which I gradually took over under her supervision. (Later we found out that immigration regulations would not allow me to work in an office role—not even as an unpaid volunteer. So I stopped doing it.) Luana was very busy homeschooling Philip and Briana, treating sick people in the mission community, keeping the household running, hosting guests, communicating with friends and supporters, and much more. I was glad to relieve Luana of part of her heavy workload.

Before leaving Germany, I didn't have a clue what I would be doing in Papua. While some people had thought that was a bit of worry, I still had been excited. I knew if God would send me somewhere, He was planning to use me somehow. Still, I was terrified at times, and this was one of those!

"Don't worry, we'll help you get going," Luana reassured me when she saw I looked dumbfounded. The matter was settled. I took a deep breath and tried to relax. I had worked in an office the previous ten years and liked it. I loved being part of this team, seeing all that happened in the office, meeting the people who used the helicopter, and being a part of this exciting work in this exciting place. I knew that having a task would help me settle in. While children were invaluable and a tremendous asset in mission work, not having to care for children gave me the flexibility to help out in any way I was needed by Helimission. I think with this arrangement and everything else going on, I didn't even have time for a proper culture shock (my friends might tell you otherwise).

I was so glad about the way things had turned out after arriving in Wamena. I couldn't have asked for a better start. Our work and presence were appreciated. We were welcomed into a team, family, and mission community.

"Imagine, if we'd have had to find our way around and learn everything from scratch, like so many people have to," I said to Hans. "I wouldn't even know where to shop and what to cook with the limited ingredients here. I'm so glad Luana is helping me with that and even feeding us!"

Brian and the family had lived through a much harder start. Many missionaries had to find their way around on their own and were isolated from friends, family, and the local community because of the language and culture barrier. The status and knowledge they had held back home didn't always count in their new setting. Hans' qualifications, however, enabled him to do his part from day one. It was also a great comfort to know that if we got sick, Luana could treat us or would know who else could help us. I marveled how their family went about life in such an unpredictable place as Wamena. "Hope for the best, but prepare for the worst," certainly was a healthy attitude, so we tried to adopt it as well.

Jan was already used to interacting with foreigners, graciously overlooking many of their (and our) cultural blunders. He became a great friend to us. Jan was also a huge help for me in communicating with Ibu Marice and even running a few errands when I was at a loss where to buy sewing needles or green beans to complete our dinner.

"Mausi, we're all going to Silimo tomorrow on the heli with the Tanners," Hans announced.

"Fantastic!" I went about making sure I had some extra rolls of film and a full battery for the camera.

We had already heard a lot about Buzz and Myrna and their two boys, who lived in that village, and it would be great to meet them and to see their situation. Buzz had worked together with Brian and Johannes, another Helimission pilot, during the drought relief operation. Buzz was a second-generation missionary in Papua, and his parents had been among the first missionaries here in the mountains. Buzz and Myrna had started a community development program teaching the local people to make crafts like carvings, baskets, and other items to sell to support themselves, their evangelists—who they had sent into different areas—and also a Christian kindergarten. Even though Buzz's parents had retired and returned to the USA, they were still involved in the ongoing Bible translation work and would sometimes come to visit.

After a twenty-minute flight through the beautiful mountains, we landed at Silimo. While Brian disconnected the helicopter battery and spun the rotor backward, to prevent a carbon lock-up in the turbine, we were warmly welcomed by Buzz, Myrna, and their two young sons, as well as people from the local Ngalik tribe. We women were even given long handmade necklaces as welcome gifts from the villagers.

"Come on in, let's have some hot drinks."

Myrna invited us into the wooden mission house, surrounded by a beautiful garden and a traditional Papuan fence. Along with the drinks, Myrna served us fresh pineapple. While sipping my hot chocolate, I looked around the cozy, old wooden mission house, which featured a rustic fireplace.

What a lovely peaceful home out here in the mountains!

Buzz introduced us to two local evangelists and told us about them and their ministry. I felt a sense of admiration and great respect for these two barefooted men.

As I would learn later, local evangelists and their families experienced many hardships. Many of them were sent from the highlands to the lowlands, which entailed getting used to the unfamiliar food and a different climate. Tropical diseases like malaria threatened their lives. They also needed to study new languages and cultures. In the traditional animistic belief system, ancestral spirits ruled over every aspect of the people's lives: the way they made their gardens, waged wars, ate and drank, treated the sick, got married, and ran their community. Fear of the spirits and enemies was a major factor in everyone's life—from birth to death. Any intrusion by outsiders was feared to bring on the spirits' wrath through landslides, failed crops, infertility of their women and pigs, etc.

Many local evangelists had been killed attempting to bring these tribes the message of eternal life through Christ's sacrifice for them. Others kept trying despite the danger, because they had experienced what a life-giving message the gospel was and knew the other tribes needed to hear them, too. While the approximately two hundred fifty tribes on this half of the island had their individual languages, stories, and traditions, the widespread animistic belief system was similar. To us foreigners coming from western countries where everything had to have a logical explanation, this worldview was incredibly outlandish. Our scientific way of thinking wouldn't make the first corner in this society. In that regard, the local evangelists—who had been brought up with a similar worldview—were way ahead of us in relating to those tribes.

Once a relationship was begun with the tribesmen, it was still a difficult task to live among them, learn their language, and present the story of the Creator God, who had sent His own Son as an atonement for their sins and who had conquered the power of the dark forces. It wouldn't have changed anything to tell these people there were no evil spirits and they could just stop worrying about all that, as secular aid organizations might. This belief and fear of demons was so deeply-rooted and engrained in their culture and identity; only a stronger power could break it. Then there was the fear of death.

Many tribes had legends about how eternal life was lost—and all of them longed for a way to find it again.

Even though their worldview was similar, I suspected it was harder for these indigenous families to go to their own people in a different area, than for us western missionaries to go overseas in this day and age. They didn't have the same support, training, technology, means of transportation, and communication we had.

"We're having some problems with the hydropower plant behind the house. Could you guys have a look at it?" Buzz asked Hans and Brian.

"Sure. Let's get to work."

The rest of us walked around the compound and the airstrip and took in the sights, sounds, and smells. Women were busy repairing the airstrip and the water channel leading to the small hydropower plant.

"That's interesting, why is it mainly ladies, who do the work?" we wondered.

"Well, that's part of the culture here," Myrna explained, "the men do the hefty one-off jobs like building the houses, clearing the land for a garden and the like, but the women do the ongoing everyday work. Traditionally, the men were responsible for warfare and for protecting the women while they worked. The ladies are used to working hard on a daily basis to provide food and they are also diligent at maintaining the airstrip."

"Protect the women? From what?"

"From enemy warriors. If one tribe has killed more people than the other in a war, a woman or child could be killed working in the garden to even out the score."

While we walked along, I tried to process all this information.

"Look at that old lady; she doesn't have fingers, just stumps! What happened to her?" Ernst asked, and we all looked at the petite elderly lady distraught. When we looked around we noticed, several other older ladies had one or more fingers missing, with only the first phalanx remaining, while none of the younger women did.

Buzz passed on Ernst's question to the lady and then translated her reply.

"When I was a young girl, my mother died. As it was our custom, my fingers were chopped off as a sign of mourning."

We were all struck by this revelation.

"So when you die, will your daughter's fingers also be chopped off?" Ernst inquired.

"No, no," the lady replied. "We know the gospel now and have stopped doing that."

Also in Wamena, I would come across many older women who were missing fingers. Not only had the death of close relatives used to be marked that way, but also that of important men in the tribe.

I had often heard people in Europe say that peoples like these, living so close to nature, were much happier than us in the western world. I became more and more convinced this was nothing but a romantic fallacy. Most anthropologists wouldn't live with the tribal people long enough to truly get through to the core of the culture. It was a different story with those who lived or grew up with them. A young friend with wisdom beyond his years would years later send shivers down my spine with his chilling conclusion:

"A friend of mine described Papua as 'the heart of darkness' as we discussed growing up and living here. But a newcomer would first be overwhelmed by the green expanse, the towering mountains, and the beautiful smiles of the people. The adventure, the laughter, and the beauty is a thin layer floating on a lake of molten fear. Eventually, one slips through the carpet into a terrifying experience that threatens to suck us into the abyss."

Walker Wisley, 13 years old, Bokondini, Ob Anggen School.

No Wrenching, No Flying—Mechanics Matter

Hans came into the cramped office. "Mausi, can you help me, please? I dropped a special washer, and now I don't have time to look for it in the grass. I need to close the cowlings before it starts raining."

Dark clouds were gathering, and soon there would be a tropical downpour, making work on the helicopter impossible. I got up from my accounting books and walked over to the helicopter. For the next half hour, I searched the grass underneath it but didn't find the special washer made of expensive aviation approved metal, but only cockroaches.

The helicopters and the men working on them needed protection from the intense equator sun and tropical downpours. The offices were bursting at their seams in the small cabin-like building too. As much as we dreaded taking on this mammoth task, a hangar had to be built. None of us had much experience in building, let alone in another country and culture with a different language.

Some maintenance jobs on the helicopter could be performed outside. Statically balancing the main rotor was not one of those. The conditions had to be right without any wind, which would have knocked about the rotor blades, making the task impossible.

"At least this time we can use the neighbors' hangar to take the rotor off," Hans told me once when this work was due again. "Last time when you were still in Germany, we hired a Caterpillar wheel loader to lift off the rotor. Man, we were sweating! One wrong move by the operator and the huge bucket could have come crashing down on the heli!"

We had to wait until all the day's work was done by the owners of the hangar next door. Then the complete eleven-meter long rotor was taken off with the help of a block and tackle attached to a pipe protruding from a roof-truss of the small wooden hangar. The helicopters were too tall to fit inside. The rotor was then carried into the storage room, along with the tools. The actual balancing was a matter of several hours. I joined Hans and Jan for this night shift. We watched the rotor seesawing and finally leveling out on a small hardened steel ball. Meanwhile, rats climbed up and down the piles of rice bags waiting to be flown to the mountain villages. The mosquitoes and the smell of supplies and rat pee didn't make the scene any more romantic. We were thankful we could borrow the hangar, but also glad when the job was completed just before four in the morning.

Helicopter maintenance was a difficult and responsible task under the best of circumstances. Back in Germany, during his training at a helicopter maintenance company, an event had shown Hans what could happen if things went wrong. That day Hans had come home from work shaken up and distraught. He had worked on a helicopter flight control component by himself. Although he had asked a licensed inspector to check his work, the machine had hurriedly been pushed out the hangar for a test flight with all the technicians on board. The customer's pilot, who had seemed unfamiliar with the aircraft, had then failed to perform the mandatory check for "freedom of controls" during the ground run. The flight around the pattern had gone well at first, but when the pilot began to descend, the collective stick needed for this maneuver was stuck. The mechanics had held their breath. After a struggle with the controls, the pilot had managed to break the collective stick free by pushing hard all the way down to the panel, where it broke with a bang. This had instantly sent the helicopter falling toward the ground! Hans' life had flashed through his head like a film while a sickening realization had hit him: "I have killed us all!"

After moments of what felt like free fall and seemed like an eternity, the pilot managed to regain limited control and land the aircraft. At the ground, the inspector had shouted. "Hans, what have you done? I thought we were dead!"

A time of anxiety, sleep disturbances, and self-doubt had followed even though Hans had later been cleared of all wrongdoing in the incident. In fact, a design error had led to the near-fatal incident. A service bulletin had subsequently been issued to deal with this problem on all helicopters of that make and model. Even though Hans hadn't caused the incident, he had been unable to find peace.

"I'm doing everything I can: I go to bed early so I get enough sleep and can concentrate on the job," Hans told me. "I work carefully, I always make sure all my tools are accounted for, and none of them are left behind in a machine which could block the controls. But everybody can make a mistake. And in this job a mistake can cost lives! Imagine if I make a mistake on the mission field and people get killed. I would definitely never want to do this job just to make a living."

It had been heartbreaking to see Hans in this condition of shock. Apart from the responsibility for lives, which weighed heavily on Hans' shoulders, there were legal implications too. The tools of all aviation maintenance personnel were marked with their initials or social security number, so if a tool was left behind in an aircraft and led to a crash, its owner could be prosecuted. In the aviation industry, with machines worth millions, time was money. Every job had to be done as quickly as possible with a narrow margin of error. Many of the workers seemed stressed, and so did the managers. The event had been a prime example of how many accidents come about, with many small errors linked together mounting to a catastrophe, which could have easily been prevented.

All we could do was ask God, who had called Hans to this work, to cover his back where he might fail. To get "back into the saddle" Hans had forced himself to go along on every flight he could to conquer his new fear of flying. After all, it was essential that a licensed mechanic would go on test flights to measure vibrations and gather diagnostic information.

Still, the traumatic stress of falling from the sky, while thinking he could have caused the death of three others as well, had taken its toll. Anxiety and panic attacks had persisted for weeks, no matter how hard Hans had prayed for God's help and peace. Other strange things had happened in the neighborhood including domestic violence and a subsequent suicide attempt in the flat below. None of Hans' attempts to talk sense into the abusive husband had worked, and there had been no peace in the house or neighborhood. None of Hans' prayers had seemed to help, and people had started to notice his changed personality.

After another terrible night of despair and feeling helpless, Hans had read this verse in the morning: "Therefore submit to God. Resist the devil and he will flee from you" (James 4:7).

Hans had realized what he had to do: "Satan, you have no right to disturb me. In the name of Jesus: Leave!" He had commanded. That very moment the peace returned, and Hans had learned a lesson in spiritual warfare. It seemed as if Satan had tried every trick to stop Hans from completing his training as a mission helicopter mechanic.

Helicopters were irreplaceable in the feat of reaching the last unreached and isolated Papuan tribes with the gospel. No matter how difficult the work would be and how much the enemy would try to stop it, it *had* to happen! While there would still be risks, a well set-up hangar would eliminate some and make helicopter maintenance much easier. With increasing flight requests and a ratio of three and a half hours of maintenance to one hour of flying, Hans had his work cut out for him.

There was a chain of people involved in reaching the unreached tribes and everybody had to do their part to make it happen. Many people back home prayed for the work and gave money. Then there were the people at headquarters and at the local offices who did their part to get visas and permits to keep operations going and communicate with supporters to keep them informed, etc. The pilots took the missionaries to their stations and delivered supplies. The mechanics kept the helicopters in airworthy condition to make that happen. And then there were the wives who kept things going at home, cooked nutritious food, made sure there were clean clothes and also kept in contact with supporters back home. My role didn't seem significant, but after I had heard that many people left the mission field because the wives couldn't cope, I started praying we'd never have to leave because of me.

I *needed* to function, so Hans could function so the helicopters would fly, and the missionaries could bring the Gospel to the people who were living in bondage and fear!

Hans and Jan at work

Wanted: Women, Land, and Pigs

The next guest who came to Wamena, and the first one who spent a night on our couch, was Brent. He came from Canada to work on dubbing the *JESUS* film in the Western Dani language (also called Lani). Here in Wamena, a different Dani dialect was spoken, but it was also a melting pot of people from different tribes. The village of Pyramid, about thirty kilometers down the Baliem Valley, was located in pure Western Dani territory.

After seeing Pyramid from a bird's-eye view on my first medevac flight, I couldn't wait to see it from the ground. So Hans and I volunteered to take Brent there by car to meet Scotty and Heidi, an American couple, who were running a program called EduVenture and knew the area well.

"Just be careful," we were warned. "Often people walk on the street, pigs run across coming out of the tall grass, or children run after a ball without looking for traffic."

Going with several vehicles would be even more dangerous, because often people would make room for the first one, but would not hear the next one, and then step back out in the street.

There was not only the obvious danger of people or animals getting injured or killed, but also the complicated and often violent situation following such cases. In the Papuan culture, a death or injury had to be paid for by the one who inflicted it, be it malicious or accidental—even if it was the injured person's fault. Payments were mostly made using pigs and sometimes cowry shells. In this day and age, the cowry shells were replaced by money in most parts of the island. People were still being killed in revenge if the matter could not be settled by other means. We heard about a missionary pilot and his family who rapidly had to be moved to another part of the island after a man had died of injuries sustained while crossing the Wamena runway and being hit on the head by the landing wheel of an airplane. We also learned that often people tried to stop cars and motorbikes on the road to demand money.

Any more happy thoughts anyone?

Still, the young man had to go to Pyramid, so we prayed and trusted God to protect us, the pedestrians, and the animals and to keep all scoundrels away.

"Daa! Daa!" A group of children on the side of the road jumped up to the driving car, giving me a fright.

"Minta gula-gula ka!" they yelled. This happened all along the way, and after a while, we relaxed when we realized they knew to stay out of harm's way and were just greeting us (Daa!) or asking for sweets (Minta gula-gula). We waved and smiled back.

Hans was used to driving on rough roads from his time in Albania. The spectacular scenery made up for being rattled around on the bumpy, narrow road. From the ground, the amazing Baliem Valley showed itself in yet another way, and it was wonderful to see the plains and the mountains, the plants, the rivers and streams, the hamlets, sweet potato gardens, people, and animals up close. Here and there was a stretch of tall dry grass blowing in the wind or a group of flat-topped trees reminding me of Africa. When we drove through such a shady little forest, we found it hosted a coffee plantation.

Wow, Lord, thank you for sending us to such a beautiful place!

After driving for over an hour, we arrived at Pyramid. Scotty and Heidi's house looked like an extended and more advanced version of a traditional Papuan *honai* (hut) with a small loft and a thatched roof. It was set on the grounds of the beautiful, tidy old mission complex. Inside the house, it was a bit dark but cozy and nice.

Pyramid was the nearest village to Wamena where the Western Dani language was spoken. The dialect of the Grand Valley people was different. Western Dani was one of the largest and most widely understood languages of this area so the *JESUS* film in this language would touch the hearts of a large people group. Scotty translated for Brent, who interviewed an elderly Dani man. We were allowed to listen and learn.

"For us Dani men, three things are most important," the man explained, "women, land, and pigs. That's what we need to survive and what most of our wars are about."

Later, we learned more about the implications of that statement. If a man had a lot of land, he needed the women to work in the gardens which would produce food for the families and the pigs. The more pigs someone had, the more wives he could buy, and the more friends he could make by giving pigs to people—thus gaining influence in the community of the clan and tribe.

A man could settle most societal or worldview matters with pigs. If someone got sick, a pig could be sacrificed to the evil spirits in the hope these would in return take the disease away. If a man killed somebody in a war, out of revenge, or by accident, he could compensate the victim's family by giving them pigs. He could buy another wife, preferably a very young one who would live long, make gardens, have many children, and raise many pigs and the circle would grow bigger. Pigs meant status, power, wealth, and security. Pigs weren't kept as a regular source of food. Traditionally, pig feasts were held only on rare occasions, like funerals, weddings, and ceremonies.

A Papuan hamlet

Often people wouldn't eat pork for a whole year. Many people suffered from protein deficiency if they weren't able to come by enough frogs, crayfish, possums, tree kangaroos, or other sources of protein. When they did consume large protein quantities during pig feasts, some ended up suffering protein shock. Apparently, this had been most severe in cases of cannibalism which used to be a widespread tradition in the Baliem Valley and had led to its nickname: Cannibal Valley. In the old days, the crops used to be limited as well, and many people had been malnourished and had suffered from debilitating diseases, large goiters, or open sores. When outsiders had started to settle in the Dani territory, they had also introduced many varieties of vegetables and sources of protein like legumes, peanuts, chickens, rabbits, and fish.

My Bumpy Journey as new "Jungle Cook"

On a sunny day in early June, a mission pilot poked his head into our office and made our day with his words and a smile. "I've got something I think you might like!"

Our five red boxes had arrived from Germany! I was as excited as a child at Christmas. It had taken five weeks for the boxes to arrive. It would be wonderful to have our things—including my fantastic kitchen machine. This piece of equipment should prove invaluable for me in Papua (and still is a blessing now). Since I hadn't known what to take to Papua and what to leave behind, Luana had sent me an email with some information and ideas. One comment stuck out: "An absolute must have for every homemaker is a good kitchen aid."

I had then asked around to find out what would be a good kitchen machine/food processor and kept coming back to this wonderful machine. In addition to blending, stirring, emulsifying, and kneading, it could also weigh, cook, steam, and grind meat. The downside was it cost a small fortune and was only available at a presentation—not from a store. Time had been running out for obtaining one of these machines before our departure, but my aunt who owned one had made inquiries.

"Sorry, Elke, there won't be another presentation in time before you leave," my aunt had learned. A few hours later she had called back.

"Elke, listen! The lady just called back, because she was asked to fill in for another presenter. You can go too, but it's tonight."

I was sure God had been working on my behalf. I had gone and signed the order form for the machine that night—just before the price went up.

I took the kitchen machine out of the box, put it in the kitchen with a big grin, and continued to unpack. We had padded the breakable items with towels and clothes and stuffed them with socks and washcloths. There was no point wasting space and weight with padding we wouldn't use later on.

"Go figure, the glass teapot is in one piece and the only thing broken is a plastic lid," I said to Hans. That night, I covered the table with a newly unpacked tablecloth and cooked a special meal in the kitchen machine: steamed broccoli, potatoes, and cheese sauce. I'm sure the guys would have thought it was even more special if there had been meat in it—but it was a start. Soon after, we got a gas stove and oven, which made my life so much easier and our meals a lot more interesting.

"Fantastic! Now I can bake bread if Ibu Marice is unwell," I said to Hans when the stove was delivered. "And I can also bake cakes. I'm kind of getting over the store-bought cookies."

I still hadn't managed to get the wood oven going, and depending on the weather, even Jan had been unsuccessful with it. It took some time and a lot of wood to heat the oven. Unfortunately, my joy didn't last long.

"What in the world is this?" I vented to Hans after several failed baking attempts. "Each time I want to bake a cake, it comes out burnt on the outside and not done in the middle!"

I got close to giving up baking altogether. It turned out I had been naïve enough to believe that whatever temperature I adjusted the knob to, would be the temperature in the oven. Once I got my hands on an oven thermometer, I found out no matter which setting I used, the temperature was always 200 °C (nearly 400 °F), a lot more than my average cake should have had. I then found out, if I kept an eye on the flame, while slowly turning the knob to where it almost turned off, I could lower the temperature, but I had to check often to see if the flame was still on. I got used to it—like so many other things. Later on, I'd learn tricks like rotating the bread and cake in the oven for even baking, covering the top with foil to keep it from burning, or putting a wire rack under the baking dishes to allow for better hot air circulation, etc.

From then on, between my kitchen machine, the accompanying cookbook, and my newly acquired improvisation skills, we would have hamburgers, steamed vegetables, sauces, soups, pizza, bread in all shapes and forms, powdered sugar, jams, cookies, and cakes. And all that even when the wood ran out. We started gaining our weight back, which we had lost while our digestive systems were still getting used to life in a different part of the planet.

"Elke, I'm getting some fish from the coast," Luana told me, "would you like some too?"

Since I had been shockingly uninterested in learning to cook from my grandmother, my experience with cooking fish was limited to frying battered frozen fish from a package—and even that had gone up in black smoke once.

"Thanks a lot, but I'm afraid I wouldn't know what to do with a whole fish!"

"Don't worry; Jan knows what to do. He can help you."

The fish was delivered and Jan, who had studied to be a quality security manager in fisheries, turned out to be our resident expert in seafood. He scraped off the scales and cut up the fish—not without the occasional grumble. We cooked some for dinner and froze the rest.

Occasionally, Papuan men came to the door to sell us crayfish they had caught in the river. Luana showed me how to open, clean, and cook them. However, as much as I liked crayfish, putting a live animal in boiling water just didn't seem right! I tried breaking them in half with a quick twist which wasn't any more fun. Once, Hans tried to help, but he gave up after sending one flying across the kitchen after it pinched him with a flick of its tail. I decided to wait for frozen prawns on furlough.

What proved invaluable for our survival were two cookbooks. One, which I had bought at the missionary sale on my first day, was bilingual Indonesian and English and not only helped me with my language study, but it also contained conversion tables for degrees Fahrenheit and Celsius, for measurements like cups, ounces, liters, etc. and ideas for substituting unavailable ingredients. The other one was a yachting cookbook, which featured lots of great recipes you could cook from a limited pantry and in a tiny kitchen with just one or two cookers. During the time when I had only one fully working hot plate (the other one had lost half its heating element), this one came in handy, and French onion soup with bread and cheese became our favorite and my signature dish. Thankfully, Luana had informed me before our departure that bringing some favorite spices was a good idea, so I had the required "Provençal's" or mixed herbs.

When I purchased huge meat chunks from the butcher and had to cut them up, I was very thankful for the high-quality knives that had come in our boxes. I then used my kitchen machine to mince some of the meat, before carefully weighing portions into bags and then I would freeze the meat.

"Oh, I'd love to dig my teeth into a steak," Hans would often say, "but then my jaws hurt the next day!"

Beef certainly occurred more in Hans' daydreams than our meal plan, as it was not easy to get and the cows were mostly past their tender age. Not being able to properly age the meat in a cooling chamber added to the toughness. Years later, I learned beef could be aged in the fridge for three days by putting it in either stainless-steel or glass bowls with a loose cover (not airtight). My attempts to do this in plastic containers had failed miserably! Hammering it with a meat mallet or tenderizing it with papaya leaves or leaf powder also helped to a degree.

Unlike meat, vegetables were plentiful and always available. Powdered milk was a handy staple and could be used in many dishes, and also as a substitute for cream or even sour cream when mixed with water and a bit of vinegar. It was also useful for making yogurt. I used it to make sauces and mixed it with water and eggs in casseroles. Eggs were available most of the time, but many of them were rotten. I learned to always buy twice as many as I needed for a recipe and to open each egg into a cup, before adding it to the other ingredients. A good way to find out how old or fresh an egg was, was to put it into water. If it lay down on its side on the bottom, it was fresh, and if it floated on the top, it was old. Before I learned that trick, I sometimes had to hold my breath while running outside when an egg turned out to be green inside. The smell was revolting!

However, sometimes a foul smell came in through the kitchen window. An old overgrown truck had been left to decay on a neighboring empty lot, just outside the window. To make matters worse for the poor vehicle and for us, people had decided to make it the public toilet.

I worked at the office most days and went home to cook lunch before Jan and Hans came to eat. I loved these two treasures for appreciating whatever I cooked (with the odd exception, e.g. tomato soup with a "pepper imbalance").

"I have no idea what happened to the rice," I said to Jan and Hans. It had turned into a gray porridge with black dots, instead of the fragrant, grainy white I had expected.

"You didn't wash the rice first?" Jan asked me with wide eyes.

"Wash the rice? Why would I do that?"

In Germany, I had used packages of clean rice, sometimes in small plastic bags to cook small portions. I had put the bags in boiling water for twenty minutes and then taken them out to find the rice perfectly cooked. What had gone wrong? First, I hadn't looked for tiny stones in the rice, so our teeth were in danger. Secondly, I hadn't washed it about five times, being careful to avoid draining the rice along with the water and the bugs. Third, this rice was the kind Indonesians used for *bubur,* a kind of porridge given to sick people or young kids. I didn't know yet that only this kind of rice was sold in pre-packed one-kilogram bags and the normal kind for regular meals was available in five to fifty-kilogram bags or got scooped out of one and into a black plastic bag on demand. We took out the bugs and ate the rice anyway, and I progressed another few degrees on my learning curve.

The flour had to be sifted because it was full of weevils. It looked disgusting to have all those bugs crawling around in the sieve, but I got used to it. Later on, I found it was best to buy a large bag of flour that didn't smell bad, sift the contents into airtight containers, and then repeat the process a few weeks later when all the weevil eggs had hatched but weren't able to lay eggs themselves yet. Sometimes we got whole wheat flour from over the border in Papua New Guinea. Sifting it would have defeated its purpose since we wanted to retain the nutrients and fiber of the bran and germ, so we put it in the freezer to kill off any bugs.

Fruit and vegetables had to be disinfected in bleach water or *PK* (potassium permanganate) for twenty minutes, and the rainwater had to be filtered or boiled before we could drink it to avoid getting sick. After a while, we got so used to these extra chores that we didn't even think twice about them (unless we had forgotten to fill the water filter the night before and were thirsty in the morning). Later, on home assignments, it even felt strange to drink tap water and only wash the salad instead of disinfecting it. Yet, people back home still couldn't quite understand, why I needed a house helper.

Fruits and vegetables weren't sold in shops, so I bought them at little corner markets in town. Sometimes, produce was delivered to our house, but not always to my delight. Early one morning, there was a knock on our back door. I opened it and saw someone slipping past me into the house from the corner of my eye. When I turned around, there he sat: a skinny Papuan man with a neon pink comb in his hair. He proceeded to put vegetables on our linoleum-covered dining room floor and didn't seem to notice the puzzled look on our faces. To get rid of him, I bought some of his overpriced vegetables and he left. About two minutes later, there was another knock on the door. The same man squeezed past me, but this time he walked straight into the living room where Hans was reading his Bible before breakfast. We didn't understand much of what the man was saying, but he pointed down toward his brown trousers. The seams of the lower portion had been neatly unstitched. Apparently, he wanted to convince us he was wearing rags and needed our help to buy new clothes. Somehow, Hans managed to escort him out the door politely.

The man kept coming, and each time he was as annoying as the first time. Sometimes, he came on Sundays, and we would tell him we didn't usually buy anything on our day of rest. He wouldn't take no for an answer and kept coming.

No Ordinary Desk Job

June 5, 2000

I went to the office to work on the accounting as I did most days. It felt like it had been decided only a few days ago that I was to help Jan with the finances for the new hangar building and already the first receipt came in.

"Oh, boy, where do I start?"

"Don't worry, we set it up together, and you'll manage," Luana reassured me. "Jan and I can always help you. Here are the books you'll need."

She handed me a numbered receipt book with several carbon pages and a thick, blank A4 accounting book. We went to the bank together and opened an account for the building process. Jan set up the accounts on the computer so we could enter all the payments for the reports to headquarters. It was a daunting task, but at least I wasn't alone. In the following days and weeks, we would have meetings with all the people involved in the building project. We discussed and decided which materials, color schemes, etc. to use. The contractor hired local workers, and some qualified tradesmen were brought in from another island. Not only did our hangar need to be built, but a small residential house needed to be demolished and a replacement built at a different spot on the airport grounds.

June 6, 2000

"Hi guys, how are ye? Have you looked outside yet?" As it often happened, a mission airplane pilot dropped into the office to have a brief chat and a cup of coffee with us. Since Wamena was the hub of the entire mountain region and was only reachable by air, many things happened right before our eyes at the airport. Sometimes, it was hard to focus on the work at hand. Also, the noise of the Fokker F-27, Hercules, and Transall planes was infernal. We went outside to have a look, and this time a huge crowd of Papuan people had gathered on the airport tarmac. Most of them were dressed up in feathers and traditional attire and their bodies were painted. Others had accessorized with white sneakers, sunglasses, or jerseys of soccer clubs.

"They've come to welcome back a delegation of Papuan politicians returning from a big Congress," one of our friends filled us in.

More groups came running from the villages around Wamena. The people were singing, dancing, running back and forth, and some were parading their bows and arrows in military fashion. I had learned from the first day on, to always have our pocket camera on me, because you never knew what photo opportunities would come up.

"Elke, this is a good day to stay home," Luana told me on the phone another day. "They're expecting a huge demonstration with thousands of warriors coming into town. If you must go out anyway for some reason, remember to stay away from crowds. Jan can make the payments if any bills should come in."

"Sure, thanks a lot."

I hung up and prayed. Demonstrations, but not of such proportion, frequently happened with warrior groups armed with bows, arrows, and spears, coming to Wamena running through the streets, hollering and hooting raucous high-pitched shrieks. We didn't dare imagine what would happen if the indigenous warriors, police, or military would start shooting to kill. The tension was running high, but so far, only warning shots had been fired into the air. Most times after we all prayed, an exceptionally strong rain shower would come down on the protestors' largely naked skin—which combined with the cool afternoon winds—dissolved the tension and dispersed the crowds.

This situation didn't give us a warm and fuzzy feeling, as Brian would put it, but seeing how well he and his family handled it helped us to stay calm too. They were prepared, alert, and trusted God with the rest. We, westerners, weren't the targets of the conflict, and we tried our best to keep out of harm's way. Other than that, the demonstrations didn't affect our daily lives too much. Brian, as a base leader, always functioned best in tense situations and he knew what to do.

"Have a backpack ready for each of you in case things come to a head, and we need to evacuate," Brian had recommended from the start. "When push comes to shove, you need to have passports, money, computer backups, some toiletries, and clothes ready to go."

I hated the thought of ever having to use those backpacks, but I was also glad we didn't have the responsibility for children or animals which would have made the situation even more stressful. It was interesting to see how the situation affected people in different ways. Some were nervous; others were prepared, and yet others were in denial that anything could happen and didn't prepare at all.

Phone conversations with my mother were a balm to my soul in all of this. She often said things like: "Nothing extraordinary is happening here, I'm just making strawberry jam."

While life here consisted of unexpected changes and uncertainty, at least back home things were still normal.

While working on bookkeeping one day, a noisy motorbike drove down the street. Suddenly, the sound changed and then died.

That must have been an accident! I jumped up from my chair and looked out the window. People were screaming and crowding in at the scene. We soon learned a motorcyclist under the influence of sniffing glue fumes had crashed into a lady walking on the street. The woman was killed instantly. The following day we saw smoke rising from across the airstrip where the lady had lived. The funeral was held at her family's home, and the woman was cremated on a wood pile in her front yard. The family demanded to be paid fifty pigs by the motorcyclist who had caused the woman's death. Until that was settled, the clan held demonstrations with war chants for several days.

There was no way of just going to work at the office, closing the door, and getting the job done. Whether you were at home, out in the streets, or at work, the things that happened around you ruled most of your day. I had to get used to the fact that the plans I made for the day usually changed before nine o'clock in the morning. Sometimes, it was frustrating.

"Don't worry," Luana said "Someone once said to me: 'If you get one thing done on your to-do list every day, be content.' There's no way you can get them all done under these circumstances."

"That's a good way of looking at it. And it might prevent us from getting stomach ulcers," I replied with a crooked smile.

Hans often commented how in Switzerland people run their lives and make plans; things work according to plan and get done. Here, however, we were often ruled by circumstances.

No matter how discouraged we were or what the week had thrown at us, some good food, fellowship, laughter, prayer, and hearing about Brian's experiences flying to the different mission stations usually picked up our morale again during our weekly fellowship nights.

What are they doing there?

I walked to the office in the morning and saw a group of men working on something in the middle of an empty garden. On my way back home to prepare lunch, I got my answer. The biggest part of a brand new honai—a traditional Papuan hut—had been erected. At night, the whole group walked past our house carrying their tools as well as bows and arrows over their shoulders and hooting and singing their impressive tribal chants. Early the following morning, the group returned. This time they were carrying large grass bundles on their heads which they deposited by the new house to be used as roofing material.

"That's amazing," I said to Jan. "They all work together and put up almost the entire honai in one day."

"Yes, but the owner is busy for several months beforehand getting all the materials ready. When that's done, the whole clan pitches in, and they erect the honai in no time."

In my culture, house building was done quite differently. People would save up money, get a loan from the bank, hire an architect, apply for a building approval at the council (which could take half a year to obtain), and hire tradesmen who would do the work. When the house would be finished, they'd invite their friends to a house-warming party. I had already learned this culture wasn't individualistic like most of our western ones had become, but rather, the family and clan was essential for every aspect of life. People here hadn't had the option of hiring others for money, but everybody relied on the community. While the women were the ones who worked in their gardens alone day in and day out, most men needed group dynamics to get things done.

In the Papuan culture, the roles of the men and women were clearly defined. Emancipation of women was still in the beginning stages. On the roads outside town, I often observed the same scene: a man walking along—his hands behind his back with an ax hanging over his shoulder. Several meters behind him a woman walked bent over under a heavy load with two to three net bags slung from her head over her back, filled with sweet potatoes, greens, sugarcane, or other vegetables, and firewood on top. Sometimes, there was also a baby in one of the net bags or a toddler sitting on the woman's shoulders on top of the pile of bulging bags. It never ceased to amaze me how much these thin, petite ladies were able to carry and how hard they worked. In this culture, a woman was valued by the weight she could carry. Helping a woman carry a load would have embarrassed her and made her feel inadequate.

Shopping, Wamena-Style

June 10, 2000

"Wow, that's probably the biggest pig I've ever seen!" I watched a dark, gray hog "decorated" with bright red dots of betel nut spit leisurely walk across the market area.

Jan, who was house sitting for Brian and his family, needed rabbit food and had taken me along to the *Pasar Baru*—the vast market a few kilometers out of town. So far, I hadn't felt confident to check it out on my own.

The market itself was huge and reminded me of a filthy train station. Crowds of people were sitting or moving between long rows of tiled, concrete tables with roofs over them. Papuan ladies of all ages and a few older men were selling vegetables, fruit, and other things. They were sitting on the ground underneath the tables on dirty old rice bags. I tried hard not to step on anybody's toes or ruin a stack of tomatoes. The produce was presented in neat piles. The fruit and vegetables looked beautiful, but I couldn't get over how dirty everything was.

Now I know why we go through the trouble of soaking the fruit and vegetables in PK!

(And we were still getting sick from time to time). Outside the market, we had seen women washing their produce in the ditches next to the road. I made a mental note: *the cleaner the vegetables look, the more dangerous they might be from contaminated water.*

When we paid for the vegetables, I was surprised to see where the money went. Most of the women put it on the ground under the rice bags they presented the vegetables on. Most male vendors would pull the change out from under their hair nets, made in the same way and of the same plant fiber, as the traditional net bags. I wondered where else money was kept and made another mental note: *I must thank Luana for advising me always to wash my hands when I come home and especially after handling money!*

My next discovery made me stop in my tracks. In between all the Papuan ladies with their beautiful brown skin and black hair, there was a white child with a nasty sunburn. The boy's hair was as frizzy as the other people's, but it was a light blond color, and his eyes were blue. The poor child was an albino for whom living at this altitude with the intense equatorial sun meant a constant sunburn.

Jan had gotten what he needed, and we were about to leave when all the vendors and buyers started running in one direction in the market. Jan went to find out what was going on.

"Looks like two veggie ladies got into a fist fight."

We resisted the temptation to go watch and went on our way.

On my next trip to the market, I hardly noticed the dirt but focused on the beautiful pineapples, papayas, citrus fruits, passion fruit, tomatoes, cucumbers, onions, garlic, cauliflower, carrots, beans, and many other varieties of fruit and vegetables representing the fertile Baliem Valley.

However, as much as I liked the variety of produce in the Pasar Baru, I rarely went. What discouraged me, apart from the distance, was the street kids who wanted to watch the motorbike or car for money and cover it with dirty cardboard to keep it from getting hot in the sun, or to carry my bags for a fee. While this happened in town as well, it was worse here.

"I watch, I watch!" about five children shouted, trying to be the first and the loudest. It wasn't that I didn't want to pay for their services, but it was sad to see them bully, push, and shove each other over a job or the payment. They were clothed in rags and had runny noses—and they weren't in school. Sadly, most of them wouldn't spend the money they earned on nutritious food, soap, or clothes, but on glue which they sniffed to get high. It hurt me every time to see these precious boys in such misery. Why were their families and clans not taking care of them?

Beauty, Hardship, and Miracles

June 20, 2000

From the battered, green Helimission Daihatsu, I marveled at the views of the Baliem River, the tall mountains on our right, and the light green hills on the far side of the river. We were driving down the Baliem Valley in the opposite direction of Pyramid toward Kurima where the strong afternoon winds came from. Heike, a single German teacher I had met on the coast, had come to Wamena with a friend. Curt, a single missionary who knew the area well, had agreed to guide them on a tour and I was invited along. Sure, there was lots of work to do at home and the office, but opportunities to get to know the area wouldn't come along every day.

We drove on, past gardens, square fishponds, and streams rushing downhill past big boulders on their way to the Baliem River in the valley below. We crossed over a giant landslide that had washed out a mountain and made its way down to the river. The almost white silt, mixed with rocks, had already dried up, so it was easy to cross by off-road car. After driving for about half an hour, Curt stopped the car.

"This is as far as we can drive. Part of the road and a couple of bridges were swept away by the river."

He parked the car on a small grassy plateau where people and several *angkots* had congregated. Angkots were the main transportation for the local people between Wamena and the villages with road access. They were battered, old minivans which would be packed with people, animals, and produce, some of the latter strapped to the roof. People from all over the mountain area would walk here to catch a ride to Wamena or beyond.

We started walking. The sky was blue, and we enjoyed the beautiful scenery while walking on the old dirt road—which mostly ran parallel to the Baliem River further down the valley. We scrambled down and up the sides of the dark, gray riverbed from a Baliem tributary where it had washed out the road and the bridge, but thankfully, the river didn't carry too much water this time. The terrain narrowed considerably after we had left the wide-open space of the Grand Valley.

"This is why Wamena gets the strong afternoon winds," Curt explained. "The wind comes through here like through a funnel."

The people we met on the way were friendly. Some were working in their gardens or carrying loads, while others were sitting around chatting or playing simple tunes on their self-made ukuleles. Others roasted corn on fires and sold it. After walking for about forty-five minutes, we left the main trail and walked up a steep footpath between the gardens. My shirt was sticking to my back under the backpack which seemed to get heavier by the minute. It was hot. I tried to control my breathing to make it to the top, all the while waving off flies.

We reached a more pleasant, level section of the path. I put a drop of ammonia solution onto a mosquito bite and hoped it was as good at relieving the itching and preventing malaria and other diseases, as we had been told. Being a cautious person, I had brought enough drinking water, some food, sunscreen lotion, insect repellent, a rain jacket, and a camera. I rather felt like a wimp when I looked at Curt, an experienced mountain hiker, who was only wearing sandals, shorts, and a T-shirt and hadn't brought anything. We came to a spot near a little stream where the path was blocked by a fence but had a little wooden crutch as a foothold to climb it.

"How funny," I said. "In Europe, we make fences to keep our animals in, and here the people use them to keep pigs out!"

All day long the pigs in Papua roamed around freely, ate whatever they found, and dropped things wherever they walked. If they managed to get into a garden, they wreaked havoc in it, hence the fortification. In the evenings, the pigs would go home to their owners and be fed sweet potatoes. Here the term "free range" was at a totally different level than in most parts of the world!

After about an hour, we reached the Polimo airstrip and mission station. It consisted of a polyclinic, a missionary house, and a school with a dormitory for women and girls. We walked over to the mission house and were welcomed and invited in by Sister Kaethe, a German lady in her early sixties. Kaethe and her Dutch housemate and colleague, Trijntje, had invited us to come to Polimo for coffee when I had first met them at the Helimission office.

We spent an enjoyable hour with afternoon coffee and good talks at the cozy mission house. I felt strangely reminded of my grandparents' house. Many of the mission houses I visited later gave me this same warm nostalgic feeling. I loved the old-fashioned charm and peaceful, quiet atmosphere most of them had where time seemed to have stood still. These places were far removed from the busy, noisy town of Wamena in many ways. In Kaethe and Trijntje's house, there were many books, and vinyl LP's, and to my utter amazement, there was a TV, a VCR player, and many videotapes of German TV shows I had grown up with. (The difference was there hadn't been the need to organize the fuel and start a generator when I had wanted to watch them, as there was here.)

"Well, I'd love to stay and chat more, but there's a major thundercloud building up overhead, and we should really get going," Curt urged. "The paths get quite slippery when it rains, and the river might flood."

The other problem was, in these parts (four degrees south of the equator) dusk lasted only about half an hour, and there were no streetlights anywhere. While packing sunscreen lotion and water bottles for a hot day, I hadn't thought of a flashlight. We certainly didn't want to lose daylight in this terrain. I had no idea then that the gentle stream we had crossed earlier was the notorious Yetni River—which was prone to flash floods and could suddenly turn into a raging torrent after a rainstorm carrying along boulders and crushing everything in its path. I shuddered when I thought of a tourist who had taken a risk against local people's advice and died a few weeks ago. Kaethe, on the other hand, had survived here for over twenty years. Some risks were worth taking for ministry, but not just for having a nice outing.

We made it home safe and dry that day after a beautiful trip to Polimo. I thought about the different situation the ladies in Polimo were in. I was getting sore muscles from a nice walk to their house, but they had to do that walk each time they wanted to get in and out of their station, while they were about twice my age. I had struggled to descend the steep slopes in dry weather on my feet instead of my bottom, while they had to get down no matter if it was muddy and wet. We were able to hop into the car, once we arrived at the road, but they had to wait for an angkot to arrive and fill up with passengers before they could leave.

Over the years, we were amazed at the perseverance and dedication of many single women who spent decades of their lives in these rugged mountains and isolated mission stations. They quietly did their work, treating the sick, delivering babies, teaching, encouraging, equipping, translating the Bible, and loving the Papuan people. They are unsung heroes, but they won't be forgotten by the people they cared for and whose lives they saved, touched, changed, and enriched.

Nowadays, missionaries often stay on the field for only a few years because of their family situation. While some of these single ladies married later, others stayed in those places for twenty, thirty, or even forty years. I couldn't imagine what sorts of hardships a life like that entailed. I had heard that Kaethe had even broken her neck once and lived to tell about it.

I contacted Kaethe while working on this book.

"Well, if you want to write about this, you have to get the whole story right with all the good that came out of it," Kaethe said on the phone.

What good can come out of a broken neck? "Okay, can you tell me?" I asked. "I'm taking notes."

"Sure. I was on a walk with two Papuans. We crossed a landslide which covered the road. I took a wrong step and fell headfirst into a riverbed. My two shocked companions let me get up and walk the two hours back to the house by myself, keeping an eye on me."

"That's unusual," I interrupted. "We've seen the way people pulled on a guy who had fallen from a tree."

"I think it was God's protection they didn't do that. We suspect this was why I didn't end up dead or a quadriplegic," Kaethe continued. "For a few days, the mission leadership and a doctor debated what to do with me, and I was flown to the coast and back to Polimo without a clear diagnosis. They didn't suspect broken vertebrae because I was still able to move my hands. So I walked around and slept in my normal bed for several days."

Eventually, Kaethe had been examined further and diagnosed with a fractured second vertebra in her neck and compression fractures of the fourth and fifth thoracic vertebrae! Kaethe had then been airlifted to Germany where she had been immobilized for three months.

"That must have been horrible for an active person like you," I said.

"Actually, I've never felt closer to Jesus during any other time in my life. It felt as if He was right beside me, holding my hand."

"Wow!"

"And the other amazing thing was I had a re-entry permit to Indonesia for three months and was able to return just in time. Otherwise, I would have lost my visa and not returned to Papua. The doctors agreed I could go back, saying that an active lifestyle would be beneficial."

When Kaethe was telling me this, she was already retired back in Germany. She still suffered some pain but was getting massages and other special treatment paid by the insurance. She also received an additional amount to her regular pension because of this work-related accident which made her retirement a bit more comfortable.

Another good outcome of the incident had been that it had given the opportunity for good talks and discussions with the Papuan people after Kaethe's return to Papua. The people there wondered why God allowed difficult things to happen. Some suspected Kaethe had done something wrong and the Lord had therefore caused this to happen to her. People discussed Bible verses and their relationships with the Lord and with this white woman—who was as vulnerable as they were after all—grew. The mission doctor was given a new computer after this incident which made his work more effective.

"I'm so amazed and immensely thankful when I see how much good the Lord brought out of this situation!" Kaethe concluded, and I wiped a tear from my eye.

"And we know that all things work together for good to those who love God, to those who are the called according to His purpose."
Romans 8:28

How to Lubricate a Cog in the Machine

Although life wasn't always easy and I had much to learn, one thing was clear to me from the day I had set foot in Wamena: this was the place for me to be! Thanks to God, our friends, and my patient, experienced mentor, Luana, I had managed to survive despite my inexperience, and neither Hans nor I had starved. I was finding my way around Wamena and was becoming more and more confident. (Although executing cockroaches I found in the pantry brought me close to my limits, I was learning to adjust to these challenges including getting used to the fact that running water in the house was not a right, but a privilege which we didn't always enjoy, due to various factors). I was busy, integrated, and fulfilled. Life was fascinating, challenging, and full of surprises.

I was very glad I hadn't been deterred by any of the people who said things like: "If you're not a missionary in your home country, you also won't be one in another country."

I had long ago discovered that God would position the people He called to use the particular gifts He had given them. For some people, that wasn't evangelism, but rather, technical or bookkeeping skills, creating a nice home, preparing nutritious meals, and many more abilities people often didn't associate with missionary work. The pioneer missionaries and Bible translators in the tribes were the spearhead of the mission effort but needed a whole "shaft" behind them. Every link in the chain to the unreached tribes counted. I had never in my life seen a single person give their life to the Lord because of my efforts. However, by freeing up Hans to do his helicopter maintenance and repair work, I contributed my part to the effort of bringing the gospel to people who never had a chance to hear it in their history.

There was no point in comparing myself to someone else, who did a better job or was better at interacting with the local people and discipling them, even though I would have loved to be able to do that more. If Hans were able to do his work, missionaries would be able to physically and spiritually reach isolated tribes, and God's Word would go out to unreached people. That was what counted more than anything. It was my calling. If I had wanted my own ministry, for which I would be acknowledged and get praised, that main goal might have suffered. My most important job was making sure things ran as smoothly as possible at home so Hans could function well. I was a small cog in the machine, but I was content because even that small cog was needed, important, and appreciated. I also enjoyed working at the office and occasionally helping with hands-on work on the helicopters was a special treat.

Then, of course, there was the other side of the coin.

"Elke, Karina had a baby boy! They named him Daniel," my mother told me on the phone in the middle of June.

So far, I had been too busy to seriously miss my friends and family in Germany and had mainly been excited about telling them about my new life in this fascinating place by phone and email (sounds easier than it was—it could take days to get a short message through). I wasn't even homesick too much. This phone call changed everything, and now I felt the separation and distance with full force. My brother's son Daniel was my first nephew.

While I could imagine the facial expressions of my family members I talked to on the phone, I had never seen Daniel, I had never held him, and I couldn't communicate with him by phone or email. I didn't see everybody's shining eyes when they interacted with him (or the dark rings under their eyes from sleepless nights). The realization hit me: I wouldn't see my brother's first child until he'd be three years old! Photos and news were a big help, but I wasn't part of the joy, the changing family dynamics, and most of all, I didn't get to see and hold baby Daniel.

I loved my new life and work. But I also had to deal with seeing poverty and misery all around me without being able to help much, since there were just too many suffering people. I saw my beloved husband weighed down under a huge workload. The difficult shopping situation, having limited ingredients for cooking, and every task taking a long time to accomplish, took a lot of patience and drained me of energy. The constant threat of unrest in town was unnerving. We all needed ways to relax and relieve stress to maintain our mental balance and emotional stability.

"If I don't get a guitar from somewhere soon, I'll go nuts," I said to Luana one day.

I hadn't been aware how much singing and playing the guitar—preferably, when nobody was around—was a stress relief for me.

"Johannes left his guitar in the storage shed. Why don't you email him and ask if you can use it as long as he is away?" Luana suggested.

I contacted Johannes, and he kindly agreed. When I opened up the case, I couldn't believe what I saw: It was a kind of guitar I had always wanted to have, but couldn't afford. God had again provided above and beyond. For over a year, I would be able to use this beautiful guitar at home, during the Sunday fellowship times, and at ladies' meetings. Downloading emails for twenty minutes on end, with the dial-up connection breaking off several times, no longer tried my sanity, but I took it as extra time to play the guitar and relax.

I loved to play all the new songs I was learning. A foul mood was no match for a praise song, and wouldn't survive the first verse. Meaningful songs brought comfort, new hope, and joy. The words I sang helped me shift my eyes away from the difficult circumstances and to focus on Jesus again. Our relationship with the Lord was the most important factor in surviving and thriving in our new life and setting. Daily Bible reading and prayer was vital for our spiritual life. For me—much unlike for Hans who doesn't really like music—songs were like the icing on the cake during my (in that case not so) quiet times.

Time spent with friends or in nature also kept me out of mischief.

Hans rarely had time for a hobby, but sometimes on Sundays, he and Jan worked on a balsa model plane kit we had brought from Germany.

Celebrating a Life Well-Lived

End of June 2000

We had received the sad news that Len, who had been a helicopter pilot with Helimission, had passed away in the USA. Now, Len's widow and children had come back to Wamena for a few weeks to pack up their house, spend some time with their friends, and bring closure to their life in Papua, which had come to an abrupt end when Len had been evacuated because of his brain tumor about six months earlier.

"What should we wear for the funeral?" I asked some friends, "I didn't bring any black clothes."

"Oh, don't worry, just regular Sunday clothes will do. People here never wear black for funerals."

In Germany, everybody went to funerals in black, the men in black suits with a white shirt and a black tie. If somebody chose to wear a bright color for a funeral (which was almost unheard of), that would be the talk of the town for a while.

When we arrived at the venue, Len's beautiful blond widow, Janie, dressed in a light blue summer dress, greeted us.

"You must be Hans. And what's your name?"

We would have been team members if Len hadn't passed away.

After the introductions, we went into the meeting hall where many missionaries from different parts of Papua had assembled. I looked around the room full of people in summer clothes and listened to the moving stories different people told about Len. He must have had a great sense of humor since there was as much laughter as there were tears during the service. Janie shared how she had lived through the time of her husband falling ill, the evacuation to the USA, and his passing. I could hardly look at the beautiful, young kids. It was heartbreaking to think they would have to grow up without their father! We regretted not having met Len. Without him and his flying experience in Papua, the start would have been much harder for the other helicopter pilots.

How nice to celebrate somebody's life, instead of just mourning.

"Can you imagine what it must be like to not only lose your partner, but also your whole life as you know it?" Hans asked during dinner.

"I know! It's bad enough when that happens in your home country, but at least people still have their friends, family, and church, the kids can keep going to the same school, and so on."

Len's family now had to pack up their life, sell their things, and leave. Nothing would be the same. Len had been the holder of the visa, which allowed the whole family to stay in the country. It would lapse in a few weeks' time. What a tough reality to face.

Balm and Poison

"Elke, one family has to go to Papua New Guinea to get their visa renewed," Luana told me on the phone. "What they usually do is go to the grocery shops there and get all the things we don't—or rarely—get here, like wholemeal flour, cream cheese, whipping cream, and the like. They have offered to bring some back for us too, so if you like, you can put an order in. We should give Kimberley the money in advance because we can't expect her to be out-of-pocket with so much money for everybody."

"Good point. Sounds great, thanks a lot for letting me know."

What a nice opportunity. I had learned to substitute ingredients, for instance using powdered milk with a bit of water instead of cream in soups and sauces, but having some whipped cream on cake or fruit would be such a treat for our palates and our hearts. And having some whole wheat bread would do our health good. I put my order in and about a week later it was delivered.

"Now, what we need to do next is write Kimberly a nice thank-you card," Luana suggested, "She went out of her way for us, and we should let her know we really appreciate it."

Brilliant advice. I hadn't even thought of that yet. Luana was forever writing thank-you cards to their supporters as well, and I wondered how she kept up with it, despite her huge workload. I found it difficult to find the time for writing our thank-you cards in the busy days full of surprises.

"Grace ends where responsibility starts," Luana often said.

Yes, I needed to make this a priority. Even though we never knew if the letters would get to their destination or how long they would take, we needed to try. (Luana had first taken me to the post office on May 24 where we had found the Christmas parcels for the team sent from Europe and the USA in November!) Some of our supporters might wonder if we were even receiving the donations they were sending to keep us on the field. We appreciated their faithful prayers and gifts so much. They needed to know what a vital role they were playing in bringing the gospel and physical help to the Papuan people. It was obvious we all depended on each other. We needed our faithful prayer supporters, and we needed each other to survive and thrive in this difficult place. Most of all, we needed God's help, provision, and guidance.

I'm sure it was a huge chore for Kimberley to do the shopping for part of the mission community, but she knew how much it would mean to her sisters and to herself to have these extra things to make life easier or just a bit more pleasant, so she did it. I'm sure Luana had more than enough to do as it was, but she always made sure I was doing fine, and things were going well with us. I could ask her or other ladies in the community for advice, often with trivial things—like figuring out what caster sugar was (we didn't use that in Germany). This would make a difference to what Hans would find on the table when he came home from a long, stressful day of work. Hans did his part with the helicopters' maintenance as well as many other tasks and thus relieved Brian, while I had started to free up Luana by taking over some finance work. We all depended on each other.

"What does supplication mean? Or petition, or to consecrate?" I wondered. I needed a dictionary for the church services and the English language ladies' Bible study. While this weekly afternoon meeting was an oasis for me both spiritually and socially, it was also demanding. I slowly learned the biblical terms which hadn't been included in the English classes at school.

Back in Germany, I had wondered how to live in the Indonesian and Papuan cultures which were distinctly different. Now, it turned out my biggest initial adjustment was interacting with people from other western cultures which I hadn't anticipated. Since we hadn't been able to learn Indonesian before coming here because of an extreme staff shortage, my communication with the locals was limited for the time being. Therefore, I relied on the English-speaking community. I was glad for the other ladies' grace toward me. I'll never know how often I put my foot in my mouth with my comments, or when I didn't know how to reply to questions or comments which seemed foreign to me. What was ruder: to say the wrong thing or say nothing at all?

Unfortunately, there wasn't always just love, support, and grace amongst us expats, but once in a while, there was distrust, envy, and negativity. It made me sad to realize that, but then again, why was I surprised? Somehow, it had been in the back of my mind that all missionaries were holy and near-perfect. But that didn't make sense, now, did it? I was here too! We were all human beings, and all of us were out of our comfort zones and under a lot of pressure, one way or another. Many were carrying emotional baggage from the past as well, and we all had to cope with a foreign culture. Just as the help and support we were giving each other were a balm for the soul — in the absence of fellowship with our families and friends back home — slander and negativity were poison for the soul and for relationships. Grace and forgiveness were vital for us to get along. Other times, we needed the courage to say, "I'm sorry" when we had been wrong.

I had a choice to make every day: would my words and deeds be uplifting, encouraging, helpful, thankful, or correcting or would they be hurtful, demeaning, and destructive?

"But no man can tame the tongue. It is an unruly evil, full of deadly poison. With it we bless our God and Father, and with it we curse men, who have been made in the similitude of God. Out of the same mouth proceed blessing and cursing. My brethren, these things ought not to be so. Does a spring send forth fresh water and bitter from the same opening? Can a fig tree, my brethren, bear olives, or a grapevine bear figs?
Thus no spring yields both salt water and fresh."
James 3:4-5 and 8-12

"Pleasant words are like a honeycomb, Sweetness to the soul and health to the bones."
Proverbs 16:24

Point X-Ray

Early July 2000

"Have a safe trip, Brian! And don't get eaten by cannibals." Brian was getting ready for an exciting flight. While we joked, we were also worried. Contacting isolated tribes for the first times was always unpredictable.

Despite all the uncertainties and tension in Wamena with demonstrations and the prospect of evacuating if things escalated, our work was continuing on. A team of missionaries was ready to be flown to the "Point X-Ray" area for a final survey before building a new mission station there. Point X-Ray was a landmark for the pilots. Three rivers in the deep mountain gorges converged into one there, making it look like an X from bird's-eye view. The word for X in the radio alphabet is X-Ray, hence the name. None of the area's tiny hamlets were marked on a map or known by name, because until two years ago—apart from neighboring tribes—nobody knew they existed. Mike, a missionary working in a nearby tribe, had heard villagers talk about people living around Point X-Ray. He had seen their hamlets and gardens on flights over the area. People from the tribe he worked in had contacted the X-Ray people but no mission work had commenced yet.

The Lord had answered Mike's subsequent prayers for missionaries to go and work amongst that tribe. Several young missionary families from Indonesia, the USA, and Canada had moved to Papua and started preparing to work in an unengaged tribe. Stephen and Tim, two of those young missionaries, had met up with Mike who had told them all he knew about the tribe and helped them on their way to find it. During survey trips to the general Point X-Ray area in 1998 and 1999, the men had made first contacts with some tribal people and even treated a few horrific injuries of people without healthcare.

For our team, the Point X-Ray area brought a new challenge. While numerous missions, churches, evangelists, and medical ministries frequently used our services, until this point, only two missionary families permanently lived in the bush and depended fully on our helicopter service for supplies. These families were working amongst two separate tribes in the southern lowlands. Without the helicopter, a trip back to town would entail several days of dangerous hiking through the dense jungle and perilous river canoe trips to reach the nearest grass airstrip where a mission airplane could pick them up.

Point X-Ray, however, was much harder to reach. To get there from the nearest airstrip on foot was impossible for the missionary families. We learned later the trip took the local people a grueling two-week hike. This planned mission station would truly be "HELI ACCESS ONLY." The newly established team in preparation consisted of three families with a total of seven young children. It was a huge responsibility for us that they would depend on our helicopter service, but we were excited nonetheless. This was what we were here for. Now, many months and preparations later, the time had come for Andersen, Stephen and Tim to find a good place to build the mission station with a potential site for an airstrip near Point X-Ray. Once houses were built, the wives and children would join them.

"What a place to take a family with young kids to," I said to Hans. "Remember all the big bugs hitting the camera and the team in the footage we saw?"

We had read about one of the survey trips in a Helimission newsletter back in Germany and seen some footage.

"I totally admire these guys," I mused. "And I'm so glad I can support the whole effort from town!"

Brian took off early in the morning and headed to the rendezvous site over an hours' flight away, to meet the survey team. This time, Tim and Stephen were joined by Andersen and Tim's father, Bonard, as well as a guide from a neighbor tribe, and airplane pilot, Nate. He would examine the possible airstrip sites. Brian would meet the team at a nearby airstrip. The team had already surveyed the area in the previous days from a Helio Courier, a light *STOL* (Short Take-off and Landing) mission airplane. They had flown low and slow over the area and found eight possible locations—two of which looked promising as airstrip sites and needed further investigation.

We couldn't wait to hear news from the jungle. We were glad when we heard Brian on the radio report everything was going well so far and the tribesmen seemed friendly. We were even more relieved when he returned safely a few days later.

"There wasn't a flat spot anywhere in these mountains," Brian told us. The only natural breaks in the thick rainforest were sheer rock walls. No wonder the tribe hadn't been reached before! Then there were clusters of wooden huts with thatched roofs (which might be blown away by the rotor wind) and small gardens. The only option had been to land in one of those—right in the "lion's den!"

The team had seen women and children running for cover between the trees and men with bows and arrows. Brian had landed the helicopter in an uneven vegetable garden. After a few tense, uncertain moments, the tribesmen had walked up to the visitors unarmed and greeted them. The ice had been broken. Some subsequent attempts to find a good airstrip site had been unsuccessful. There hadn't been a suitable place to land near any possible airstrip sites which had been located during the preceding airplane survey. The good news was that the tribesmen hadn't objected to the missionaries staying with them for a while. So Brian had returned to Wamena and planned to pick them up again in two weeks' time.

We kept praying and waiting for news, just like the men's families on the coast. Stories of missionaries being killed, like the five men in the Auca/Waodani tribe in Ecuador in 1956, and Stan Dale and Phil Masters in 1968 were on everybody's mind.

When the time got closer for Brian to pick up the survey team, he had an idea.

"These guys have been hiking through the jungles, probably eating instant noodles and jungle food for over two weeks," Brian said. "How about you women prepare some lunch packages which they can find in their seats when they get into the heli."

Great idea! I loved the way Brian always thought of ways to encourage people. How exciting to serve these courageous men in a small way. We got to work. Besides preparing food, I asked God to help me find some encouraging Bible verses. I don't remember all four of them, but the Lord brought me across the following verses:

"And everyone who has left houses or brothers or sisters or father or mother or wife or children or lands, for My name's sake, shall receive a hundredfold, and inherit eternal life."
Matthew 19:29

"Behold, I give you the authority to trample on serpents and scorpions, and over all the power of the enemy, and nothing shall by any means hurt you."
Luke 10:19

On July 21, Brian picked up the team from Point X-Ray, and Tim and Stephen stayed at Brian's house that night. They joined us for our weekly Helimission fellowship night. Of course, we were dying to hear about their experiences.

"Wow! That was tense when we first landed. The women and children had run for cover, which left only armed warriors." We hung onto Tim and Stephen's words.

That would be scary, no kidding!

"Anyway, we exited the helicopter and then something happened that we wouldn't have guessed: the men put down their bows and arrows and walked up to us unarmed. They extended their hands to snap knuckles with us and kept saying: 'Abba, abba, abba, abba, abba ...'"

"Yeah, just as in 'Abba, Father.' That gave us some confidence."

I had seen people snap knuckles like that. This greeting, comparable to a handshake in our culture, was practiced all over the Papuan highlands. Two people extend the bent index and middle finger of their right hands, linking with the other's fingers and while pulling away there is a popping sound.

"The first three or four nights we slept in tents on the jungle floor. Man, that was cold and wet. But then the men had mercy on us and invited us to sleep in the men's hut by the fire."

"These people were unreached all right," the two continued. "They basically made everything from things they found in the forest or grew in their gardens. There wasn't a single piece of clothing. The only evidence of contact with the civilized world were a few worn out broken pieces of machetes and knives and a few steel axes that were worn down almost to the handle. They must have traded these with people from a neighboring tribe a long time ago."

"There wasn't a nail anywhere. The thatch-roof houses were all tied together with vines. No cooking pots."

"But it was amazing to see how sharp the bamboo pieces were, which they used for cutting. And you should have seen how quickly they can get a fire going with a piece of flint!"

Stephen had been pleased to discover that some injured people, who he and Mike had treated the previous year, had healed surprisingly well. This had helped the people to trust the foreigners.

"It took a while to get started with learning a few words of their language. I picked up a rock and tried to ask what the word for rock was. Then I pointed at trees and pigs, but I kept getting different answers from people. It was really frustrating."

What a task to learn a language that had never been studied or reduced to writing before. No dictionaries!

"But then one day a guy we hadn't seen before, came in and excitedly pointed at my camera saying something," Tim continued. "So I memorized the phrase he had used and tried again, pointing at rocks, trees, pigs, etc. while saying those words, and then I finally got the same answers from everyone."

What a breath of fresh air it was to spend time with these two after dealing with all the big and small problems here to somehow keep the helicopter service going. These pioneer missionaries were the main reason we were here and they deserved every bit of our efforts and support.

A Fiery Welcome

Early July 2000

Finally, we got another addition to our team. A Canadian couple with their eight-year-old son arrived in Sentani–incidentally, just at the time when an angry mob was busy rolling fuel barrels down the street and burning down the market and a few other buildings. What a welcome!

"Finally, we're not the new kids on the block anymore," I said to Hans with a big grin.

I was able to help Luana prepare the house and orientate the wife a bit. She had been on the mission field before and was already quite experienced. Jan's mother, who knew English well, came to Wamena from the coast to teach the new family some Indonesian, and I was invited to sit in on some lessons. So far, I had learned from books and language tapes by myself and had picked up words in conversations. It was great to learn a few basics, which made it a lot easier for me to make sense of the language. Jan's mother was a friendly, energetic lady who also worked for Helimission on the coast and helped us in many ways when we were in Sentani.

The new family settled in quickly and understood more of the language every day. I enjoyed their company and hearing about their experiences. However, the demonstrations and unstable situation in town made it hard for the family to adjust.

What's Worse than a Toothache?

Mid-July 2000

It was a complicated, drawn out process to get work visas in Indonesia, so we had been given a business visa which needed to be extended every month until our long-term visas would be ready. This meant a monthly trip to the coast for Jan and us involving a hotel stay and finding a car and driver, etc. but also the opportunity to shop for ourselves and our team members. Shortly after returning from one of those trips, my tooth started aching. My ultimate nightmare! There wasn't quality dental care available in Wamena.

Getting a dental checkup was one of the most important things before going to work in an underdeveloped area. I had been late asking for an appointment (which took several weeks to get) before leaving Germany, but God had intervened on my behalf. A friend had called me after I had told her about my predicament. "Elke, my son had a dental appointment this afternoon, but now he's sick. Do you want to take it?"

Did I ever! Not that I normally enjoyed trips to the dentist, but this had been the time! A young dentist had checked my teeth and taken X-rays that afternoon before replacing an old filling. Two days later, the newly-filled tooth started aching, and the senior dentist allowed me to come for an emergency appointment. His words hadn't left me feeling reassured: "The filling is probably too close to the nerve. Either it will calm down by itself, or you'll need a root canal. But there's no time for that before your departure."

I left the dental surgery close to despair.

Lord, you know where I'm going, and there's no good dental care in Papua. You need to help me!

I had tried to chew on the other side, which had worked—until a tooth on that side started hurting as well. Good grief! What could be wrong when the dentist had checked all my teeth and taken an X-ray scan less than three months ago?

Lord, why did you allow that to happen? Please help me.

At the same time, Hans got sick, and to add to our misery, we had problems with our water system. Some pipe connection was broken, and we couldn't turn on the water pump to get water into the house without flooding the shed in the process. Dear Ibu Marice showed me how to get water straight from the tank in the yard, and we used pitchers and bowls to haul water into the house. Hans' blood got tested for malaria, and when the result came back negative, Luana brought antibiotics which Hans had to take every six hours—even at night. Along with the medicines, Luana brought a delicious warm meal since she was delivering food to the new family anyway.

I have no idea how she does it besides all her normal work and homeschooling!

Brian and Alex came as well and glued our plastic PVC water pipes.

After a few nights with minimal sleep and new water problems, Hans got better. The relief was not long-lived.

"Luana, I've got a problem," I said on the phone. "Last night, Hans finally slept through the night, but I couldn't sleep. The toothache is wandering all around my jaws. I sure hate the betel nut stains everywhere, but I'm so desperate, I'm ready to try chewing some. I can't eat, and I'm getting hungry."

"Don't worry, I've got good painkillers. I'll drop them off soon. I'll also ring Bob on the coast. He's a pilot and mechanic, but he also does dental work and did a beautiful job filling Briana's tooth not long ago. Maybe he can help you."

"Thank you so much!"

Bob, this man of many talents, had a small dental practice at the international school in Sentani. However, there were no more flights to the coast that Friday afternoon and on Saturdays it was hard to get flights anyway.

Aduh! ("Aduh" was one of the first words we learned in Indonesian. You could pronounce it mournfully for several seconds, sounding like "adooooooooooo," or short with a sense of shock like "adooh!" and there were all kinds of variations in between. For instance, when you saw a child spilling a drink, a plane crash, or heard a shocking story from a neighbor this word would be appropriate.)

Luana called back and made my day.

"Elke, good news. We can go to Sentani, after all, tomorrow. Geerten is flying to the coast with the family and can take us along. Bob has agreed to see you after sunset."

Hope!

On Saturday, we rode the helicopter to the airstrip our friend Geerten was flying the Cessna from. The painkillers had kicked in, and I was excited about sitting up front in the Cessna 206. I'd get a clear view of the landscape during the flight which would include a stopover in the mountains.

"Down there is Panggema," Geerten pointed out while we were heading for our first stop. I had read about this village in the first book I had read on Papua and resolved to read it again now after having seen the location of much of its plot. In Germany, it had seemed worlds away. I thoroughly enjoyed the flight until anxiety kicked in when we approached the runway of Pronggoli. Geerten flew a heart-stopping turn between the steep mountains before landing on the grass strip. I decided I liked the slow helicopter landings better. These mountain airstrip landings seemed more like controlled crashes to me!

We picked up a young Asian missionary lady and headed for Sentani. Soon, we left the mountains and flew over the lowlands toward the coast.

"Hey, Elke, would you like to fly the plane?" Geerten asked. This unpleasant toothache story got better and better. I took over the control yoke, and Geerten explained to me how to pilot the plane. Who would have thought that what had almost caused me to despair yesterday, was now turning into an adventure? Flying the airplane turned out to be quite similar to steering a ship. For eight years, sailing on tall ships had been part of my life. While I had given that up for going to the mission field, aviation had become a part of my life now instead.

Bob, the American pilot and mechanic, met us at the dental clinic at the international school after sundown. His son, Gary along with his lovely fiancé, Wendy, had come along to assist. I can't express how thankful I was to Bob for agreeing to see me. Just being there made me feel better already. I looked around the room, which had all the equipment you would expect at the dentists—only a few decades older. I was about to ask Luana if she thought Bob had any anesthesia when I saw a hammer lying on a counter and decided it might be wiser to keep my mouth shut, as the expression "mallet anesthesia" came to my mind. After hearing about my symptoms, checking my teeth, and taking an X-Ray scan, Bob gave his diagnosis. "The tooth is dying. Could you go to PNG, Singapore, or Jakarta to have a root canal done?"

My heart sank. I couldn't even think of living with this pain any longer and was quite hungry by now. Besides, in those days, there weren't several flights to Jakarta per day, but only two per week. I also didn't have a visa which would allow me to leave and re-enter the country. We had come all this way, and I still couldn't get the tooth fixed?

"All right then, I'll start the root canal."

To our huge surprise, Bob pulled out all the medicines and equipment for the job. We surely hadn't expected him to do more than regular fillings or pulling teeth.

"Are you afraid of this or are you tough as a horse?" Bob asked, holding up a syringe.

"I'm definitely not tough as a horse, so please, give me the shot!" (I was relieved he wasn't going to use the hammer).

For about two hours, the kind man worked on the bottom of my mouth, taking out the filling—occasionally mumbling something about 'the Germans always putting so much plastic in there'—and cleaning out the rotting roots. The smell coming out of the dying tooth was revolting.

"I'm fo forry you have to endure wat howwible fmell," I tried to express my concern for Bob when he removed his fingers from my mouth for a minute.

"If that's the worst you've ever smelled, you are very lucky," he replied matter-of-factly, and I was relieved he didn't seem to feel sick as a result of helping me. (When I smelled gangrene a few years later, I knew what he meant).

The four people, who weren't having work done in their mouths, were joking around which made the experience go by a lot faster. When Bob was done with the painstaking job at that late hour, I was pain-free and more thankful than I had ever been to anybody in my life. Bob was my new best friend.

"That should do for now," Bob said after he had put the medicines and temporary filling into the tooth, "but I don't think I'll be able to finish off the job. You'll need at least one or two more sittings. I'm going to the USA for a couple of months, and I will ask my dentist friends what they think."

I was fine for now, and I would worry about the rest later.

"And by the way, the reason for the pain on the other side of your mouth is a huge cavity and your packing food in there. The young dentist probably didn't see it on the X-Ray, because it was hidden behind the filling. Come back next time you're in Sentani, and I'll fix that for you."

(When he eventually did, he even commented on "last week's beefsteak," which he found remnants of in the cavity. How embarrassing, especially considering Bob was a vegetarian by conviction).

"Keep using the antibiotics and apply a hot washcloth three times a day, then you should be fine soon."

Although Bob had made a few rather sarcastic jokes, he was the gentlest and most concerned dentist I had ever met. I paid him about twice what he asked to cover the materials, which was only a fraction of the cost for a root canal done in most other parts of the world. I also promised to try to replace the German-made medicines and material he had used for the root canal.

The next morning, Luana and I flew back to Wamena. I was so relieved and happy to be pain-free! I was incredibly thankful to God and all the people along the way who had taken care of me. Here, almost at the end of the world, the Lord had helped me in ways I couldn't have imagined, using a pilot/mechanic of all people.

Now the question was: Who could finish up the root canal? I would have never guessed the answer.

The Big Serpent Turns in the Ground

Luana and I returned to Wamena on Sunday. After this week of illness, excitement, and limited sleep, Hans and I decided to have an early night. The rain was pelting down on the roof which always made us go to sleep fast.

"Whoa!"

We had been in bed for a few minutes when it felt as if a giant had gotten hold of our bed and was shaking it violently from side to side. An earthquake! I pulled the covers over our heads thinking in case the roof collapsed on us it wouldn't hit us so hard. Hans tried to get out of bed, but it was impossible; he kept getting thrown back into bed. We felt helpless.

The tremor stopped, and we got up with shaking knees and pounding hearts. Things had fallen off the shelves, and the lamp was swinging from the ceiling, but nothing seemed damaged or broken. We put on rain jackets and went to check on Ibu Marice. We found her in the backyard in the driving rain. She looked shaken up and gesticulated that her heart had been making extra beats. Then we noticed the water barrels had fallen off their wooden frame.

"Are you guys all right?" Jan, who was out, asked us on the phone.

"Yeah, nothing damaged too badly. Good to hear you're okay too!"

Briana phoned next.

"There will be aftershocks, so if you don't want to be outside in the rain, stand by the front door. Doorframes are a safer place to be."

The rain eased up and this time we heard it coming: a thundering rumble mixed with people's screams got closer and closer until it hit us. We held on to the doorframe for the ride and watched the house next door shaking. The aftershocks—Hans counted nine of them—became less intense, and we felt it was safe enough to go back to bed. We slept in our clothes and with the doors open, just in case.

What a weekend!

The next morning, the men got the helicopter out early to be ready if anybody needed help. Earthquakes often triggered landslides on the steep mountainsides which sometimes took out gardens, destroying the livelihood of a whole family or hamlet. Entire villages could be buried by landslides. Airstrips could be damaged by earthquakes as well, so airplanes couldn't always be used in affected areas.

"I managed to get onto the earthquake website," Brian told us. "It said the epicenter was close to Angguruk and it was a 5.5 on the Richter scale."

Hans and I looked at each other.

"It certainly felt stronger than that!"

We learned the way an earthquake is felt and affects an area depends on the depth in which it occurs and other factors. Our friends in Pyramid later said they had seen the ground move in waves, while it had felt more like jolting back and forth at our place.

All the remote mission stations were called one-by-one on the HF radio, to make sure nothing bad had happened. One station didn't come in. Had the earthquake maybe caused a landslide and devastated the village? Brian flew to the station to check, and we were relieved to find the people had only forgotten to turn on the radio.

We took a quick drive around town on our lunch break and talked to several people. We were glad to find there had been only minor damage and no casualties. There were very few two or even three-story houses in Wamena. Some buildings had cracks and some bigger structures, like a large rice warehouse, had sustained more considerable damage with walls collapsing.

New Guinea is part of the notorious Pacific Ring of Fire which means there is frequent seismic activity. It is only a question of time when the next earthquake will strike in any area. Over the years, we would have many small tremors. When we started having regular Internet access, we'd check the epicenter location and the magnitude and pray for the people there. Although those little tremors made us nervous, we found it interesting how they affected us differently when we were sitting, standing, walking, driving, or even which direction we were facing. Sometimes, we were woken up by a jolt at night and heard the glass panes of the louver windows rattle. Years later, we were in Jakarta on the third floor of a high-rise building when an earthquake struck. That was the second most intimidating one after our first experience.

We later learned the tribal people had theories about the cause of earthquakes, some involving a giant serpent turning around underground. Their way to try to stop it was to jump up and down to let the snake know it was time to "knock it off."

Carjacked

Beginning of August 2000

An eventful month had gone by, and it was time to get our visas extended. This time our transport to get around on the coast was an old van with several benches—as usual without air-conditioning. The drivers were two young small, skinny guys (probably weighing in at around one hundred pounds) from Sulawesi, another Indonesian island. Obviously, they didn't have a lot of driving experience. They drove slowly and carefully—which wasn't a bad thing—but then stalled the car on a steep hill. Eventually, we made it to Jayapura.

Once again we sat in the immigration office's waiting room and filled out the forms with Jan's help. The humid heat made us tired and thirsty. We anxiously waited, wondering if the person in charge was in today, or if we would have to return the following day, and whether our visa extension would be granted at all.

The antibiotics I had taken for my root canal, combined with the equator sun, had given me a painful, itchy rash on my fingers, so I wasn't looking forward to giving fingerprints. There was no use debating whether fingerprints ever changed and if this was really necessary, rules were rules (now, it's done electronically, once and for all). When we were finally called into the office, the lady pressed my sore fingers onto the ink and the paper. I bit my lips and tried not to flinch too much. We were fine to stay in Papua for another month, what a relief.

Our next destination was the police station where we had to get registered and fingerprinted as well and got our *Surat Jalan*, the travel permit we needed to go back to Wamena and to travel to places.

"That's strange," Jan said when we got outside the police station.

"You're right, we haven't ever seen a traffic jam in Jayapura before, have we?" Hans remarked (things have changed since then).

We went to the wonderfully air-conditioned *TMF* (The Missions Fellowship) office with the friendly staff where mission organizations received assistance with money transfers, ordering materials, getting airplane tickets, etc. There we learned a ship with refugees from conflict-torn Ambon, in the Maluku Islands, had arrived. Their relatives and friends were coming to collect these scared, traumatized people—hence the traffic jam.

After more errands, we started the trip back to our hotel in Sentani which normally took at least an hour. We were hot and tired, but still on time for my five o'clock dental appointment. Everything was going according to plan—until we came around a bend in the road. There he was: a dripping wet, muscular Papuan man, dressed only in a muddy pair of underwear, who had probably just climbed out of Lake Sentani. When the man staggered onto the road and pointed at our car, we could see he was drunk and held rocks ready to throw at the car.

"What are you doing? Keep driving!" Jan urged our two timid drivers from the back when we noticed they slowed down.

"No, no," they argued, "he lives in our neighborhood. If we don't stop now, he'll come after us later!"

We got nervous. The man came to the co-driver's locked door. The guys cracked the window a bit and tried to slip money through the opening. The man took the money and ripped it up. To everybody's horror, he proceeded to slide his hand through the crack, push down the window, and unlock the door. In stark contrast to our skinny drivers, he had the frame of a boxer, and his face looked like it had taken many punches before. He shoved one guy over and sat in the front seat of the car, not paying any attention to the three of us in the two back rows. We stayed quiet to keep it that way. The man incessantly talked at the drivers. Jan, who sat on the bench behind us, was calm with his arms crossed and his eyes getting smaller and smaller while he observed the scene, probably steaming inside. The man started harassing and intimidating the terrified drivers.

"Jan, what is he saying?" we whispered over our shoulders.

"He said: 'Today the refugees from Ambon come here—tomorrow you Indonesians here in Papua will be the refugees.'"

The two guys were close to panic and tried to give the intruder more money. Again, he took the money and tore it up. Then he commanded them to start driving. This wasn't good. I looked at Hans and Jan who were still calm. Our driver pulled out, and now we weren't just in danger of an intoxicated, aggressive man who had become a carjacker, but also of having a traffic accident! The driver, who had demonstrated his lack of driving skills to us all day, now started speeding on this curvy road. My worry, anger, and heart rate went up another notch when the guy grabbed the steering wheel from the side and jerked at it. Thankfully, we stayed on the road. While the man threw things from the car out the window, he discovered a lighter and tried to set fire to the dashboard and then to the driver's shirt. We were praying quietly in the back, but couldn't do a thing while the man kept poking and harassing the young men and interfering with the steering wheel. I fought the overwhelming urge to punch the man—which probably wouldn't have helped the situation. By now, we were getting closer to the hotel, and I was worried about my dental appointment. The drivers slowed down to pull into the hotel complex, but the drunken man commanded them to keep driving. My heart was pounding. For the first time, Jan spoke up: "*Masuk!*" (Enter!) He commanded the driver, but the carjacker was still closer to him, so he kept driving.

"Should we grab him?" Hans asked Jan under his breath. Before they could take action, the man suddenly told the guys to stop and he got out. What a relief! We drove back to the hotel.

After that experience, the trip to the dentist felt like going to a party. I still had time to brush my teeth and freshen up before Gary and Wendy, who had assisted Bob with the root canal, picked me up. Once again, they assisted Bob with repairing my tooth. I was happy to see these dear people again and thankful to get the aching tooth fixed as well, but I can't say I was sorry when that day was over.

After spending two more days on the coast buying a second car for Helimission, doing some serious grocery shopping, and enjoying a candlelight dinner (the electricity company had added the romantic atmosphere) at Bob's family's home, it was time to return to Wamena.

As we had already experienced, bookings with the two commercial airlines which flew the noisy Fokker F-27 turboprop airplanes were not very reliable. In addition to the frequent technical problems, the weather could always bring about schedule changes or cancellations and sometimes the previous day's stranded passengers had to be flown first before the ones who had booked for any given day. To our delight, we managed to get tickets on the "adventure airline."

We leaned back in our seats and prayed for a safe flight while the plane took off. We were ascending over Lake Sentani, and the landing gear was being retracted. With wrinkled foreheads, we watched through the dirty, oil-streaked windows how the wheels went up halfway, stuttered as if there was not enough hydraulic fluid to fully retract them (Hans' diagnosis), and down, and up, and down. The plane took a turn over the lake and landed at Sentani airport again. At least the landing gear had locked in the down position, and the landing went well (there was always a reason to be thankful).

After a long wait, we were told the problem couldn't get solved quickly, so we looked for another ride in a cargo plane. There were no seats available on the passenger plane that day and our luggage had already been sent up with the first flight anyway — including our swimming clothes and our partly perishable groceries. Oh well. We got another ride in the cool Transall. The plane was vibrating and shaking this time, water was dripping onto our heads, and we didn't have a window to look out of, but who cared? We were going home!

Wrenches, Pencils, and Arrows

"I'm so looking forward to having our own hangar," Hans said while digging for a spare part in a box. "All these parts in neat shelves with labels ..."

"And desks for everyone," I added.

It would be great to have the helicopters—and the guys working on them—under a roof, protected from the scorching sun, strong winds, and tropical downpours.

We'd have to keep dreaming of a hangar for a while since we were still waiting for building permits and the actual hangar construction couldn't yet start. To use the time, a makeshift carpenter's shop was set up where doors, window frames, and the like were pre-fabricated. The men were going about their work with flying, maintaining the helicopters, paperwork, and running the base, while I enjoyed getting into the bookkeeping for the base and the hangar project. I enjoyed meeting people from all over the world who came to the office for flight requests and other business or simply to say hello.

The tension in Wamena between the indigenous Papuans and the *pendatangs*, the transmigrants from other Indonesian islands, was palpable. Groups of demonstrating warriors kept coming to town by the dozens and hundreds in their war paint armed with bows, arrows, and spears. It was an experience when a group of them ran past us with their chants and war cries. Groups from different areas had different styles of chants. It's hard to describe the sound and force of dozens of male voices shouting "*OWA-HO!*" in unison while running past nearby. It felt like the ground was shaking and the air vibrating.

We tried our best to steer clear of crowds and always looked into a street before entering it to make sure we wouldn't get caught up in a crowd of demonstrators. While driving through town, Luana and I often simultaneously locked the car doors when we saw people who didn't look trustworthy. However, in the darkness and rain, it was sometimes hard to see.

"Why do you think they're running?" Hans asked Jan, while the two were driving from the house to the hangar in the dark.

"Oh, probably just because of the rain," Jan replied while rolling up the car window. People always seemed to run when it started to rain and one could never be careful enough not to hit anybody who ran out on the street in front of the car. Hans switched the headlights to high beam.

"Whoa!"

A large crowd of warriors armed with bows and arrows was filling up the street completely like a wall, running toward them. It was too late to turn around or to back off. Hans pushed the pedal to the metal and tried to reach a side street between the car and the warriors, through which they could escape—if they reached it faster than the mob.

Bang, bang, bang!

Arrows pelted the car. Hans' maneuver must have appeared like an attack to the Papuans, so they started shooting and hitting the window Jan had just rolled up.

"That was close," Hans said while pulling some arrows from the radiator grill after safely arriving at the airport.

Our Own Wheels — and Other Things that Kept Us Rolling

Late August 2000

"Elke, here's a package for you and Hans," Jan said while holding up a cardboard box. We were surprised to find a colorful, nylon motorcycle jacket, a white open-faced helmet, and two rear-view mirrors inside. Oh, what a teaser! When would the rest of the motorbike follow? A few days later, we heard that the motorcycle would be on the next cargo flight. It had taken about seven weeks to get the machine. Finally, we could stop borrowing other people's motorbikes. We were allowed to use the Helimission car whenever it was available, but we needed a reliable mode of transport for everyday use. A motorbike was the best solution in our case, and besides, it would do so much for my happiness level.

"I'm so glad I learned to ride a motorbike in Germany already and not in this chaotic Wamena traffic," I said to Hans. I hadn't been a natural at riding and might have ended up in a barbed wire fence or a sweet potato field while learning, as had happened to others. Now, I could concentrate on staying alive in traffic while controlling the bike without thinking about it.

Who would have thought God had started preparing me for the mission field many years back, without me suspecting it? I hadn't been sure which career path to choose after school, so my father had suggested a business school and getting a moped for the commute. At hearing the word moped, the boring-sounding option had jumped straight up to first place. (I had fallen in love with motorbikes at the age of thirteen. I love horses, and after being devastated when I had developed an allergy to horses, motorbikes had somehow become a substitute. You might catch me petting my motorbike occasionally, but I stop short of offering it a carrot). With the humble old 80 cc Zuendapp my dad had then traded for a couple of old speakers, I hadn't exactly been a cool rider, but I enjoyed it nonetheless and subsequently had gone on to ride bigger motorbikes.

It turned out mission preparation didn't start at a Bible or language school—neither of which I have been to yet. God can use anything we learn in our lives, the good, the bad, and the ugly. My father's idea that I could learn bookkeeping at the business school, saving him money for the accountant, didn't pan out for him, but both my riding and bookkeeping skills came in handy now on the other side of the globe!

It had taken us a while to decide what motorbike to get. The variety of bikes on offer was limited, and 200 cc was the maximum cylinder capacity allowed by the government. Off-road bikes with a reliable four-stroke engine weren't available. We also didn't want to stand out with the biggest and fanciest model, appearing even richer than we already did amongst the people in Wamena. After much thought and prayer, we decided to order a silver Honda Mega Pro 1600 (a bit of an overstatement, since it had a 160cc engine). This model had beautiful lines and promised to be simple to maintain and reliable.

Here it finally came out of the airplane: our beautiful, *black* Honda with yellow, orange, and red markings. Oh well, it wasn't the color we had ordered, but it ran beautifully and was comfortable. The slightly curved, but flat tank, was perfect for hauling loads like net bags full of vegetables, twenty-kilogram bags of rice, trays of eggs, or even children if more than one person needed a ride. That would have been unimaginable in our home countries, but was common practice in this part of the world.

While it had been hard for me to sell my beloved Honda 750 Africa Twin before leaving Germany, now the money bought us a much smaller but more suitable Honda Mega Pro. We rode around the airport grounds to try out the bike. However, we steered clear of the runway to avoid risking an arrow in our backside. After dangerous incidents with people on the runway had gotten out of hand, guards had been put in place. The guards were indigenous Papuans armed with bows and arrows and dressed in black. Everybody knew they meant business. For instance, if the guards would find people wandering about on the runway, often drunken or high from sniffing glue, they would put them into barrels full of cold water for a while until they sobered up. One could debate whether their ways of doing things were ethical, but the fact was they worked.

I loved my new freedom and mobility and enjoyed every time I could ride my bike (about four times a day) to the office, shops, markets, banks, etc. When I rode the motorbike, I thanked God for it and prayed for protection for myself and everybody around me. The people on the road made sure I kept my wits about me when they jumped into the road wanting to sell me a newspaper or wash my bike with dirty water from the ditches. None of that had ever happened to me in Europe.

Street life here was so different from back home: It never ceased to amaze me that people did everything in groups instead of splitting up to reach more potential customers. Here were five healthy young men sitting at the same intersection, selling the same paper, all yelling: "*Cepo-Cepo-Cepos!*" (For Cenderawasih Pos, the local newspaper) and on another intersection, there were four or five boys with pumps to inflate flat *becak* (bicycle taxi) tires.

Hmmm, how many becaks will have a flat tire exactly at this spot?

Money Makes the Blades Go Round

I stood at the bank's cash counter nervously looking over my shoulder at about twenty-five customers who watched me stuffing my backpack with bundles of bank notes. I was so glad I no longer had to walk to the office, but could just hop on the bike and get out quickly! Luana and I had opened a bank account specifically for the hangar construction. Bills of several thousand dollars were coming in for cement and metal roofing and needed to be paid in cash. The biggest bill in the Indonesian currency was 100,000 Rupiah (at the time approximately US $13, which made counting out the cash box a big job).

We always had to be several steps ahead with the finances. We'd estimate upcoming expenses for the building site, fuel for the helicopters, and other ordinary or extraordinary operational costs. We'd then request a money transfer from Headquarters in Switzerland. It took weeks for the funds to get through the banking system. The money we received in flight payments was like a drop in the ocean. Since the missionaries and churches wouldn't have been able to pay the full price for the expensive helicopter operations, Helimission had decided to heavily subsidize the flights with the help of their supporters. The helicopters made a vital difference to ministering to isolated people groups, so they had to happen, no matter what the cost. In remote pioneering locations, missionaries only had to pay for the fuel. While this was still a significant amount, it was only a small fraction of the true operating costs for the helicopter.

"I better go on my round to the kiosks and buy *Beng-beng*," (my favorite local chocolate bars) I said to Hans.

The workers had started preparing the wood for the hangar and supplies came in, so I paid the bills and every two weeks the workers' salaries. It was nice to meet them and learn their names. Some workers were local Papuans, while most skilled workers came from Manado in northern Sulawesi.

Wamena had no road access to the coast. So like the cement and other supplies, the money had to be flown in from the coast. Since the shipping cost the same for a bundle of Rp.100,000 bills as for Rp.1,000 bills, the banks seemed more reluctant to order the latter. Since the financial institutions couldn't supply me with enough small bills, I had to find more creative ways to get the right amounts ready. I took some large bills and bought something small like Beng-beng one at a time at different kiosks until I ended up with enough change to complete the payroll.

I had paid all the expenses for today, and now I needed to make all the entries into the accounting books. I had just laid out and ordered all the receipts on the counter, opened the A4 accounting book, and started to write when the door opened, and two men came in with the large architectural plans, heading for the counter. I put the receipts into the book, grabbed my writing utensils and calculator, and moved into the corner. I sat down on a stool in front of the fridge, put the book on my lap, and started to write, trying not to drop anything or get distracted by the men talking. Hans came in.

"Oh, Mausi, could you please move over? I need to get something from the fridge."

Next to some drinks, the fridge contained glue, sealant, and other chemicals used in helicopter maintenance. I closed my books again and desperately looked around the tiny office full of people. How could I ever get my work done like this? Brian came in and saw I was close to tears.

"How about you use my desk while I'm out flying?"

I was very touched by that offer—and since Brian was usually inundated with flight requests, there was enough desk time left for me. How we longed for that hangar to be finished with enough work space for us all.

Building Permits, Papuan-Style

"Jan, what's going on? Why are the men sitting on the ground and not working?" Hans had asked on a July day when returning to the airport after his lunch break. The hangar building permission had in the meantime been granted, and the work on the building site had commenced. Hooray! However, as we had learned by now, not everything in Papua was settled by the rules and regulations of government departments. Our building project was no exception.

"Some clan came and claimed they were the land owners," Jan reported after talking to the men. "They threatened to kill the construction workers if they kept building before we pay them for the land." No wonder the workers' enthusiasm had been dampened!

The airport authority owned the land, and Helimission had leased it for twenty-five years. However, a piece of paper in some folder hadn't been very comforting to the workers when they had faced men with machetes, bows, and arrows. The issue needed to be dealt with.

We then learned the Indonesian government had acquired the land from the local people before developing the airport. We even found records stating the clan leaders had received money. However, it was impossible to verify whether this money had been passed on to the individual garden owners since Papuan people traditionally don't use paper records. Instead, they remember things for a long time, including scores in tribal wars.

We had looked for ways to resolve the issue so the building process could continue. The head of the airport authority hadn't been reachable as he had left the island for two months and didn't have a deputy. Jan and Hans had gone to pay the clan leaders several visits.

One of them had been difficult to reason with. The other two had been friendly.

"I know Helimission is doing great work here and is really helping the Papuan people," one clan leader had stated. The picture of a Helimission helicopter on his wall had confirmed his words. "I'm happy to help in any way I can. I suggest we write a letter for all the clan chiefs to sign, stating we don't want any money for the land Helimission is using. If anybody then comes to demand more money, you can show it to them and refer them to us."

What a relief! One down—two to go. There was still the particularly difficult fellow, and this "nut" was not to be cracked easily. A couple of meetings had already left him angry, and Jan and Hans frustrated.

It was now late August and a meeting was called with all three clan leaders. I stayed home and prayed on my knees while the talks were held at the office.

"Praise the Lord; it's done!" Hans told me afterward. "The other two leaders reasoned with the guy for a while and eventually, he gave in and signed the letter. For appreciation, they were all offered a short helicopter ride around the airport and a Helimission sticker. He was happy."

The sticker would grace the windshield of the man's car for years to come. He became fond of Helimission and never caused problems again.

Finally, the building project could progress. Shortly after, the head of the airport authority also returned, more papers were signed, and the matter was settled.

From then on, when various people came to claim the land was theirs (for some time on a weekly basis), we showed them the letter and sent them away. Some other organizations were forced to pay huge sums for their land several times over the years, after threats to burn down all the buildings and other violence.

Unsettling Advice

"We don't know if things will escalate, but it is definitely getting tenser, and we need to prepare," Harry, the base manager of another organization told us during a contingency meeting between several organizations. The indigenous people had started to raise the prohibited Morning Star flag of their independence movement in several places, and the police and army were forcing them to take these down.

"Every person needs to have an emergency backpack, not heavier than five kilos, containing their passport, travel money, documents, computer back-ups, toiletries, and a set of clothes."

Even though Brian had often talked with us about a scenario like this and we had our bags packed from the start, this talk made me feel uneasy.

"We'll need the weight of every person in each family, so in the case of an evacuation, we won't have to weigh people before putting them on an airplane," Harry continued.

This sounded serious but also reasonable (I guess vanity came after safety).

"We have come up with an alarm code system. The highest code means you need to be ready at any time to leave the house on five minutes' notice."

Now this announcement felt like a punch in my stomach area! How could we ever be prepared like that? I hoped and prayed the situation would calm down instead of all these scenarios happening.

"We also need an alternative means of communication; in case the phone connections will be shut down."

People suggested walkie-talkies, talked about frequencies, etc. Every organization had at least one satellite phone.

"We have come up with evacuation points."

The man proceeded to tell us all where we had to go in an emergency so we could be picked up by helicopter if the roads to the airport would be blocked off, or if the airport would be closed. This all reminded me of war movies I had seen.

"You should also explore side streets and garden paths leading to your pick-up point. There might be roadblocks and riots on the main streets."

I was glad Brian and Luana had gradually given us sound advice and taught us about precautions in scenarios like that. Otherwise, this meeting would have definitely freaked me out. At least people were dealing with the situation sensibly and making solid plans.

While walking or riding through the streets from now on, I would keep my eyes peeled for hiding places and side roads.

A familiar, but unexpected sound, made me jump up from my accounting books and run out the office. All I saw were fighter jet tails doing a low flyby over Wamena. Back home in Germany while growing up, I had found those planes fascinating, and I had watched the movie *Top Gun* several times. But these planes were not on a training exercise. The prospect of being on the receiving end of their payload certainly took the fun out of watching them!

"You know what to do when you see them dropping things, don't you?" Brian asked us. I gave him a blank stare. "You throw yourselves to the ground."

I nodded and looked at the hedge or anything to hide behind. Thankfully, it never came to that.

We went back inside but soon we heard people screaming in the street. Through the window, we saw a panicked crowd running down the street as the planes came back for a second flyby. Because of their incredible speed, we hadn't heard the jets coming before they were already overhead.

"It doesn't make much sense that they're trying to outrun fighter jets, now, does it?" I asked Hans.

Most Wamena people had never seen such planes before, and the infernal noise must have terrified them. A little later we went up to Brian and Luana's house. Philip had identified the fighter planes as F-16 jets and had already pulled out cards with all their technical data.

Can you shock this boy with anything?

Well, he had already experienced an evacuation by a truck with combat helicopters flying overhead and by ferry in a severe storm along with Hans during a civil war in Albania.

Soon after the F-16's appeared, five Hercules C-130 military transport planes circled simultaneously above Wamena. Hans watched as dozens of soldiers parachuted out of them filling the gray sky.

"That really felt like war," Hans told me when he came home. The situation didn't look good and the military presence was increased.

Fluffy Feathers and Flying Rocks

End of August 2000

"Keep the door closed, or MG will get the chick!" a big sign said on Brian and Luana's office door when we went there for a visit. Apparently, the "security system" with a night guard and dogs had once again failed. During the previous night, thieves had broken into the yard and stolen all the chickens. When Luana discovered the theft in the morning, she had found a chick struggling to hatch from an egg. She helped the baby bird get out from the eggshell and kept it warm in her hands. She had turned a shoebox into a makeshift incubator by adding an electric heating pad. Now the problem was to keep MG, the cat, away from the chick.

"We just don't have the time and energy to keep the little thing alive. Will you take it?" Luana and Briana pleaded. "We'll give you chicken feed and the electric pad to keep it warm."

I hadn't ever raised chickens before, but I loved animals and figured the chick wouldn't have a chance to survive the week with MG in the house, so we took it home. We were instantly smitten with the fluffy, tiny bird, which, of course, the guys didn't admit to.

"Let's name him AGM, short for Ayam Goreng Mentega," Hans and Jan agreed with each other, smacking their lips while thinking of their favorite Indonesian chicken dish. They tried to annoy me by checking the tiny little thigh for meat, commenting how they couldn't wait to eat it, but when Jan thought nobody was looking, he often checked on the chick and held it in his hand. I doubted either Hans or Jan could ever eat it. The other side of the coin was it was noisy and left droppings all over the house when we let it run around. It came running after me, thinking I was its mother and even ran up my body to snuggle up under my hair when I was sitting on the couch. AGM outgrew the shoebox, then a water bottle box, and eventually, moved into a large carton.

We had known from the beginning; we would only stay at our first house temporarily while the missionaries who usually occupied it were away. Most Indonesian houses had a kitchen only featuring a kerosene cooker and cold tap water as well as a common Indonesian bathroom with a squatting toilet/shower and a cold water basin. Turning a house like that into something we spoiled westerners could cope with and function in, would be a major challenge for our tiny team. There were no advertisements for empty houses in newspapers, no housing agents or any other easy way to find accommodation. The hangar project, helicopter maintenance, and flight program left no time for door-to-door house hunting.

But once again, God surprised us with an unexpected solution: a fully set up mission house became available to rent! However, we were shocked and saddened about the cause for the vacancy of the house. All the agencies' missionaries were losing their visas because they had been falsely accused at the immigration department. There was nothing to be done. Although the lovely couple who lived in the house had just returned from their home assignment, they had to pack up again and go back to Australia. Some things were hard to understand.

The kind, helpful couple made sure everything was in good repair and taken care of before they left. The house was fully furnished (slightly old-fashioned by now but who cared!), had electricity, a well-developed hot and cold water system, a bathroom with a sit-down toilet and shower, mosquito screens on all the louver windows, and a fenced-in yard—all we could have wished for. The floors were even tiled!

The backyard not only featured established fruit trees (one with grapefruit-sized lemons), but also an Indonesian-style thatched gazebo with benches around a table. A shed behind the house was separated into a little workshop, a small storage room, and a laundry. The place was a godsend in this time of turmoil and constant overload for Hans. We loved to live in the middle of an ordinary street where the house with its low metal roof and black wooden boards didn't stand out from the others in the neighborhood. The experienced house helper of the previous occupants was happy to stay on and work for us. It was sad to leave dear, faithful, Ibu Marice behind, but she was working at the other house so we couldn't ask her to come with us.

Our new home

By now I had come to terms with having domestic help and appreciated the freedom it gave me to work at the office most days. A level of cleanliness that came close to our standards back home would have taken me all day to achieve without help. Louver windows and unsealed sidewalks were a recipe for a dusty house, making it necessary to sweep daily and mop at least twice a week. The washing machine wasn't fully automatic, and it had to be filled with water by hand. Washing laundry was an active job for two to three hours about twice a week.

Shopping took a long time, too since the grocery stores didn't sell vegetables or meat which I had to buy elsewhere. Sometimes, eggs were sold out, and I had to look for some all over town. The only bread available at the shops were sweet, white, sandwich loaves which were often moldy when I bought them. So I rather baked my own bread—after sifting the weevils out of the flour. Even with a house helper who worked three to six hours five times a week, I still spent more time on housework than I would have in Germany without a helper. The lady was able to cook a few meals which would be a tremendous help for me on days when I couldn't leave the office early to cook.

Another employee happy to stay on was Nius, the night guard, who had a little place to live behind the house and kept the yard neat and tidy as well. In this tropical climate, plants grew incredibly fast, and we might have harmed ourselves if we had cut the grass with a machete, as was the local way of doing it. Nius was a gentle, friendly man, and we seriously wondered how he would scare away burglars. He had obligations at church, including playing music and was often gone in the evenings. Still, the set-up at the house was perfect for us.

We moved our four suitcases, the five red boxes plus the other items I had bought at the missionary sale. The cardboard box with the chick was supposed to move last. Jan would continue house-sitting at the other place. Tired, but happy about finally settling into a more permanent home, we went to sleep in our new bed. Soon we slept like logs.

CRASH!

Our hearts were racing as we jumped up in bed. A man was yelling and rattling on our front door. He had broken a front window. What should we do now? We didn't have anything to defend ourselves with and were sure the raging man would be inside the house any minute to kill us! Even if we had known the phone number of the police station, we couldn't have communicated with the officers.

There was no trace of the guard. I tried calling friends, but nobody picked up the phone at two o'clock in the morning. Eventually, Tom, the single pilot, answered and agreed to come. There were no other sounds from the man outside, but we were scared to go out fearing he might still be in the yard. Finally, Tom arrived with his neighbor, Curt, bringing a big wooden club. They checked every corner of the yard. By now, the guard had come out of his door, looking sleepy and remorseful. He hadn't heard a thing. The lock on the gate had been pried open. We found a large river rock, weighing about four pounds, stuck in the mosquito screen in our living room and shattered glass on the floor. Tom had to get up early to fly, so the men declined my offer for a cup of tea and headed off, leaving the club with us. (It remained next to our bed for years to come and was joined by an air rifle later on).

"It's time to get a dog," Hans said. "I'm sure it will be less traumatic to be woken up by a barking dog than by the sound of glass breaking."

"You've got a point there. Let's start looking for one."

It was Helimission policy anyway to have guard dogs.

I couldn't go back to sleep. Dogs barked in the neighborhood, and I was worried the angry man was still around. There were more sounds that worried me, but they turned out to be the wooden rafters cracking and big beetles flying against the tin roof between the house and the little sheds in the back.

What's that now?

My heart raced again. All the dogs in our neighborhood started howling! Then there was another eerie sound which turned out to be the voice of the imam at the nearby mosque. It was four thirty in the morning—time for the Morning Prayer. In our old house, we had never heard the mosque or the dog concert going with it.

A Somersault of Events

Early September 2000

Brian came to our new house. We were just unpacking our boxes and suitcases and putting things away into their new places.

"Hi, Brian, come in. What brings you here?"

"Why don't you sit down," Brian suggested.

Then he dropped the bombshell.

"I'm sorry, your new visas aren't finished yet, and the immigration department has refused to extend your temporary ones. You have three days to leave the country."

We were glad we were sitting. Three days! It sometimes took longer to arrange to leave Wamena, let alone get tickets to travel the four thousand-kilometer journey to Jakarta and then getting an international flight to leave the country.

Our life in Wamena felt like a boat trip on a river, and we never knew what to expect behind the next bend. Most days we were paddling in rapid, white water, constantly trying to avoid hitting huge boulders. Some days we were paddling along on a calm, sunny stretch (those days were few and far between). Right now, we were going over a waterfall.

Nobody knew how long it would take to get the new visa, so Papua New Guinea, which was the closest neighboring country, was ruled out right away as we wouldn't have been able to make good use of the time there. The best place to go for all eventualities, whether we'd receive the visas or not, was Singapore. Arrangements were made and—all but miraculously—we got all the tickets to leave

Indonesia within the three days. We were glad our chick could stay with Jan. We repacked the suitcases we had just unpacked and were on our way.

Three whirlwind days and five flights later, we arrived in Singapore. Here we were, in the bustling, clean, commercialized cosmopolitan city of Singapore after spending the last four months in an underdeveloped, remote mountain town in the far east corner of Indonesia. Instead of the wide-open Baliem Valley, surrounded by beautiful mountains and virgin rainforests, we were now surrounded by the tall city concrete and glass jungle of an island city-state.

Thankfully, Mr. Junius, a board member of Helimission Indonesia, invited us to stay at his apartment in Singapore for free. We were very thankful for the good accommodation and prime location near the main shopping street. We tried our best not to be a burden or disturbance to the two young women who lived in the large apartment, along with four dogs. However, we didn't always succeed.

"I don't believe it! I locked myself out of the bathroom," I said to Hans. I had accidentally turned the little button in the knob which could only be opened from the inside. No matter how embarrassed I was, I had to call the maid for help.

"*Tidak apa-apa*" (no worries), she reassured us and without much ado climbed out the bedroom window at the fourth floor, onto a ledge in the façade of the thirty-six story skyscraper. She disappeared through the bathroom window further down the ledge and opened the door from the inside. We watched with our mouths open.

The second time I did it myself.

Spending time in a fascinating city like Singapore could have been a nice break for us, but the building project in Wamena was still stressful. Sweat dripped from Hans' forehead in the humidity when he returned from the ten-minute walk to the Internet café where he had gone to check his emails. He found one from the building contractor. During previous discussions, the man hadn't seen the need to put columns into the walls to support the roof but claimed the walls would be the load-bearing structure. Now he had changed his mind and wanted to put them in—exactly where the windows needed to go. To make matters worse, he demanded new drawings by the next morning in time for the foundation to be poured.

There was no landline phone available to us, and Skype hadn't been invented yet. Our mobile phone bill became astronomical, but at least the thirty construction workers kept working, and Hans was able to give Brian repair advice for two broken down helicopters. The other task Hans was finally able to tackle was studying for the Indonesian air law examination. This was a requirement to get his Swiss helicopter maintenance license validated to an Indonesian one. Without this, he wasn't able to release the aircraft into service by signing off work on the helicopters.

Hans was busy; I was not. But boy, was I homesick! This was not what I had bargained for. When I couldn't be in Wamena, at least I wanted to be with my friends and family. My whirlwind life of the last four months had come to a screeching halt. What should I do now? What was there to do in Singapore that didn't involve spending lots of money? I felt stuck.

"Elke, what do you think? Will you come to Germany for a week if we pay for your ticket?"

I couldn't believe what my mother was just asking on the phone. It was an amazing thing to hear a sentence that opened so many possibilities: it wouldn't have been the last time I had seen my grandmothers when we left four months ago; my brother's son, Daniel, wouldn't be three years old when I'd see him for the first time ... Hans agreed. He would be studying most of the time anyway. So once again, we tried to get a flight on short notice, but most of them were unaffordable. My hope sank. Another phone conversation with my mother made my day.

"Elke, listen. Michael found a decently priced flight for you. We can pay it from here."

Everything was arranged, and with a big smile, I skipped back from the pay phone to the apartment to pack my suitcase. Singapore was so much more beautiful all of a sudden!

"I'm sorry, madam, but the payment hasn't come through yet, I can't give you a boarding pass."

I stared at the friendly, Asian lady behind the check-in counter.

I had come this close to seeing my family and now this! I had learned the appropriate expression for what was happening to me from my American friends: Emotional roller-coaster. Having a rather steady temperament, I wasn't used to so many emotional ups and downs. After what seemed like an eternity, and about seven trips to the help desk, the payment was confirmed, and I was on my way. Only one thing dampened my joy: I missed Hans already and felt bad for him, having to stay behind.

So Familiar, Yet So Strange

When I walked into my parents' house and the grocery shop in Grebenstein, I was overwhelmed by a familiar feeling. I had experienced the phenomenon before, after returning from my first sailing trip on a Russian sail training ship. Back then, I hadn't had an expression for the experience yet: Reverse Culture Shock.

When I had first boarded the Russian four-masted sailing ship, *Kruzenshtern,* this colossus of steel, wood, canvas, ropes, and ratlines, I had been awestruck! I had never been at sea for more than a few hours and had never met a Russian in my life before, so I had been apprehensive. However, the Russian crewmembers had proved to be friendly and welcoming, and I had loved every minute at sea. What I had admired most in the crew was their warm hospitality and ability to improvise and make do with whatever materials they had, instead of waiting for perfect circumstances to come up.

I had met nice, interesting people from various countries; eaten Russian food; climbed a mast for the first time in the sleet, and temperatures of 4° C/39° F; and I had my first serious adrenalin rush in the process. I had been scared but loved it. One night, there had been gale force winds that could have stranded the ship (which I had been blissfully unaware of at the time). I'd had my first encounter with cockroaches, found a pen friend for life in one of the young Russian cadets, scrubbed the deck, learned sailors' knots, and much about the life and work on present-day sailing ships. I had gotten sore muscles from climbing the masts and calloused hands from the rough ropes. A fellow trainee had had a schizophrenic attack, started packing up our clothes in his bag, and wanted to leave the ship. Instead of getting picked up by a boat for a special mission, as he had anticipated, he had been picked up by an ambulance. Just to name a few things which had happened during that week.

That sailing trip had turned out to be an incredible cross-cultural experience and looking back, probably my most important preparation for the mission field. However, when I had gotten home to my life of comfort and routine, my head had been spinning, and for several days I had struggled. My steady life had been seriously shaken up, and for a while, my thoughts had still been on that windjammer in the Baltic Sea, headed for Russia and an uncertain future. When I had walked through my parents' spacious house with nice furniture and a big TV, I realized we were rich and privileged compared to most Russian crew members who sometimes didn't get paid for several months, were separated from their families for long periods, and had to live in tight, confined spaces—some together with several others with limited privacy.

In Wamena, just like on the *Kruzenshtern*, right away I had been sucked into the activity, excitement, and adventure, without much time to slow down and think. Having to fly one hundred fifty-five miles and drive for an hour along a dangerous road for a chance to buy a two-kilo block of cheese (if there was any) had become an accepted inconvenience. Going to our local grocery shop in Grebenstein now made me tear up. There was a well-stocked refrigerated section with scores of different types of cheese—chunks, sliced, and processed.

In Wamena, we lived in a nicer house than most indigenous Papuans, and we had electricity and hot running water which was a luxury, but apart from that, the house fit nicely into the neighborhood. Here in Germany, all the houses were large and solidly built with all the conveniences. All roads were paved, there were sidewalks and streetlights, but there were hardly any people in the streets. I hadn't been used to anything else all my life, but the last four months had changed me profoundly, and I looked at everything from a different perspective.

"This is amazing," my German dentist kept saying while looking at my teeth after hearing the hair-raising story of a helicopter and airplane ride and a pilot/mechanic filling a tooth and even doing a root canal on me.

"I won't even touch this filling; it's perfect."

Four months after my exasperated prayer when coming out of this dentists' surgery in Grebenstein (just before going to the jungle for what I thought would be three years with a time-bomb of a tooth in my mouth), I had come around full circle. The dentist who had made an effort to fit me into his tight schedule took X-Rays of the tooth with the root canal and finished it up with his state-of-the-art equipment.

When I walked out the dentist's surgery this time, I couldn't help but marvel at what God had done. A few months earlier in Wamena, desperate and in pain with a terrible toothache, I had almost been angry with God for allowing this to happen, even though I had trusted Him. I would never have imagined in my wildest dreams how He would solve that problem. God had now sufficiently convinced me He was able to take care of me wherever He would send me. I was even able to obtain the root canal medicine kit from my German dentist, which Bob had asked me to get for him.

One week of waiting for news on the visa turned into two. Hans and I missed each other, but we decided to make the most of this opportunity, so I stayed another week. It meant the world to me to see my relatives, friends, and church family, and to share with them about my new life in Papua, and all that had happened in the last four whirlwind months in that incredible part of the world. I kept tearing up when I looked at baby Daniel, my precious little nephew. What a gift it was to see and hold him—and even to be there for his christening!

"Where is Mr. Schulte?" (name changed) I asked someone at our little church fellowship.

"Oh, haven't you heard? He passed away."

That wasn't the only sad thing that had happened in the last four months without us knowing. While I could understand, people didn't feel comfortable writing us about challenging things or were too affected even to think of us, it felt as if we had been left out. Other problems had been more severe—the church had changed forever, involving much grief and pain. This all was hard to process. The church was very small, and everyone sorely felt it when difficult things happened, or people left. At least in this matter, a friend had taken the time to write us a letter and fill us in.

I had also noticed how my friends had moved on with their lives and some were only marginally interested in my new life. I was no longer an insider. My grandmother was admitted to the hospital, just before my departure to Singapore. I wondered if my visit and impending departure had upset her so much as to make her sick. A piece of news from Wamena made me shed a few tears too: When I called the Helimission office in Wamena, I was told AGM had died. My poor little chick!

However, the joy of seeing my friends and family and being able to share about my new and exciting life outweighed all the sad things. After this special time, I never felt the same homesickness I had before.

When I got back to Singapore, I was happy and relaxed and up for some sight-seeing. Hans, on the other hand, wasn't feeling too well and was not as enthusiastic about exploring this great city, especially since he had already traveled all over it while looking for materials he needed to buy and going to the Internet café to stay in touch with the work in Papua. Hans was also disillusioned by the great variety of wonderful looking food, which was expensive, sometimes very spicy—or downright deceptive.

"I bought this beautiful Danish puff, filled with sweet, creamy vanilla custard—or so I thought—and do you know what it tasted like?"

"What?"

"Garlic sauce."

I burst out laughing. Hans didn't think it was funny. He had eventually resorted to familiar cheap, western fast food, which had given him an achy stomach. Hans was ready for a change in diet, but we didn't feel comfortable interfering with the two ladies' use of the kitchen. I discovered a food court with great Asian dishes and Hans reluctantly came along.

I now fully appreciated the sights, sounds, and tastes of Singapore. We traveled around on the superb MRT (subway), walked up Mount Faber in the tropical heat and humidity and looked over to Santosa Island with its amusement park. We admired the cities' grand colonial-style buildings and bridges and walked around the Boat Quay, marveling at the contrast between the ornate houses, built in previous centuries and the clear-cut modern skyscrapers behind them. There would have been so much more to see, especially in the ethnically diverse parts of town, but fortunately, time ran out.

When our visas were approved, we went to the Indonesian Embassy and got our papers. Hans had just finished studying the material for the Indonesian Aircraft Maintenance and Legislation test, and we were off to Jakarta where he was able to sit and pass his exam. (Another eight months later, he eventually received the paper and was henceforth licensed to sign off the logbooks of the Indonesian registered helicopters for release to service. This had been a huge hurdle to overcome and the time away from Wamena hadn't been wasted).

Going Home! Or Are We?

October 6, 2000

"Not again," Jan sighed after trying to check us all in to fly the last leg from Sentani home to Wamena. He had spent a few days with us on the coast to take care of our immigration paperwork until it was completed. We were all eager to go home finally. How different this trip to Papua had been from the one five months earlier. It seemed like enough had happened to fill two years and for the first time in my life the word home wasn't reserved for a place in Germany anymore.

"What is it *this* time?" we asked.

"Well, apparently they had technical trouble with the plane yesterday, so now they need to take yesterday's cargo up to Wamena, before taking passengers. They said to try again at eleven this morning."

We had gotten up with the birds, made our way to the local airline, and were once more looking for a Plan B to get to Wamena. As usual, we went to the Transall C-160 operator to ask for three seats on their cargo plane.

"Bad news, guys," Jan told us with a concerned look. "The Transall isn't going at all today. Apparently, there's some serious trouble in Wamena."

"Oh no! I hope the others are okay. What do we do now?" We looked at each other perplexed.

"Maybe you guys should just check back into the hotel," Jan suggested, and we reluctantly agreed. It was unlikely that any other airline would go to Wamena under these circumstances. Thankfully,

Going Home! Or Are We?

there was still a room available at the hotel. We phoned our friends in Wamena and Briana answered.

"Whatever you do, don't come to Wamena!" she urged us. This sounded serious. There was nothing we could do, except wait and pray.

The situation in Wamena, which had been brewing all this time, had now blown up. Eventually, our team was reunited at the hotel in Sentani, after our second helicopter had landed in the dusk, following a busy day of evacuating people from Wamena. We were filled in on what had happened. The whole Wamena mission community was evacuated.

While we felt immensely for our friends who had gone through all this, we were very thankful that Jan, Hans, and I had been spared the trauma of going through the dramatic evacuation and horrific scenes. Apparently, it had all started when some indigenous Papuans had raised the prohibited Morning Star flag of the independence movement, and government forces had forcibly taken it down. A group of warriors from the Kurima area had then come to town and started burning houses of transmigrants from other parts of the archipelago and killing people with machetes and axes. It hadn't taken long for the whole town to erupt into riots and violence.

Later, we heard that thirty dead bodies had been counted at the hospital alone. Many of them had been killed in gruesome, atrocious ways. Those were the official numbers, but most likely many casualties were never reported. We heard of dead bodies floating down the Oue River and getting caught in the hydroelectric power station. This situation had turned into a full-blown massacre. Brian had flown scores of people to safety by helicopter, while fighter jets had flown in and out of Wamena around him.

Victor, a young Indonesian man who had been hired to keep track of the building materials, had helped with fueling and loading the helicopter. He had always been shy around us westerners and lacked confidence. On that day, he had risen to the occasion and proved to be an excellent man. Disasters and crises often brought out the best or the worst in people, and we had struck gold with Victor.

Even though we missionaries hadn't been the primary target in those riots, the situation had still been dangerous: bullets didn't ask about nationalities, and one had missed friends of ours by inches when it had passed between father and son. While we were glad we had been spared all that trauma, it felt wrong not to have been there with our friends and so many local people, caught up in this madness. Since we were just returning from Singapore, we still had our suitcases full of clothes, while the others had been evacuated with nothing but their five-kilo emergency backpacks.

I spotted another familiar face at the hotel.

"Tanya! Are you and the family all right?"

"Yes, we're fine, the children and I came down on the Kamov. Gerhard stayed behind to take care of the cows and the house."

Tanya was the Russian wife of Gerhard, the German agricultural development worker who worked in Wamena. They were friends with the Russian crew of the Kamov transport helicopter. Tanya went on to tell me about the chaotic scenes that had taken place and how Gerhard had taken her and the children to the airport, forcing the car over obstacles in the road.

"It was horrible. With us in the helicopter was an Indonesian family. The mother had been killed and the others injured. The little boy's chin was split with an ax."

I felt sick to my stomach. It was hard to come to terms with what human beings were capable of doing to each other. Even little children had been killed or maimed.

While we were displaced to Sentani, our team kept the flight operations going. The new missionary team and their building supplies were flown to the Point X-Ray region to build their houses amongst the Moi tribe. Besides mission flights, the pilots also made several trips back to Wamena and surrounding villages to take injured people to the hospital.

While everybody was still shaken up by the events in Wamena the previous week, more bad news came in: one of our pilot friends crashed a Cessna 206 mission airplane at the challenging Ninia airstrip on landing. When the emergency call came in, Brian was flying in the area with a valuable passenger.

"Hotel Mike Echo estimated time to Ninia eleven minutes. I have a doctor on board."

Thankfully, nobody was critically injured. But all of our nerves were ready for a break!

"I can't wait to get back to the beautiful highland weather," I said to Hans.

We were drenched in perspiration because of the hot, humid air and the relentless equatorial sun burned our skin. My feet ached from standing on the ladder. Still, I was glad to do something useful by assisting Hans with a 100-hour-inspection. Helicopters required constant maintenance, so the work had to go on. There were always panels to remove, parts to clean, or other work to do that didn't require special training.

Zooooooom!

I tried to scramble down the ladder, but once again the fighter jets were already overhead when we heard them coming. Thankfully, they didn't drop anything during their low pass over the airport. When our heart rates went back to normal, we continued working but couldn't deny the fact that the tension was rising in this town as well.

Curt stopped near the helicopter and told us that all the expats of the EduVenture team had been evacuated from Pyramid.

"I'm so glad everyone made it out," I said, but it felt hollow. My thoughts went back to the people in Wamena. We all knew not *everybody* had been able to leave. The local Papuan people didn't have the option of evacuating. Nor did most transmigrants. All their lives, families, and homes were in and around the Baliem Valley, and we all hoped they were all right.

"Hans, can you please check out the tail rotor of Mike Foxtrot? I've had some vibrations," our Canadian pilot requested after returning from a flight. Hans went to take a look.

"Mausi, you can fix that," he said and handed me some toilet paper. I looked at him perplexed. One glance had been enough for Hans to see what must have caused the problem. After lubricating the tail rotor generously, the pilot hadn't wiped off the excess grease. By the centrifugal force the grease had spurted out and onto the spinning rotor blades, causing the imbalance and vibrations.

I climbed the ladder and started wiping the thick reddish-brown grease. There was so much that I quickly ran out of toilet paper. I made my way to a mission aviation hangar.

"Hi, guys, could you spare me some toilet paper?" I asked the pilots who handed me a nearly empty roll.
"Sorry, but that won't be enough, do you have more?"
"Is it that bad?" One man asked, looking concerned.
"Oh yes, it's bad."
"Do you need medicine?"

Nobody knew when we would be allowed to go back to Wamena. While we were able to make good use of the time, we all longed to go home. One afternoon, all the missionary ladies from Wamena met for a time of sharing about how they had gone through the evacuation. It was helpful to be able to talk, listen, and to hear how this traumatic event had affected them all. Talking through it also helped me to process the events. I felt slightly out of place because I hadn't been there. But we all had lived with the tension building up in Wamena for months, and it had become a part of daily life. The possibility of evacuation had always been lingering.

"It really took me a while until it sank in that *this is it*," one friend shared and several others nodded. Some had fled from their homes on motorcycles with their backpacks on, trying to get around the obstacles and roadblocks and to the airport. I was thankful the Lord had spared us this traumatic experience, but I felt for my friends who had gone through it all.

Everybody had handled the situation differently. One lady had been in denial that anything would happen and frantically had to pack her backpack at the last minute, while another had been wondering matter-of-factly where they would go and what to take: "Snacks if we wait it out in a mountain village or swimming suits if we go to the coast."

"Well, one thing is for sure: I won't save any goodies from home for a special occasion anymore. I'll just eat them while I can. Who knows what will happen tomorrow?"

Our Canadian family was struggling. They hadn't expected to take their young son to a country with civil unrest. They felt that Wamena wasn't the right place for them.

Simon Tanner, who was to take over the leadership of Helimission from his father, came from Switzerland to talk to us, encourage us, and assess the situation. The decision was made that the Canadian family would leave us. It was hard to see them go. We had gone through difficult times together as a team and as friends. We also desperately needed people for the ever-increasing workload. However, their decision was understandable. They didn't want to expose their son to any more danger and trauma, after being greeted by a riot with burning buildings in Sentani upon arrival, and subsequently going through disturbing events, including an earthquake, a massacre, and an evacuation.

Before Simon got onto the airplane to start his long trip back to Switzerland, he had some final words for us. "I had this impression last night I'd like to share with you: God wants us all to be like an arrow, aimed at one goal without getting sidetracked."

This made sense. There were so many good things we could do and get involved in because there were needs everywhere. But the main reason for us all to be in Papua was to bring the gospel to the isolated people who had never had the chance to hear it in their entire history. This had to remain our main focus, and many other beneficial things would follow in its wake. In our case, good was the enemy of the best. Despite our current unsettled situation, we could continue doing just that. We assisted our new friends in moving to the Point X-Ray area to study the language and culture of the Moi tribe. Another milestone had been reached.

About two weeks after the evacuation, the mission leaders of various organizations declared the situation in Wamena as stable. Their personnel could return, provided Helimission would return to Wamena first, so in case the riots would resume they could be evacuated by helicopter. Brian and Hans were the first ones to return to Wamena by helicopter. During the first night in the house by himself, Hans had a very uneasy feeling, but everything stayed quiet.

Finally, the day had come, and I was going home too. This time I didn't have to wonder if our usual "adventure airline" would have a seat for us, but we women and children were taken to Wamena by my new best friend, Bob, in the Pilatus Porter STOL airplane. Although

I was extremely thankful for his dental skills, I much preferred sitting in an airplane seat than sitting in a dentists' chair. While I had a big grin on my face, because I was finally going home and I would get another first flight in a fascinating aircraft, Jan didn't look happy, to say the least. He stood next to the airplane in the faint light of dawn, longing to go to Wamena as well. Since he was not an indigenous Papuan, Brian had decided he was to stay on the coast until he was convinced Jan would be safe. I felt sorry for him, and the team wouldn't be complete until he'd be back in Wamena too.

The Aftermath of a Tragedy

When I got out of the Pilatus Porter, after landing in Wamena, I took a deep breath of the cool, fresh mountain air and took in the magnificent view of the gray mountain wall on the far side of Wamena. It was such a relief to be back home. After we had gotten three days' notice to leave Indonesia, it had taken six and a half weeks until we were able to return to Wamena, but here we were.

There was no pretending nothing had happened. From the plane, I had seen the charred remains of houses in the part of town where the massacre had started. The whole town was eerily quiet, and the streets were all but deserted. The site of the old market that had recently been reused by ladies to sell fresh produce was fenced in and a spot where the prohibited Morning Star flag had been flown was empty and showed signs of a recent fire.

Nius, our guard, had stayed at our place throughout the riots and also operated the church's HF radio which was the only means of communication with the mountain villages. We sat down with him and listened to his story.

"It was bad. Rumors were going around that the transmigrants were killing Papuans everywhere, so the Papuans were about to kill the transmigrant schoolteachers in the villages. Over the radio, I told them this wasn't the way it happened and pleaded with them not to kill anybody."

In doing so, he had most likely prevented more bloodshed and saved many people's lives.

"With the closed gate, nobody even tried to get into the yard here; everybody just ran past. With the shops all closed and boarded up, it was hard to get food, so I took the bag of rice you kept in the storage shed and shared it with some people."

We were thankful that he had been safe and even able to help others, and that our house was untouched.

When I went to my usual grocery store, there were a few new faces.

"What happened to your other staff members?" I inquired, fearing for the worst.

"They were scared and went back home to their islands," I was told. At least they were safe!

I couldn't imagine what the situation must have been like for the transmigrants. Many of the terrified Papuan people caught up in the events, had fled Wamena and gone back to their villages, but the transmigrants hadn't had a safe place to run to. Even before October 6, people had sold their houses cheaply to escape from the rising tension. When the violence had erupted, people had apparently offered their houses and cars for a ticket on any aircraft leaving Wamena—anything to get out of Wamena alive. Many had barely escaped the attacks with their lives, while others had lost family members.

Stranded people whose houses had been burned, had sought refuge on the military base. Scores of armed soldiers and police officers were patrolling Wamena and mixed with the frightened population. Buzz, who was probably half a Papuan in his heart after having been brought up here, didn't only help the indigenous population. While we were stuck on the coast, he had stayed in Wamena and also reached out to the transmigrants. He had gone to the mosques and the emergency accommodation locations and listened to people's stories. When his family had safely returned, they went and visited the people together. Their sons, Ben and Dani, even gave some of their toys to the children. Most of the children had lost loved ones, their homes and everything in it and their lives would never be the same again.

"*Selamat datang!*" (Welcome) We greeted the women and children who came to join us for a ladies' meeting at one mission house. This was the first trip out of the military compound for some. Even though the streets were quiet and safe, they were still too traumatized to go out on their own. After enjoying some food and playing games, we talked about the terrifying events that had left the women homeless. "I want to leave Wamena as soon as possible," a timid young lady with a scared look on her face said. "At least I managed to save our wedding photos," another one shared.

We hoped the group had gained some confidence for leaving the compound after this outing.

"How about we all go and visit the refugees at the military base, spend some time with them, and bring food?" Buzz and Myrna suggested at the Sunday church service. Whoever in the mission community was able to make the time, went along. We walked into the large hall in the middle of the compound and found scores of people—men, women, and children sitting on dirty, thin mattresses on the floor. What a way to spend several weeks! By now I was able to communicate a little bit in Indonesian and felt comfortable enough sitting and talking with them.

"They beheaded my wife before my eyes," one man told me. The refugees told one terrifying story after the other, but the people seemed glad someone was interested in their situation and stories. There was no way I would be able to comprehend what had happened nor the impact it had had on people's lives.

Home Sweet—Sour—Home

After all the temporary housing, travels, and disruptions, I was glad to be here to stay. There was still a lot of setting up to do. I enjoyed the hot running water in the bathroom and kitchen; the beautiful, easy-to-clean tile floors; the yard with flowers and fruit trees; and especially the giant lemons. We had a spare bedroom and a study which doubled as an extra guest room, and I looked forward to hosting our first overnight guests.

The house had a woodstove, and we also had the gas stove Helimission had provided. When the woodstove was in use, it heated the water for washing dishes and showers. For times when it was not in use, an electric water heater had been installed. A small chest freezer, microwave oven, and electric water kettle were part of the house's inventory as well. Along with my kitchen machine which could cook and steam, our kitchen was now crisis safe; it was safe to assume there would always be either gas, wood, or electricity. Thanks to the freezer, I could bake more bread, buy larger amounts of meat, poultry, cheese, margarine, or processed meats on the coast, and was less likely to run out of any type of food. Hosting guests would be a piece of cake from now on.

Dry and canned foods could be kept in the outside shed where I found large, metal storage cans, in which I could store rice. However, I soon found any food kept outside the relatively sealed house would have to be rat proof. I knew ants and cockroaches would chew through freezer bags. Now I found out plastic containers were impenetrable for cockroaches and ants, but no match for rats. Only the metal storage cans kept rats out. However, their lids weren't completely sealed and didn't keep ants or tiny bugs out. Storing food was turning into a science of sorts. I needed to keep checking if the aging freezer was still running and the electricity supply continued. Over the years, we lost at least two freezer loads full of food, which was heartbreaking, and cleaning it out was disgusting. It was such a shame to bury all the precious meat, cheese, bread, berries, etc.

"Bunga! Bunga! Buah! Buah!" Incessant children's voices were intruding into my dream. I managed to open one eye and could make out it was 5:30 a.m. The sun was just rising, and since it was Saturday, I wasn't planning on getting up for another hour or so. By now, I knew enough Indonesian to know the children at the gate wanted to sell flowers and berries. I sighed, turned around in bed and hoped they would give up and go away. They didn't. The only way to have peace and quiet again was to go out and talk to them, so I put on some clothes and went outside. I couldn't resist buying flowers and fruit.

In the following weeks, I tried various tactics to keep the children from coming so early, but nothing worked. I told them it was useless to come before seven a.m., and I wouldn't buy anything, but then again, how would they know the time? They didn't have watches. I learned there were several groups of them, and they knew that who came first sold first. Sometimes we were lucky, and they went to other people's houses before ours, and we got to sleep in a bit longer. No matter what time, the produce was worth getting up for. The flowers brightened up the house, and the berries were fantastic for desserts and jams.

The young berry and flower vendors weren't the only ones who came to the house at the crack of dawn. Since the missionaries who had previously occupied this house had to leave the country, it was difficult for the church members to stay in touch with the mission in Australia. There were no Internet cafés in Wamena yet, and international phone calls were expensive. People kept coming to the house with messages which I wrote down and emailed to the mission in Australia. I'd then pass on the return messages to the church.

The church's Ladies Association also needed a go-between, and I was happy to help out in the same way. I enjoyed having a cup of tea with the ladies and hearing what was going on in their ministry and lives, now that I had become more fluent in Indonesian. Finally, I was beginning to communicate more with local people and building relationships.

Cloudy With a Chance of Flying Cars

Late October 2000

I was on my way to the office. The previous night's rain had stopped, and brilliant rays of sunlight appeared through gaps in the cloud blanket. A car flew past under a low cloud layer.

What?! A car?

A closer look revealed a long line leading into the cloud and the noise gave away that the heavy Kamov helicopter was flying above the cloud layer, suspending the car. The unusual pair was on the way to Mulia, a mountain village being developed into a regional capital. A road between Wamena and Mulia was under construction. I had always thought roads were built first, and cars would come later, but this was Papua—one unusual place! The Kamov was a powerful cargo workhorse of a helicopter. A commercial company was temporarily operating it out of Wamena for heavy lifting. The need for helicopters was endless in this vast, rugged, mountain area with very few roads.

Our hangar building project was well under way and taking shape now, even though it had taken several weeks until most transmigrant workers had returned after the riots. Everyone was working long hours from before dawn until after sunset to keep the office and flight program running. Maintaining the helicopters in airworthy condition at all times was vital for life-saving medivac flights and for keeping the mission stations going. However, achieving this while working in the open field, exposed to the elements, and in a very under-developed setting was difficult. Hans always had to be a step or two ahead with ordering spare parts. During routine inspections, Hans often found parts that needed replacing. If a replacement part wasn't in stock, the helicopter might sit idly on the ground for three months—the minimal time it took to get a part ordered and delivered to Wamena if all went well. The pressure was on. Problems at the building site were putting more strain on Hans' nerves.

Everybody was stretched to the limit. Brian was the only pilot at the time and he also served as the base manager. Jan had to make sure visas and permits were in order, the bookkeeping was up to date, and the bills paid. We were all glad that Alex, the young, bright, gifted Papuan worker, was assisting with so many practical tasks like refueling the helicopters and helping with the helicopter maintenance.

"My goodness," I said to Hans and Jan. "Is there a day when you can just keep working on your stuff?"

"Hasn't happened yet!"

One day, the major interruption was a Fokker 27 airplane full of passengers with a locked up wheel blocking the runway. The men rushed to help the airline personnel remove the cracked brake disk. When that was done, the plane could be towed off the runway and the other planes circling in the holding pattern could finally land. Another time, the team had to fly to Silimo by helicopter to cut up a crashed Twin Otter airplane blocking the runway. It was then pulled off the airfield and pushed over the edge with the help of the villagers so that other airplanes could land again.

The next task was to remove the damaged Cessna 206 which had been blocking the Ninia airstrip since the crash. The mission airplane was badly damaged, but parts of it could be salvaged, so the decision had been made to take it back to Wamena by Kamov helicopter.

"Surely, that would be a good story for the Helimission newsletter. Don't you maybe need someone to document the recovery with photos?" I suggested, half-jokingly—one could always try, right? To my utter amazement, Brian said I could come. By now I was so fascinated with the Papuan mountains and helicopter flying that I always hoped for another opportunity. It was close to addictive.

In the morning, I was ready with my camera and several rolls of slides.

"Sorry, Elke, one of the Russian crew members would like to come along," Brian informed me. "He says he's never been in a light helicopter before." How disappointing!

"But they said you could get a ride in the Kamov instead if you like."

Wow! Brian had probably negotiated this, thinking I'd be unbearable for days if he had given my seat away ... Anyhow, good deal! What were the odds of getting a ride in such a special aircraft? And besides, I could practice a bit of my rusty Russian.

The principle of "form follows function" had left little room for esthetics on the Kamov Ka-32. This was heavy duty Russian engineering. Since I came along to take photos and this cargo helicopter only had tiny windows in the back, I was allowed to sit in the co-pilot's seat. (Hans still thinks the female-and-blond-hair-factor was not to be discounted as the reason for the Captain's decision to give the co-pilot a flight off). Using the footholds, I climbed up into the cockpit where I had an excellent view through the large windscreen and the bubble windows in the doors.

Hans joined Brian and the others in our helicopter going ahead to hook up the plane to the Kamov. On the previous day, they had already prepared the plane by tying wood to the wings to spoil the aerodynamic lift of the airfoil. This would prevent the pilot-less plane from flying on its terms while hanging under the Kamov which would be dangerous.

The pilot ran up the turbines of the Kamov and its two sets of rotor blades started swooshing over the cabin in opposite directions. They were installed on the same rotor mast, so the counter rotation made a tail rotor unnecessary. The powerful machine was shaking first and then vibrated strongly. We took off straight into the air, lifting up the long line before picking up forward speed toward the South Gap. The friendly captain and I talked about the beauty of Papua, and he pointed out some interesting places.

Beeeeep!

Along with the horn, a red light lit up on the caution panel and my heart sank to the bottom of my stomach. When a horn and light would come on in one of our single-engine helicopters, the cause might be low RPM of the rotor, or engine failure and the sound might likely be one of the last earthly sounds you would ever hear. I looked over to the pilot who looked surprisingly unfazed.

"What's the problem?"

"The hydraulic system," the pilot replied nonchalantly and pressed a button. The sound stopped.

Beeeeeeep!

How can he be so calm? Isn't the hydraulic system a pretty important component?

By now we found ourselves totally surrounded by clouds and the pilot flew a circle to find a way out. I was convinced my time on earth was coming to an end. I remembered a helicopter of the same type had crashed in Papua the year before. I started preparing to meet my Maker any minute now. Finally, we broke free from clouds, saw green mountains around us, and soon Ninia was in sight.

Thank you, Lord!

My mind switched from emergency mode to photo reporter mode.

"Can I get out to take photos when we land?" I asked the pilot.

"No, sorry, we can't land because the rotor downwash would blow away all the huts."

He briefly hovered over the wreck and then turned away from the airstrip. I thought this was just to assess the situation. I looked down through the bubble window and saw the plane suspended in the air below us. I hadn't even felt a tug on the helicopter when it had effortlessly lifted this heavy load! No doubt, this pilot had done this before. I took photos of the unlucky Cessna flying over mountains, valleys, and rivers for the last time. It's unfortunate mission pilot watched and filmed from our Helimission Long Ranger which followed behind us. After a smooth flight, the Kamov pilot carefully put down the Cessna in front of its hangar. Then all available men and children pulled the wreck into the hangar cheered on by Archie, the airport dog. Later, we discovered the airplane pilot had filmed the wreckage recovery in standby mode, for which he got teased for a long time.

After that episode, we sometimes got together with the Russian helicopter crew.

"So, did the hydraulic system get fixed?" I asked the pilot.

"Oh, no, not to worry, we have three of them."

Hmmm, that would have been a useful bit of information, while I was mentally preparing myself for my imminent demise!

The flight in the Kamov had been an exciting break in between my daily tasks of working at the office, buying food at shops and markets all over town, washing, cooking, baking, and writing to our families, friends, and supporters. The latter was often neglected since it was important, but not urgent and there were always plenty of urgent matters to attend to first. I constantly had a guilty conscience toward our faithful supporters who helped keep us going with their prayers, encouragement, and financial support. However, while I was busy and could barely keep up with work at the office and home, nobody's life depended on my work, and I had a house helper. I enjoyed life in Wamena and felt more and more comfortable and at home, while Hans was losing weight and felt worn out. We both got sick frequently and were underweight.

While the hangar building progressed, the next challenge came up: the annual "Certificate of Airworthiness" Inspection of both of our helicopters by the Indonesian government. This document was the basis on which any aircraft was allowed to fly in this country. If the inspector wasn't happy with the paperwork or the helicopter's condition, he could take it out of service with a devastating impact on Helimission's work and the users of the helicopter service. The pressure was on. This was the first such inspection since registering the helicopters in Indonesia and we didn't know what to expect.

Hans pulled out all the logbooks and other documentation of the helicopter due for inspection and got to work. The documentation had to be adapted to Indonesian air law—which Hans had studied during his time in Singapore—and brought up to date. With this addition to the already heavy workload, Hans had to work almost day and night.

If only there were more people to do all the work!

The day of the inspection came. Hans and Brian loaded up all the logbooks and paperwork and flew to Sentani. At a hotel, they set up an office with a tabletop photocopy machine, scanner, and printer and got to work with the inspector. Two days later, the inspection was passed, and the men were able to return to Wamena. After this marathon of long work hours, pressure, and tension, Hans was totally exhausted and came down with a terrible stomach flu. Tests revealed he was suffering from amoebic dysentery (a type of bloody diarrhea caused by parasites) and he recovered quickly after taking the right medicine. However, the stomach pains persisted. Nonetheless, Hans resumed his daily schedule.

Lake Habbema—Almost

Mid-November 2000

It was our weekly Helimission fellowship night when Brian received a phone call. My ears perked up when I overheard him talking about going to Lake Habbema, a lake in the mountains at an altitude of three thousand three hundred meters or eleven thousand feet above sea level. I'd often look up to the mountains, wondering when I could explore them. Each time I flew in an airplane or helicopter, I wondered what it would be like to be on the ground on the mountain roads or in the jungle. I wondered what the sounds and smells would be like without the deafening buzz of the engines, rotors, or propellers and the smell of plastic and electric cables.

Brian sounded excited. "Let's make it a guy's thing!"

That's when I lost it.

Since I didn't know the culture and language too well yet and didn't have any off-road driving experience, I couldn't drive out of town by myself. Now there was a group of people planning to drive up into the mountains and jungle to that beautiful lake—and it was for guys only?

When Brian realized how upset I was, he said we could probably invite the mission community to go on the trip, including the women. I was embarrassed that my emotions had gotten the better of me. In Germany and Switzerland, people would openly say how they feel and what they think, but I would slowly learn that in America, people were not as direct. Our American friends sure had to put up with a lot from me. But I was still happy that I would get to go to the mountains.

A few days later, the Daihatsu rattled upward out of the valley. Some friends had joined us, and we enjoyed the view of Wamena and the surrounding area. The Baliem Valley was flat like a lake with mountains of different heights and shapes surrounding it on all sides. We were thrown around in the car on rough stretches of the rocky dirt road. I was glad Hans was driving and not me—especially on the steep sections and while crossing rickety, narrow bridges. He had lots of experience driving in off-road situations. I didn't dare watch when the guys in front of us nearly came off their motorbikes, while I was busy enough just hanging on for dear life in the car. It took the men strength and skill to dodge the rough rocks and pick the right track in the steep, narrow, gravel road. In some parts, it was dug out of the mountainside and therefore prone to landslides.

We passed by beautiful sweet potato and cassava gardens and met people carrying wood and heavy net bags. We came across little logging parties camped on the roadside. Wooden boards, which the Papuan men had cut in the forest and carried down the trails, were stacked up by the roadside. From there, yellow, dump trucks would take them to town for sale. Around every sharp bend, there was another stunning view of the Baliem Valley, side valleys, or hamlets. The higher we drove into the mountains, the cooler it got. Soon there were no more gardens, but only forest. The trees looked different from the ones in the valley, and many were overgrown by epiphytes, moss, and lichen.

We drove into a cloud and were enclosed by thick fog. The bizarre tree shapes looked eerie in this cold, dark scene. It felt as if we had entered into another world. I wouldn't have been surprised if a dinosaur had come out of the woods. I was so excited!

The view behind the next bend made me swallow hard: a large landslide had covered the road! Part of it had broken away, and Hans drove across the section carefully so we wouldn't slip off the side into the precipice. Next, Hans made the Daihatsu plow through the mud and past tangled branches and rocks. Now it was Jan's turn. His motorbike bucked like a horse when he maneuvered it through the woody, rocky mire.

We came to a fairly decent stretch of road and saw the remnants of a small campfire hunters must have made. The convoy consisting of a car and several motorbikes stopped. We made a fire and ate lunch. We were out of the clouds now and had a clear view of the forest and the interesting plants. Apart from our voices and exotic birdsong, it was quiet, and the air was cool and fresh. After enjoying our picnic, we had a look around the area, before driving further into these mysterious foggy mountains. Some road sections were so steep that the guys had to walk next to their motorbikes because the engine wouldn't carry the weight of the bike and them uphill in the thin air at this altitude.

Behind the next bend, we didn't find the thick, green, cloud forest we had expected, but gray and black barren trees sticking their branches in the air as if asking for help. What a desolate sight. During the drought a few years back, much of the forest had burned, but unlike this part, most of it had recovered.

After three hours of driving, we reached a grassy plain between the mountains partly covered by a cloud. The landscape colors gave it the impression of eternal autumn. The road was still winding, but it was rather flat now. There was no lake in sight yet, but looking at our watches and counting the remaining daylight hours, we decided to turn back. It was disappointing we hadn't seen the lake, but what an awesome adventure this was anyway. (On a later visit, we realized we had been next to the lake, but it was hidden under the cloud we saw on the plain).

This was the most remote and isolated place I had ever been to and its melancholic beauty left a deep impression on me.

The descent on the steep, rocky, muddy road was even scarier than the ascent! The men on the motorbikes were getting stiff arms and necks from keeping their bikes on the road. Suddenly, the convoy stopped. Ahead of us, we saw a group of young Papuan men who had appeared out of the forest with bows and arrows. Negotiations began. The people wanted us to pay money for using the road which they claimed to have fixed with their hands. It didn't look as if anybody had fixed anything, but the bow and arrow pointing at us made the men look very convincing in their request. Grudgingly, we handed over some money, and they let us through. Being threatened like this left a bitter aftertaste with us after such a beautiful trip.

Reentering Wamena with the bustling market, cars, bicycle taxis, and people everywhere, was a stark contrast to the lonely, silent, cloud forest.

This must compare to what astronauts feel like when returning to earth from outer space.

I was sad this excursion was over but so happy and grateful to the men for letting us women and children come along.

Hans and Elke at Lake Habbema

A Field Day for the Greenhorn

November 2000

"Hey, Elke, there will be room in the heli tomorrow when I pick up Hans and Buzz. Want to come along?" Brian asked after returning from his flights. What a question!

Ever since Hans had come to Papua, he had wanted to go along to a village for a *JESUS* film showing. His time had come, and Brian had taken Buzz and him to the lowland village of Suru-Suru by helicopter. Buzz's ministry supported evangelists in that area, and an airstrip was under construction.

With the overwhelming workload, it was easy to lose sight of what it was all about. The purpose of our work was not just flying helicopters and building hangars after all, but to assist the faithful missionaries and local evangelists who brought the gospel to isolated villages in the jungle. It would be good to see the impact our work had on people in the bush.

Hans had repaired the generator, gotten the film showing equipment ready, packed a mosquito net and lots of repellent, and gone off on his adventure in the morning. I was so excited to go along on the pick-up flight the next day that I could hardly sleep that night. The flight was combined with an airstrip check in the foothills of the mountain range. The pilots had to find their way around thick clouds and steep mountains. Flying was a tough job in this part of the world with the ever-changing weather. When the landscape was in plain sight again, unobstructed by clouds, many mountains and valleys looked so much alike that it was hard to tell which one it was.

Thank God for GPS!

I marveled at the landscape. Towering mountains were covered in trees, grass, ferns, and shrubs, even on near vertical slopes and divided by deep gorges in which white-water rivers thundered toward the lowlands.

Surely, nobody can live in a place like this.

I could hardly believe it when I saw a little plume of smoke coming out of a tiny hut on the mountainside to our left.

How can anybody live on a slope that steep and sleep without fear of sliding down the mountain together with the house and garden?

A little further, we could see almost exactly that scenario had happened. A hut was still clinging to the mountain slope, but the garden below it was gone with a neat line on the top where the first row of sweet potatoes had been. What were the people eating now?

We landed in Paro which was situated between the gray peaks of the Sudirman Range and the flat, hot, steamy lowlands. The mission airplane pilot, who had come along to check the newly built airstrip, got out the pogo stick and other equipment to check the surface of the runway, its *crown* (convex shape allowing rain water to drain), the ditches next to it, and also to measure its length.

I looked around. Most houses were built on stilts and in the traditional way, but there was a lot of construction going on with planed wooden boards, nails, and corrugated steel. I was surprised to see a transmigrant worker amongst the indigenous population. I walked behind the helicopter to get it into the picture together with the scene of the airstrip check.

"Why did you go to the back of the helicopter?" Brian asked me.

Oh no! Now, I realized I hadn't even thought about the rule that you NEVER go to the back of a running helicopter with a tail rotor! During short stops on the ground, it was more economical to leave the turbine engine running to avoid the accumulation of start cycles. This would lengthen the time between maintenance intervals and conserve time and battery power needed for the startup. Shutting down would require time to cool down the engine and warm it up again before take-off. In between, the rotor needed to be turned backward by hand to prevent carbon buildup which could otherwise lead to a turbine module lockup. However, the problem with the running helicopter was the tail rotor spun at such a high speed that it was barely visible. Therefore, it was a real danger that people might walk into it and get killed while the aircraft could get out of control. With the excitement, rotor wind, and noise around a helicopter, people often didn't think clearly — including me. Even though I already had some experience with helicopters, I sometimes wanted to eagerly jump out after landing before I had unstrapped the seatbelt. Other times, I would be stopped after a few steps outside because I still had the headset on which was connected to the Intercom with a cable. (Later, I felt less stupid when Luana said, "We've all done that.")

The Papuan people quickly became emotionally charged, and if somebody was injured, the people often turned violent against the person responsible for an injury. Somebody being struck by the tail rotor would have been an extremely unpleasant event. Even though I hadn't been very close to the tail rotor, I was glad I didn't get injured, and Brian didn't rip my head off for making such a basic mistake. From now on, it became my mission not only to take photos for newsletters and presentations but also to keep people away from the tail rotor. Sometimes we even had to grab and manhandle a person.

The airstrip check was completed; we took off and waved good-bye to the people of Paro. It was still difficult to find a way between the clouds. Buzz radioed us, "I'm not sure if you'll be able to get into Suru-Suru. We're in the middle of a massive downpour."

Thankfully, by the time we had found our way through the mountains and the clouds, the weather had cleared up. The rugged mountain range enclosing us minutes earlier now gave way to the completely flat lowlands. They were covered by a green rainforest carpet as far as the eye could see and all the way down to the Arafura Sea. What a contrast!

We landed at Suru-Suru in beautiful sunshine. With us in the helicopter was a Papuan evangelist who wanted to work in this village. Hans and Buzz, along with some villagers, greeted us. The airplane pilot got to work again and checked the progress on the runway. The rain shower had only brought temporary relief and soon it got hot and steamy again. Hans showed me around the little village.

"I can't wait to sleep in our soft bed at home. I slept on the floor of the hut over here. The problem was that a rooster was sitting underneath the floor boards and crowed all night."

"I'm sure you fancied roast chicken," I teased, "So, what did you get to eat?"

"Well, before we showed the *JESUS* film, we were invited to a *bakar batu*, with a pig and vegetables. They also had sago and cooking bananas." (Bakar batu is a traditional feast where stones are heated in a fire and placed in a pit in the ground, alternating with layers of leaves, vegetables, and meat until the food is steamed.)

It turned out this had been an interesting trip back in time. Even though we had lived in Papua for several months and had some interesting experiences, our lives were somewhat comparable to our lifestyle back home including sleeping in a bed inside a house with four walls, taking hot showers, working in an office and on aircraft, and preparing (albeit with a little more effort) and eating familiar food. This, on the contrary, had been the all-Papuan-experience for Hans.

"So, what else did you do all day?"

"Sweating, mainly. We took a bath in the river, and Buzz went in a canoe with some other guys. Man, you should have seen them all standing up on that narrow dugout canoe and paddling on the river. I have no idea how they managed not to tip over."

Hans was clearly out of his comfort zone. Buzz, however, who had grown up with bakar batu's and canoes and knew two tribal languages, fit in perfectly except for his outward appearance.

"It was amazing to observe the people who watched the *JESUS* film," Hans reported. "I guess the whole village turned up and this must have been the first movie they've ever seen. You should have seen the reactions during some scenes. They didn't have the film in the language they speak here, so they turned down the volume and an evangelist narrated. The people were so excited; they talked until deep into the night."

Hans pointed to a simple wooden structure on stilts with a tin roof.

"Look, that's the school building over there. This morning all the children lined up in front of the building until their teacher called them in. Apparently, he isn't even a government teacher, but a motivated Christian from another area, who is doing the job."

We walked past another building.

"You wouldn't believe it. The people here have such a different way of life," Hans shook his head, "you know what happened to me this morning? While the rain was pouring down, I sat under the roof over there. A naked guy walking by saw me, and sat down next to me. You know what he did?"

"No, what?"

"He sang a little tune 'lalala' while staring into the rain. Then he fell over asleep, and when he woke up again he sat up, kept staring into the rain, and singing 'lalala.' I couldn't believe it."

Hans had a lot on his plate with overseeing the building site and keeping the helicopters up and running to international aviation standards in an underdeveloped setting with constant interruptions and unforeseen problems. He always had to think ahead of schedule and plan carefully. He knew each mistake or any negligence could have deadly consequences. Life in this village seemed to be so different from all that. No stress, no deadlines. Of course, there was so much more to life in a community like this than met the eye and it would have taken a long time living with the tribe to comprehend it all.

While looking around the village and taking photos, I couldn't help notice how unwell most people looked. Many had enlarged stomachs caused by chronic malaria, worms, or malnutrition and also skin diseases which affected large parts of their bodies. We came across a simple, wooden, church building which contained teaching material MSF (Doctors Without Borders) had used to educate the people about hygiene and nutrition. While on the outside, the people still lived the way their ancestors had, they now had a simple school, were getting medical attention, and spiritual input. The latter gave them a choice between their animistic belief in ancestral spirits and all that entailed and the gospel of Jesus Christ.

Soon the men were finished checking out the airstrip site, and it was time to go. The ground had been soaked through by the rain, and it was obvious it wouldn't be suitable for airplane landings yet without better drainage. We loaded up the *JESUS* film equipment and off we went again, back to the mountains. After about an hours' time, we were back in Wamena with all the cars, motorbikes, and bicycle taxis. Hans was back to work in the hangar, and I had to think of what to cook for lunch.

Often it was hard to take in and get our heads around all we saw and experienced. The contrast between our lives and the lives of the people in the jungle tribes was about as stark as the contrast from the flat steaming hot lowlands to the tall, rugged and sometimes snow-capped mountains. Hans had gotten a glimpse of what life in the jungle was like.

"Buzz is like a fish in the water down there, but I think I'm quite happy working on machines," he concluded.

If we all used the gifts God had given us, we would complement each other and get the work done.

Buzz later said to Hans: "Actually, you did pretty well. Another westerner I took here had such a culture shock that he banged his head against a wall."

After returning from his jungle trip, Hans' stomachaches flared up again and wouldn't go away. Something had to be done, but what? Friends suggested Hans should go to Jakarta for a gastroscopy. With all the work that had to be done and the expense and logistics of the 3,500-kilometer trip in mind which would take at least two days and four flights one way, we prayed even harder for Hans to get better.

Before we could make any arrangements in that direction, Hans noticed he didn't have any stomach cramps when he didn't have chocolate milk for breakfast. What a relief! Since moving to Wamena, Hans had never had trouble with his daily chocolate milk, but the unhealthy diet while he was by himself in Singapore and the ameba afterward must have had a negative impact on his gut flora, rendering him lactose intolerant. When Hans got a bad cold soon afterward, it didn't even faze him—now if only he wouldn't get those terrible stomachaches anymore.

Guardian Angels on Overtime

On the building site, things progressed and we were happy to see the rooms in the office tract take shape. We—along with our friends back home—prayed for safety and solid progress, but when working on such a comprehensive project, accidents were bound to happen. One day the dreaded phone call came: Hanly, one young worker had fallen off the seven-meter high roof rafters into the office tract where wood and tools were lying around everywhere. Also, there were nails sticking out of the wood and all kinds of other hazards Hans had been warning people about, but to no avail. We all thought Hanly must have broken most bones in his body when falling on such a ground, but guardian angels must have dampened his fall.

Even though he was badly bruised, had a light head injury, and was in a lot of pain, the X-rays showed no broken bones, and soon the lucky young man was able to leave the hospital. I was more than a little surprised to see him in his work clothes at the next payroll!

Soon after, Hans pulled into the driveway at the hangar after his lunch break and gasped in horror. One worker was dangling by his hands from the ridge of the hangar roof, while his friends—eight meters below—were trying to reposition the ladder he was supposed to be standing on. The man couldn't be bothered to climb down and back up again just to move the ladder over by a meter. To make matters worse, the heavily-built Dani man wasn't hanging on the bricks, but on the render. This was too much for Hans' nerves which were already stretched like guitar strings. He gave the men a good rant.

"Oh what a day," Hans said, his elbows on the table and head in his hands.

"What happened this time?" I enquired.

"Twice today I stopped someone from drinking battery acid. There was a group of young village men building the fence around the hangar as a church fund raiser. There was so much going on that I forgot to tell them where to get a drink of water. When I finally went over, I could only scream when I saw a guy trying to peel off the inner seal of a bottle with his teeth. It was battery acid!" The bottles, which looked much like drinking water bottles, were ready to be loaded into the helicopter and flown to a mission station—that's why they had been in plain sight.

Hans had already warned people of electric cables sticking out of walls waiting to electrocute somebody, wearing sandals or walking barefoot in between nails, wood splinters, and lose rocks. He felt like fighting a losing battle. This was a showcase of why some occupational health and safety rules in our home countries had gone overboard in the other direction with strict regulations. We wished a bit of common sense would prevail.

Burning Both Ends of the Candle

"This is driving me nuts," Hans vented. "If only I could concentrate on either thing: maintaining the helicopters or overseeing the building project. Doing both justice at the same time is impossible."

It hurt me to see my dear Hans in a bind every day. He tried whatever he could to keep up with the demands, but there weren't enough hours in the day. He got up before dawn each morning, read his Bible, and prayed for strength and wisdom for the day, safety for the workers and the helicopter operations, and for God's help to carry the impossible workload. He then had a little breakfast because I made him eat, even though his stomach felt like it was tied in a knot every morning. He worked long hours Monday through Saturday night and sometimes night shifts, to get the helicopter up and running again for the following days' flights. If only there were more people to share the workload!

The helicopters required three and a half hours of maintenance per flight hour. In addition to the work at the office and hangar, there were sometimes problems with the Helimission car which Hans needed to attend to or things broke at the houses. On some Sundays, he only got up for meals but slept most of the day to get enough strength for the new week and all its challenges. When we had our single friends over for brunch on Sundays, we would sometimes find Hans asleep on the couch, after we wondered what had happened when he didn't return from the bathroom.

"Don't take things so seriously, Hans. Have fun and relax." "Maybe if you'd set your priorities better, then you wouldn't be so overworked," was the advice of well-meaning people. Others suggested he should pray more and have faith.

Now setting priorities better would be difficult. Whose priorities were more important? The sick or injured people in the mountains waiting for a medevac to the hospital? The missionaries who relied on the helicopter service for food supplies and to get in and out of their remote locations? The construction crews, consisting of about twelve workers at the time, who needed materials and decisions? The people who wanted to kill the workers at the construction site because of land disputes? The guerrilla fighters who were causing unrest? The earthquakes? The burst water pipe at home? The immigration officials requesting another set of fingerprints to renew permits? Perhaps, the answer was not as simple as saying no to requests. Everybody on the team had more work on their hands than they could handle.

"You Helimission people don't fade away, you burn out," a friend remarked, and it certainly seemed like the men were burning their candles at both ends without any staff reinforcement in sight.

Helimission was in a unique situation. Unlike other aviation organizations using airplanes, of which there were several, Helimission was the only organization in Papua which used helicopters for mission work, search-and-rescue missions, medical evacuations, church support, and community development. Even though all ministries not related to pioneer mission or medevacs were put on the back burner, the need by far exceeded the capacity. It was very difficult for Helimission to find enough suitable personnel for their bases at the time.

Just as the construction workers were lax with health and safety precautions, they were not too particular about the building plans at times. One evening, after the work on the helicopters was done for the day, Hans went to check the progress on the building site. The wall had gone up—without a window. The next morning, Hans went to the contractor to go over the drawings again and asked for the planned window to be put in.

"Pak Hans changed his mind. There needs to be a window now," the foreman then told the workers.

"Hans, don't worry too much. To us, relationships are more important than money. God has blessed us, so we'll be able to pay these bills too," was the sympathetic response from headquarters when Hans reported yet another cost overrun. The contractor's cost estimates had proved inaccurate. Building supplies that had been delivered would disappear and needed to be replaced. Only the third delivery of window glass panes was intact. The first two had been dropped from the airplane's cargo hold on to the tarmac where they shattered. New estimates came up—each one higher than the previous one.

Since the workers had finally returned after the massacre, the hangar building was slowly gaining momentum, but with new problems. This time the contractor threatened to shut down the project and send the skilled laborers back to their islands if we wouldn't comply with his demands. Hans, in turn, demanded a new cost estimate before any concessions would be made, as by now the projected money was nearly used up with the building being far from completion. After another standoff with the contractor, Hans finally shut the project down.

Off With a Bang

Early December 2000

It was time for Brian and his family to go on home assignment for half a year.

"What will we do without you guys? And what if we get sick, who will treat us then?"

I was worried.

"God will provide," Luana answered, and I knew she was right. Still, it was hard for us to imagine them not being there because we were such a tightly-knit team. The responsibility weighed heavily on us, and I would have to do the finances without Luana's help. Thankfully, Jan was still there, which was a comfort. By now I got by in Indonesian reasonably well and was able to pay all the phone and electricity bills, do banking and related transactions, and pay the bills for building materials and the workers' salaries. Brian and Luana had taught us well, and God was more than able to help us with all the big and small problems we would encounter.

"Pack your bags; we've booked you flights and a hotel in Timika for a long weekend," Brian and Luana announced. We gave them a blank stare. We knew this was too generous to accept, but we also needed a break, so we gratefully accepted.

Our friends had realized the work, excitement, and stress of the past half year had taken a toll on Hans' health and well-being. There was no good place to rest and relax around Wamena at the time, and we couldn't afford to fly somewhere to get refreshed, so they stepped in and helped. We had to fly to the north coast and then across the breadth of the island to the south coast since there were no direct flights to Timika, but it was worth it. Poor Hans was sick in bed most of the weekend, but he still enjoyed the rest, tasty food, and watching TV news. I spent a lot of time on the screened-in balcony reading a book while listening to the jungle sounds right next to the hotel and went swimming in the beautiful pool. It was wonderful just to sit down for a delicious meal and not to have any responsibility for a few days.

Back in Wamena, we invited Brian and the family for one last meal together, before their departure. Philip brought his leftover firecrackers and fireworks to use up after dinner. I sat on the motorbike under the tin roof and watched the men fiddling with the lighter from a few meters' distance.

BOOOOOM!

"Brian!" Luana screamed. We all expected to see Brian's hand ripped to shreds. We were extremely relieved to see he was all right and his glasses, which the blast had sent flying, were intact too. Something had been seriously wrong with that firecracker! It hadn't been the best idea to sit under a tin roof, and I was glad my eardrums hadn't ruptured. Immediately, we heard bells ringing at the police station. Our neighbor cautiously popped his head up from behind the fence, and two minutes later an armed soldier poked his head around the corner of our house. He then waved to his comrades to follow, just like movie scenes. We should have known better than to use firecrackers a few weeks after bloody riots in town. The soldiers came closer and looked relieved to see a few puzzled-looking westerners. Everybody had a good laugh when they realized what had happened and then went back home. The next day our neighbor saw Hans on the street and called out: "Hello, Mister Boom!"

Redefining Christmas

So far, every Christmas season of my life had been traditional and mostly the same.

On each of the four Advent Sundays, we had lit another candle on the beautifully decorated Advent wreath made of aromatic pine twigs. We had baked delicious Christmas cookies, stored them in pretty tins, and enjoyed the smells of fresh baked cookies, vanilla, and spices.

We had walked through the dark, neighborhood streets to look at the pine trees lit up by light chains in the front yards. On the weekends when it snowed, we had walked or driven through the winter wonderland (not that we always had a white Christmas, though), before returning to the beautifully decorated, warm home and enjoying fresh brewed coffee or cinnamon and clove flavored fruit tea, marzipan stollen (Christmas fruitcake), gingerbread, cookies, nuts, and mandarin oranges.

We had gone to the town center where Christmas lights were suspended over historical timber-framed houses on the main street and to the decorated shops to buy presents for each other. I loved the Christmas markets with the pretty booths selling everything from woolen socks, hats, and sweaters; through scented candles and soaps; to roasted almonds, gingerbread, and mulled wine.

On Christmas Eve, my family always celebrated with a wonderful meal, then read the Christmas story from the Bible by the fresh pine Christmas tree with real candles, and exchanged presents afterward. We had also gone to the beautiful gothic church for a festive Christmas service and gotten together with my aunt and her family for coffee and fancy cakes. On Christmas day, we had always had a wonderful goose dinner and afterward spent time with my grandmother and my father's large family. This had been the time we met all our aunts, uncles, and cousins from different parts of Germany and caught up with them.

Now all that happened on the other side of the world. I walked through the dusty streets in the midday heat and wondered what we should do for Christmas. Brian, Luana, and the kids had been our family here in Wamena, but they wouldn't be here either. And besides, since when was Christmas celebrated when it was warm? (I hadn't been to Australia yet). The seasons didn't even change for Christmas. When we had left Germany in May, I hadn't thought of bringing recipes for Christmas cookies or Christmas music CDs. When I asked my mother to email some recipes, I found most ingredients weren't available in Wamena. We didn't have an Internet connection fast enough to download recipes or music yet.

Thankfully, Luana had been able to help out once again. Along with lots of books and other things, she had also loaned us homemade Christmas decorations. Luana and Briana had created colored candles by melting crayons into the wax of locally available plain white candles and used them to make beautiful centerpieces. I decorated the house the best I could by getting out the few Christmas decorations I had brought from home and adding some I found at the local hardware store (next to PVC pipes, screws, engine oil, and office supplies).

However, there was one thing I refused to do: buy a plastic Christmas tree. At home, we had always had a fresh pine tree effusing a wonderful fragrance which we had set up and decorated it in the afternoon of Christmas Eve. I decided having a plastic tree would be worse than having no tree at all.

Famous last words! In the end, I missed having a Christmas tree so much that the following year in October I bought the first fake one I saw appear in a shop.

For Christmas Eve, we invited Gerhard to join us. He was lonely because his family had gone to Germany for medical treatment. We had a nice meal and exchanged presents and stories. It felt good to have another lonely soul around on this special night. After dinner, we went to Kevin and Allyson's house. Before going on furlough, Brian had picked up the family from their steaming hot lowland jungle station, so they wouldn't be without a way out in case of an emergency before the replacement helicopter pilot would arrive. So they used this time for a break. They had invited us to sing carols with them, their children, and some other guests and to enjoy hot drinks and Christmas goodies. Allyson played the keyboard, and we sat around the Christmas tree and sang carols. Now it felt like Christmas had come after all. On Christmas day, we were invited to Kevin and Allyson's house again, this time for a real turkey dinner. They had invited other missionaries from their organization too. Everybody contributed to the feast, and we had a wonderful time of fellowship and enjoyed the special meal. It turned out to be a lovely Christmas, and we were able to talk to our families back home on the phone.

I had survived the first Christmas away from home—with God's help and the help of generous friends who had opened their house to us and others. How good it had been of Kevin and Allyson to include us. Here in Papua, our families were the people with the same goal we had. They had come from all over the world so the unreached Papuan tribes would hear for the first time in history the real reason we celebrated Christmas: Jesus Christ, the Son of God, had come into this world to carry our sins to the cross and to reconcile us to God.

Of course, we missed our families. Sometimes, however, I wondered if they missed us even more, because now there was a gap where we had always been, whereas we were in a new situation. While we had gone through numerous difficulties, we had also gained a life of fulfillment and new friends who had become additions to our family. People say, "Blood is thicker than water," but Jesus' blood connecting us is thicker yet.

"And everyone who has left houses or brothers or sisters or father or mother or wife or children or lands, for My name's sake, shall receive a hundredfold, and inherit eternal life." Matthew 19:29

On New Year's Eve, most of the Wamena mission community went to Pyramid to celebrate. Hans and other friends went by car, and

Jan and I joined them on motorbikes. My type of fun: a motorbike trip through a beautiful landscape.

"Jan, why do you wave at everybody?" I asked when we stopped, "You can't possibly know all these people."

"Well, it never hurts to be friendly, but in case you break down out here, it definitely pays to be friendly to people, so they are more likely to help you get back on the road."

Another good survival strategy. Many people sped by pedestrians giving them a fright, which I found appalling. We rode on, dodging deep potholes and hardly had time to admire the beautiful views. Many of the women on the roadside would not look at us but instead turned their faces away until we had passed. Many women looked sad and burdened, not merely by the heavy loads they were carrying. I loved to see their faces light up when we waved at them. It became my favorite sport from then on: getting Papuan ladies to smile. The children who played by the road didn't need any further encouragement, they waved at us and smiled anyway, yelling "Daaaa!" at the top of their lungs.

At Pyramid, we stayed in the crude, small, wooden cabins at the conference center. In the evening, we had a barbecue, sang, prayed, and welcomed the year 2001 together and entrusted it to the Lord. We were thankful to have survived the year 2000 and didn't need any more fireworks.

"It feels totally unreal to think we've only been here for eight months," I said to Hans. "I hope next year will be a bit less eventful."

"Unlikely," Hans replied with a sigh.

Whatever the new year would bring, if the Lord would give us the freedom, strength, finances, and health, we would continue to do the work He had given us and trust Him to do the rest. And we would keep praying for more workers to join the harvest!

I remembered a verse we had memorized at the ladies' Bible study:

He who observes the wind will not sow,
And he who regards the clouds will not reap.

As you do not know what is the way of the wind,
Or how the bones grow in the womb of her who is with child,
So you do not know the works of God who makes everything.

In the morning sow your seed,
And in the evening do not withhold your hand;
For you do not know which will prosper,
Either this or that,
Or whether both alike will be good.

Ecclesiastes 11:4-6

Beauty and Tragedy

January 9, 2001

"Hi, Elke, would you be able to go on a search flight tomorrow morning early?" our single pilot friend Tom asked me one afternoon in early January. "A Navy plane is missing, and we still need observers."

"Oh no, that's dreadful! Yeah, sure I'll be there. Do you have any more information?"

"We're having a briefing at the office in ten minutes, why don't you join that to find out more."

I went to the office where Harry, a Dutch mission pilot, filled us in: "Okay, here's what we know. An Indonesian Navy CASA plane with nine people on board took off from Timika around eleven o'clock this morning and was on its way to Sentani via Wamena, but it never arrived here. Apparently, most of the passengers are high-ranking government officials."

Nine people! I hoped they were all right.

"About the search flight," Harry continued. "Airplanes have crashed during search-and-rescue operations. That's why we always have two pilots in the cockpit to ensure we're not getting ourselves into trouble when searching for a crashed plane and not taking care of flying the plane safely. So we need you guys in the back to carefully scan the terrain for anything unusual. Don't just look for the shape of an airplane. It might be badly damaged or broken apart. Also look for smoke, evidence of a fire, or marks in the terrain or the trees."

Oh dear, this sounded very serious and difficult. I wondered if I was the right person for the job. What if I missed something? I had seen searches like that in movies, and so many times the planes had flown right overhead, and the desperate people still hadn't been found.

"We'll go up with two planes," Harry interrupted my anxious thoughts. "We'll take off with the first light at five-thirty a.m., so come a bit earlier. Any questions?"

What a terrible thought: nine people might have died in the crash! I hoped and prayed I wouldn't mess up and miss something. The poor people! If they had survived, they had a terrible night ahead of them. Depending on the altitude where they had crashed they could be in danger of dying of hypothermia.

It was impossible to start the search this late in the afternoon in this part of the world. Clouds obscured much of the rugged terrain already, and we'd soon run out of daylight.

The next morning at five-fifteen a.m., I was ready with a bag containing chocolate bars, drinking water, tissues, and a small camera. It was still quite dark and cool. Our pilots were Harry, who had brought a visiting relative as the second observer, and Tom, the one with the family.

We prayed together and then took off with the first light. The sun rose over the mountains and flooded the beautiful valley with its brilliant light reflected by the fog which covered the ground but revealed shapes of trees. We left the grand valley and entered the high mountain range on our way south.

"Whatever you guys see, just tell us," Harry urged us observers. "It's better to get a closer look right away than to miss something or to have to go back later."

The sun now illuminated the ridges one after the other. I felt guilty. How could I enjoy this breathtaking view so much, while we were looking for a missing plane with nine passengers who might be severely injured or dead?

After a while of flying over the rugged, partly forest-covered mountains with deep ravines and rushing rivers, the scene changed dramatically when we entered the forest-covered plains of the lowlands, spreading as far as the eye could see. How could we possibly find a downed airplane in these deep gorges or amongst millions of trees, which could swallow a small airplane and hide it from view?

God help us—and those poor people in the plane! I silently prayed as the hopelessness of the venture sank in. We would need a solid strategy and divine intervention to find the plane in this vast area.

First, we landed at a lowland village situated on the flight path of the missing plane. I got out to stretch my legs and look around. Even though it was still early in the morning, it was already hot and humid. Like I had already noticed at Suru-Suru, the people looked different from the highland tribes.

"Okay, the people say they heard a plane fly over at around eleven a.m. yesterday," Harry announced after talking to the villagers.

We flew to the next airstrip on the flight path of the missing airplane, and again the people confirmed hearing the plane fly over. In the third village, however, the locals hadn't heard the plane.

"That probably means the pilot entered the mountain range somewhere between Kenyam and here."

We got back into the plane and headed for the valley running from Kenyam up into the mountains to the village of Mbua. My eyes scanned and scanned the terrain, but after all I had seen so far, I wasn't optimistic we would find the airplane. Some ravines were so deep and had steep walls; we might have missed the plane even if we had flown directly over it.

"If we do find a plane, we'll have to verify first it's the one we're looking for or if it is an old wreckage from another crash. There are airplane wrecks all over the island, and many have never been found," one pilot explained.

Never been found—how hard must that be for the families? The uncertainty ...

"What's that down there?" The pilot turned the plane toward a ridge on the mountainside. We saw smoke and a small bright light shining at us. The pilot circled down and now we could see a few men flashing a mirror at us, reflecting the sunlight. Did they know where the plane had crashed and wanted to tell us? We weren't able to land anywhere near to talk to the people, so the pilots reported the sighting and its position by radio, so our helicopter could check it out. We flew on and landed at the Mbua airstrip for a brief break

Beauty and Tragedy

and to ask the people if they had heard or seen anything. It was a relief to get out of the plane again, stretch our legs, and relax a bit after concentrating for so long with the pressure of knowing peoples' lives might depend on our vigilance. We had some snacks and drinks and used the mission house bathroom. Nobody lived there at the moment, but it still looked nice and cozy, and there were family pictures on the walls.

We took off to continue the search but soon had to turn back to Wamena because the clouds were building up and the fuel would soon run low. It was so disappointing that neither we nor the other search plane had found the missing aircraft and didn't have any information for the families who were desperately waiting to hear news of their loved ones. There was no hope of the weather improving, so the search was called off for the day and would be continued the next morning. The two search airplanes had been in the air nearly four hours by the time we reached Wamena. The pilots met with an Indonesian government team to discuss the findings and further proceedings. I was asked to come along as an observer again the next morning.

The pilots had just finished the pre-flight inspections using flashlights in the dark. Johannes who had come back to Papua with his new wife, Laura, to fill in during Brian's absence, was getting the helicopter ready as well.

"We have an idea now where the airplane crashed," a pilot informed me when I got to the airport at the crack of dawn. "A Papuan guy who was walking over the mountains from Wamena to Silimo heard the plane circle and crash in the high mountains."

Oh dear, this was probably the cold regions above the tree line with freezing nighttime temperatures. There wasn't much hope of finding survivors after two nights in those conditions, but at least we had a hope of finding the wreck. This time I was in the other plane with the single Tom and another pilot.

We weren't in the air long when we heard on the radio that the first search plane had found the wreckage. It didn't look good. The previous day we had mostly flown over forest and villages, but now we entered the cold, barren, unpopulated regions at more than 3,000 meters/10,000 feet above sea level with peaks reaching heights of more than 4,700 meters/15,000 feet. I was awestruck. Sharp ridges of sheer gray rock pointed toward the sky. Some slopes were covered in light green grass and low shrubs. We flew past a huge waterfall rushing down the mountain towering next to us. We approached the crash site and over the intercom I heard the pilots commenting on the plane's condition. I still didn't see anything remotely resembling an airplane, only white limestone rocks scattered across the mountainside. Tom handed me a video camera.

"Here, try to get some footage of the plane. You might get a better view from the back."

I still had no clue as to what I was supposed to film, so Tom pointed it out to me. It appeared some scattered white objects weren't rocks, but plane parts, and now I discovered there was gray paint on some of them. I was shocked. Although I had been briefed before about what to expect, I wasn't prepared for this. Nobody could have survived a crash like that. The plane had hit the side of a mountain not too far below the ridge. I tried my best to zoom in on the wreckage, but we were too high above it, and the plane was shaking badly from the turbulence caused by the morning sun warming up the mountainside. The pilots circled several times while I filmed the area. This footage would give the recovery team an idea of the terrain they would have to deal with.

When we circled away from the wreck, we left the mountain shade and caught a glimpse of a vast high plateau bathed in the golden light of the morning sun. I noticed several plant clusters looking like mini palm trees with black stems (later I learned they were fern trees). After this breathtaking sight, we were back over the wreckage, and I tried once again to get usable video footage. The biggest recognizable pieces were a wing tip and the cargo door of the CASA C-212. There was nothing else we could do, so we headed back to Wamena to hand over the videotape to the SAR (search and rescue) team so that the recovery operation could be planned. When we descended from the cold, barren heights, we came to what looked like an enchanted forest. The trees were still wet from the night's rain, and the raindrops on the leaves sparkled in the sunlight like a million diamonds. I was mesmerized.

If only I could go there!

I thought of the gigantic waterfall as well but knew most likely I would never be fit enough to hike up there into the cold, thin air.

When we got closer to the Baliem River, I recognized the mission station of Polimo and knew we were already close to home. It was surreal to think that in a few minutes I would go about my normal daily tasks. In Wamena, the ordinary and the extraordinary constantly co-existed.

I still struggled with the fact I was enjoying this incredible flight into a different world so much, while I thought of the reason for it. It was only eight o'clock in the morning when we landed. And somebody had to tell nine families some heartbreaking news.

A Concrete Alibi

February 2001

"Sorry, Mausi, I won't be able to come home for dinner tonight," Hans told me one day. "It was decided the floor needs to be poured all at once without interruption. That can take a while."

"No problem, I'll bring you some food."

While the hangar construction project had been on hold, some problems had been resolved, and construction had recommenced. A maintenance pit was inserted for cars and for access to the helicopter fuel tanks, and now the concrete floor had to be poured. A machine had been organized and flown in from Sentani along with an operator. The concrete was supposed to get polished before it totally dried to give it a smooth finish. Hans stayed at the hangar from the early morning until midnight to oversee the work.

The following day two Papuan men and a woman showed up at our house.

"Your husband has run over our dog with the car. You need to pay compensation."

"What? I don't know anything about an accident with a dog."

I phoned Hans who came from the hangar to help clarify the situation. It turned out the accident had occurred on the previous day when Hans had been at the hangar for the pouring of the floor. He hadn't used the Helimission car that entire day, so he had a "concrete alibi". When the people persisted that we were guilty of causing the premature death of their canine, Hans got impatient.

"So where is the dog? And I don't just want to see a dead dog; I want to see a flat and ran-over dog."

"That's not possible; we already buried it."

Now we knew something wasn't adding up. From what we had learned so far, a dog would most certainly be eaten and not buried. To prove there had been a casualty, they proceeded to pull a black dog tail, attached to a necklace with a wire, out of a bag. I felt nauseated. It turned out the people hadn't actually seen Hans' face but had been told by others that two westerners in a green car had run over the dog. (We weren't about to tell them about our friends who drove a green car). When they saw they weren't going to get any money from us, they left, and Hans could return to work.

On one of the following days, I came across a black dog without a tail, which would have matched the tail on the necklace. This made me think all kinds of thoughts.

She Came, Saw, and Conquered

(For dog lovers only)

"She's yours if you can catch her," our Australian friends said about a beautiful sand-colored terrier crossbreed we had seen on the airport grounds for several days. It turned out her name was Freckles, and she had arrived on a plane from a remote mission station to live with our friends, because Jessie, her owner, couldn't take her along to Australia. Jessie, a wonderful Australian nurse, was retiring after thirty-five years of faithful and invaluable service in Papua.

During the first night we had spent at the new house when someone had tried to break in, we had resolved to get a dog. So far we hadn't been successful at that. Our Canadian family had given us their puppy when they left, but soon after it had disappeared. I hadn't been able to find it anywhere, and we never found out if it had run away or had been stolen. Our friends had already told us that dogs often got stolen because their meat fetched a good price on the market or at restaurants. Coming from a culture where dogs were kept as pets and companions, guide dogs for blind people, hunting, or rescue, but never for food, this piece of information had taken me a while to digest.

Freckles was a bit cautious around people but friendly. She followed me to the car. When I got in first and called her, Hans was able to lift her and put her into the car with me. Later, we realized how dangerous that had been. The other family hadn't been able to take Freckles home because she had bitten the father and son when they had tried to catch her. To our horror, we heard she had even bitten

Jessie when she had put her on the airplane for the flight from the village to Wamena. Oh, my! Freckles was fine during the car ride and arrived at her new home without incident.

Now we needed to figure out how to care for the dog. What did she eat? Dogfood wasn't available in Papua, and our Internet access was too limited to look up information. Where should she sleep? We were told she was used to sleeping inside (which later turned out to be false), so reluctantly we got used to the thought of her sleeping by the back door next to the woodstove. That was as far as she was allowed in. During dinner, we noticed something moving under the table: Freckles. Oh well, why not? It didn't feel right that she had to stay in a corner by herself. Hans had another nasty stomachache, so he went to bed early. After a while, he noticed something next to the bed, opened his eyes, and looked straight into the expressive, brown eyes of Freckles who had put her front paws on the bed to check on him. How could you resist a dog as cute as this one, which even checked on you when you were sick? She slept under our bed that night.

"If we ever have kids and are as consistent with them as with this dog, we'll make terrible parents," we concluded.

The next day, Freckles found a hole in the fence hidden within the thick hedge and got out. We had lost Nicky just a few weeks earlier and couldn't lose another dog! I was about to prepare fish for dinner, so I grabbed a piece to use as bait and ran after her. I sweetly called Freckles offering her the piece of fish, trying to lure her back. She would look back and walk about three meters in front of me, always keeping her distance. We were quite the sight—a dog leading the way through narrow paths I had never noticed before, and a strange white woman with a piece of fish in her hand pursuing her and talking funny. I hoped nobody would see me (fat chance!).

About an hour later, Freckles walked straight back to the house as if she had lived there all her life. I was relieved and annoyed at the same time.

Freckles turned out to be no ordinary dog indeed. You could pet her for minutes on end, and she'd roll over on her back to get a belly rub and then all of a sudden she would jump up, give you a shocked look with raised eyebrows, put down her ears, and disappear around the next corner looking over her shoulder twice. Then she would come back and stick her head around the corner to see if you had noticed she was not amused. This happened several times, and when she did it, we would count till three before she peeked around the corner again.

"Nobody accused Freckles of not having personality," a friend kept remarking. Our dog with an attitude.

"Is Freckles here?" Hans asked and stuck his head under the bed.

"Grrrrrrrrrrrr!" The whole bed vibrated.

When I was in the bathroom, Freckles would guard the door and not let Hans walk down the hallway. Obviously, this dog had protected a woman for most of its life and hadn't had a male master. Another one of her quirks was she despised being bathed. None of our tricks to bathe her worked. Once, I even stooped so low that I distracted her with meat before pouring a bucket of soapy water over her. Bad idea! She was peeved at me all day. When Hans came home for lunch, he noticed Freckles sitting on the wrong side of the house — indicating, we were "on the wrong side of Freckles." In the evening, she still refused to eat or lie on her sleeping mat outside the back door (where we had moved her by now). Having turned into very strange dog owners, we both squatted down next to Freckles and talked to her apologetically until she decided we had sufficiently repented and came to sleep on her mat.

If somebody had told us before how strangely we would behave after just a few weeks of owning this dog, we would have been insulted. Freckles knew how to get what she wanted from us. A look from her pretty brown eyes under the expressive ever-moving eyebrows, combined with a frown and whimper, and looking to the screen door and back to me, made me open the door for her. Maybe the poor little thing needed to go to the bathroom or wanted to come back in because she was feeling lonely. How could I refuse?

BANG! The sound of the screen door made me spin around. I still caught a glimpse of Freckles who had heard some noise outside, jumped up, bolted toward the screen door, and forced it open so hard with her front paw that it hit the outside wall.

"That was the end of me getting the door for you ..." I murmured.

When she wanted to get back in, she would softly tap the screen door with her paw to make it bounce off the frame so that she could stick her nose in and effortlessly get inside.

Despite her diva-like attitude, Freckles was what she was supposed to be: a watchdog. We woke up with a start when Freckles, who was inside the house, barked. There was a stranger outside our bedroom window, and the guard was nowhere to be seen! Our hearts were pounding as the terror of our first night in the house was fresh on our mind. However, this time we had a means of defense! Hans opened the door.

"Freckles, xsssss-xssssss!"

That's what had worked to make Freckles chase chickens out of Jessie's garden and would work to chase potential thieves out of ours. She would charge and click her teeth to scare away humans or animals or nip them a little bit, but she wouldn't bite hard.

"Bapak! Bapak!" the intruder called the man of the house for help, and it turned out, he was drunk and disoriented, but not at all aggressive.

"Your dog bit me, you need to pay," the man said when Hans called back Freckles and got to him. He gently walked the drunken man out of the yard.

"It's late now, let's talk about that tomorrow," Hans negotiated, hoping the man would forget, especially since he didn't have a dog bite wound to show us. The man stumbled into the bush and then fell into the ditch. Hans had to pull him out again, and we hoped he would get home safely. Most likely, he hadn't intended to come into our yard but stumbled into it by holding onto our gate (the lock was broken), swinging into our driveway with it.

Before going back to bed, Hans found a new lock, which he put at our gate. We felt so much safer with a dog, especially since the two-legged guard had failed once again. When he turned up in the morning, he said he had been at church a little longer and didn't have the key to the new lock yet. He was visibly embarrassed when Hans told him he had locked the gate at four a.m.

Freckles had good instincts, but it was hard to explain to her who to scare off, or when and why, which caused us of a bit of a headache. She had a mind of her own. The guard put up a sign outside the house saying: "Beware of the mean dog." This didn't help the elderly, illiterate Dani lady who came to our house to sell limes. She was totally unprepared when our overeager watchdog charged at her. The lady, who didn't know Indonesian, still wanted to sell her produce and planted herself by our back door, gesticulating the dog had bitten her. However, she wouldn't show us the bite, claiming it was under the skirt. When the guard wanted to investigate further, the lady gave him a good spank and a rant in Dani. To hopefully bring this situation to a good and quick end, I bought the entire contents of her net bag and she was satisfied. (She wouldn't have been if she had truly been bitten). We drank a lot of limeade that week.

During her last visit to Wamena before retiring, Jessy shed some light on Freckles' erratic behavior. It turned out the growling under the bed stemmed from a feud with the village kids who had often poked her with sticks when she lay under Jessie's house. The children had teased her a lot, but one day Freckles had struck back. She was seen triumphantly dragging a girl's grass skirt through the village. No messing with Freckles!

Soon we also discovered why our dog had been so keen to go on her walks: her belly became bigger and bigger. She had been in heat, and now she was pregnant. There was no way to have a female dog sterilized in Wamena. Five cute but noisy, active puppies were born and eventually we found homes for all of them—even the interesting-looking one.

Progress!

March 2001

Finally, our team received reinforcement. Ex-marine, Andrew "Andy", with his wife, Tammy, son, A.J. and daughter, Tiffany arrived from the USA. Andy had spent part of his childhood in Papua, as his parents had been missionaries in the southern lowlands. We desperately needed help, especially with flying and maintenance and were happy about the arrival of the nice family.

Buzz and Myrna organized a trip to the waterfall picnic area a few kilometers outside Wamena and brought two cakes: one to welcome the new family and one for my thirtieth birthday.

"To your next thirty years in Papua," Buzz saluted.

I thought about that for a moment and smiled. *Yes, I would love that!*

We hadn't been here a whole year yet and had faced difficulties I couldn't have imagined. Life often was far from easy, but one thing was for sure: I loved living in Wamena and the work we were doing. I loved the mountains, the people (most of the time), our team, and the Indonesian food. Most of all, I loved that tribes, which had never heard of Jesus Christ before, were being reached with the help of our helicopter service, and sick people in the jungle villages were receiving medical help.

In all the difficult circumstances we had encountered until now, the worst possible outcome for me would have been having to leave Papua. I often grinned when I remembered a remark from a colleague at work: "Oh, you wait. You'll soon wish you were back at the council office."

I hadn't yet! This place was where I was meant to be. Papua had gotten under my skin and stirred my blood. I had never in my life felt this fulfilled.

I frowned when I thought of Hans' different situation. While he also loved his work and was fulfilled, He was under immense pressure. Sure, life wasn't a walk in the park for me. I often struggled to balance the cash box at the end of the week because of my accounting errors. It was a challenge to come up with tasty meals with the limited ingredients, which had to be flown in from the coast or searched for at different shops and markets. Sifting weevils out of flour or killing cockroaches wasn't pleasant. There were countless opportunities to offend people—Indonesians or fellow missionaries of different cultures, etc. But unlike Hans, I never had the stress of knowing lives depended on my work.

Shortly after arriving in Wamena, I had heard a high percentage of missionaries who prematurely left the field, did so because of the wife. From then on, it had been my prayer I would never be the reason we'd have to leave.

"Don't worry, the rain won't get here, we've all prayed," Ibu Marice, who now worked for our new family, reassured me. She had seen me look at the clouds, which were gathering all around. I smiled at her and admired her childlike faith. She was right; it didn't rain.

The hangar project neared completion. Ernst and Simon Tanner, our mission leaders, were traveling in Southeast Asia, so it had been decided to hold the hangar dedication early, so they could join in the celebration. In true Papuan manner, a Bakar Batu (traditional pig feast) was put on. Nothing else would have done the occasion justice. The hangar filled up with guests from the government, different mission organizations, local churches, the workers, and friends. Besides the pork and vegetables steamed on hot rocks in the cooking pit, there was also food suitable for our Muslim guests to eat.

There were speeches and much thanksgiving to God for seeing this project through despite all our shortcomings, rising costs, problems getting supplies, riots, and evacuation. We also thanked God that nobody had been seriously injured in the process, although there had been much potential for it. This hangar had turned out big, but God who saw the future knew how we would soon need all the space and more.

"We don't want this building merely to be a roof for the helicopters," Ernst said in his speech. "We'd like it to be a place where missionaries and local evangelists can come and get practical help as well. We'd like it to be a monument of God's love to the people."

This project had been a long and daunting task, but it warmed our hearts to hear these words, which reflected our thoughts, and to think of all that could be done under this roof. Later on, Brian brought back lightweight film projection equipment from Jakarta. Over the years, the *JESUS* film would be shown to tens of thousands of people in many places all over the highlands and into the lowlands, using helicopters, cars, and motorbikes, which all started at this hangar.

Besides numerous practical projects, the hangar would also become a central pivot point for pioneer evangelization, with helicopters going in every direction to discover and reach isolated tribes. Alex and Victor would often fix generators, chain saws and outboard engines from the mission stations as well. In the years to come, all the new mission stations that opened with the help of our helicopters would get a stall in the *gudang* (storage room), to store goods before transport. All the hard work and troubles had been well worth it.

"Tammy, your quiche was fantastic," I said patting my tummy during one of our weekly fellowship nights. For an inexperienced cook like me, it was always a challenge to keep up with the delicious meals the other ladies cooked for those occasions. I couldn't cook most of my favorite recipes from home because the ingredients weren't available. Tammy had a gift of making simple but delicious meals with locally available ingredients. Andy had plenty of funny, interesting stories of growing up in the jungle and at boarding school. I enjoyed hanging out with the family. After hearing Andy talk about the situation of the medevac patients who were frequently flown to the hospital, Tammy started visiting them. She found out what the patients needed and got to work, starting what would be dubbed

"Tammy's Closet." She collected and bought baby clothes, toys, blankets, towels, and other items the patients needed.

Slowly, I was getting ahead with my—so far informal—language and culture study. I was happy to be invited to join the language sessions of the new family with a Papuan tutor most mornings before the children started school. I already knew enough Indonesian to get by from listening to language tapes and conversations with people on the streets and at the office, but it was good to get the basics right, fill in the gaps, and get to the next level. Unfortunately, the young tutor soon left and also the next one wasn't able to consistently teach us. It remained a challenge to get good language training in Wamena.

Most Indonesians were outgoing and friendly (overlooking unintended insults) with a good sense of humor. They appreciated and encouraged our attempts to speak Indonesian and were frequently rewarded with a good laugh. Mixing up words like *rambut* (hair) and *rumput* (grass) when trying to find a hairdresser were favorites or mixing up *kelapa* (coconut) and *kepala* (head). *Berdosa* (to sin) and *berdoa* (pray) were a minefield combination, which resulted in a missionary asking the congregation to bow their coconuts and sin. What made another church shake with laughter was someone mixing up *keledai* (donkey) and *kedelai* (soybean). The thought of Balaam riding a soybean was too much to ignore politely!

The transmigrant program of the Indonesian government had the objective to disperse people from the overpopulated areas and all over the archipelago, including Papua. Because of its centrality in the middle of several mountain tribes, Wamena was a melting pot of people from different cultural backgrounds and their distinct languages. Therefore, everybody was used to making sense of strange accents and incorrect grammatical structures, as most people spoke Indonesian as their second or third language too. Sometimes it was handy not to understand everything. People often came up to us with requests such as wanting to move in with us, entrusting their children to us for several years so we could make doctors out of them, or requesting a medical procedure from Hans at his toolbox.

Other times we understood all the words, but they made no sense to us.

"My wound is not healing," a Papuan man complained. "There is a guy in another village who has something against me."

The more we understood, the more we grasped how different our cultures and worldviews were. While we thought of cleaning and dressing the wound better, applying ointment, and perhaps taking antibiotics, the man thought his enemy had put a curse on him preventing the wound from healing. While we'd usually try to find out the right medicine and dosage for an ailment, sometimes we overheard Papuans discuss amongst each other which pills were most potent, the red ones or the white ones. (There were brilliant Papuan nurses and doctors, but the general population often struggled with medical concepts as these were relatively new to their society). A more traditional Papuan form of treatment was to drain the *darah kotor* (dirty blood) which was believed to cause sickness. This was done by cutting different body parts until they bled heavily. We often observed people who put white adhesive menthol-patches on their faces or tied a string around their heads to relieve headaches.

Once, a Helimission worker told us he wouldn't come to work because his arm was painful and he was scheduled to get cut by a health worker. "He worked really hard yesterday," Hans told me, "I bet you he has achy muscles, so I suggested he'd give it a few days!" Two days later his symptoms "miraculously" disappeared, and he thanked Hans and was glad he hadn't gone through with the unpleasant procedure.

Darah kotor was mostly a Papuan "disease." The most commonly mentioned illness of the transmigrants was *masuk angin* (entering wind). The cure for this ailment which could have symptoms like a stiff neck or back, flatulence, or the like, was a massage or *kerokan*—scratching the area with a coin coated in oil until the skin was covered in red or blue stripes.

Little-by-little, we learned more about the Papuan worldview. Traditionally, Papuan people lived in little hamlets with a house for all the men and boys from a certain age on and other houses for the women, children, and pigs. The houses were made of wood. Some were thatched with grass, others with leaves or bark. Some houses were round, some oblong, and some rectangular. Fences made of rough wooden boards, tied together with vines, surrounded the hamlets. They were topped with grass and peat as rain protection and also to mark boundaries. The gardens were surrounded by fences to keep the pigs out, which roamed around freely during the days and came home to sleep and to be fed in the huts at night. One thing was a mystery to us and eventually I got up my courage and asked a friend. "How in the world do Papuans multiply when the men and women sleep in separate huts?"

"You have probably been told not to leave town together with a person of the opposite gender who you aren't married to, right?"

"Yes."

"That's the reason. Papuan couples meet up in the forest or the garden shelters. They're not only used as protection from the rain showers."

"Oh!"

Taking the Unseen Challenge

April 2001

Work on the new mission station in the Moi tribe at Point X-Ray had started, and Andersen and Tim had already moved in with their families. Now the task was to cut lumber and build a house for Stephen and his family, who had returned from home assignment in North America. Our pilots had flown in a team of Papuan chainsaw operators from town to cut wood for building the house.

Soon we received disturbing news. Although the most influential tribesmen had previously given the missionaries permission to build their houses, they were now telling them to leave. They claimed the spirits were angry because the building site was situated right on a sacred "spirit trail." In their eyes, the only way for the missionaries to stay would be by sacrificing a pig to the spirits. The team was in a dilemma. They couldn't sacrifice to the tribes' spirits which would have broken the first of the Ten Commandments and expressed that the missionaries had the same fears tribespeople did. However, if they didn't do that, the people would be scared, fearing the spirits' revenge—namely people and pigs dying. What should the team do? What if someone in the tribe died and blamed the missionaries? Would the tribesmen kill them in revenge?

When the missionaries told the tribal leaders the Great Spirit who had sent them was stronger than the spirits they feared, the leaders deliberated amongst themselves. They told the missionaries they could cut wood at the site, but they would also have to carry the consequences. The team prayed and resumed their work, along with their helpers from town. Strange things happened: tools and chainsaws broke down one after the other in impossible ways while in use at the site. The generator died and then a planer melted into a clump. The Papuan chainsaw operators who had been flown in from town were terrified, and the missionaries were puzzled. While the latter weren't afraid of evil spirits, their understanding of the local language was so limited they couldn't yet explain to the tribal people that God wanted to set them free from their fear.

Additional disturbing problems arose, and the confusion about the whole situation reached into the midst of our team.

"Our work isn't a fight against flesh and blood," we concluded. There was a struggle going on in the unseen world. The people had lived in fear and bondage throughout their entire history and the spiritual rulers, principalities, and powers, which the Bible talked about weren't giving up this territory lightly. Although we knew about these things, we hadn't experienced such drastic manifestations in the seen world.

"We need to get serious about praying for the remote mission stations," Hans and I concluded. "How about we start a weekly prayer meeting at our house where we specifically pray for the mission work in the jungle?" It seemed essential not only to provide a flight service to the missionaries but also to support them in prayer. The following Tuesday some friends came to our house to pray. We wrote to the missionaries on remote stations and asked them to email us their prayer requests (transmitted by satellite phone or radio). Our team—especially the pilots—belonged to the ones who were in the closest contact with the teams out there. Some situations and problems the missionaries encountered were sensitive, so they couldn't write about them to their friends and supporters back home. This challenge was for us!

Apart from a few exceptions, we met and prayed every week for years to come (and the prayer meetings still continue as I write this). While we meant to bless the teams in the jungle, we were blessed in turn. We learned about the daily struggles on the isolated stations and felt more connected with the pioneer missionaries. This boosted our motivation to keep the helicopter operations running and gave us a sense of satisfaction. We'd be on the edge of our seats hearing of tense situations and delighted and encouraged by the breakthroughs made. This all spurred us on to give our best in our work—even through the hardest of times. Being just a taxi service to and from the tribe would never be an option for us. We felt like part of the greater team beyond organizational boundaries.

"If we were to run out of food or have other problems and the helicopter couldn't come, we wouldn't even try to hike out," the Moi team told us. "It takes the local people a two-week hike through the jungle to the nearest village airstrip."

We thought about the slippery slopes, raging rivers, snakes, and leeches. The pressure was on: this mission station truly was heli-access-only! We'd definitely do our best and pray faithfully to always have a helicopter running. When circumstances made that impossible, we prayed harder for the health and safety of our friends, who were now stuck in the jungle until our machines were sorted.

With this close connection, we also learned more about the worldview and life of the tribal people. Some of their customs and beliefs boggled our minds.

"The people here never bathe from birth to death," our friends reported. Later, we learned they believed evil spirits lived in the water. This also kept them from drinking when they were sick or pregnant—which had negative consequences. They would only get fluids from fruit and vegetables during pregnancies. The tribe didn't believe there were natural causes of death. Sickness and death were attributed to evil spirits, curses, and witchcraft from other individuals, mainly women who were then punished for their alleged crimes— usually by death.

It was frustrating for the missionaries at Point X-Ray that this belief didn't leave much room to treat the sick. Instead of letting the missionaries help them treat wounds, bites, or diseases, the tribal people would turn to their ancient treatments, like giving the sick person deep cuts all over the body to cause bleeding which they believed would rid the evil spirit. Some people bled to death needlessly while the initial cause, e.g. a centipede bite, wouldn't have been strong enough to kill an adult. With the lack of hygiene and medical care, open wounds would get infected, posing a risk of blood poisoning and a slow, agonizing death.

This was disturbing for us to hear and for our friends in the tribe to witness. How tragic that these people came so close to hearing about the freedom in Jesus Christ and His gift of eternal life, but then died because of their ancient belief systems with deadly rituals and taboos! Over the next few years, the team would find out that about eighty percent of children died before reaching the age of five. Numbers seemed to be declining fast, and at this rate, the tribe was in danger of dying out within a few years' time. This had happened to other tribes where nobody had gone to help.

The missionaries felt the pressure to study the tribe's culture and language as fast as possible. They wanted to communicate God's message which would give people the option of freedom from fear of spirits, acknowledging natural causes of death, adopting hygiene practices, accepting medical care, and stopping self-harming and revenge killings.

Apart from spurring us on to give our best, the jungle stations' reports made us more grateful for the way we lived. Life in Wamena wasn't a walk in the park, but it was much easier than jungle life without shops, medical care, phone lines, or Internet services. There were no restaurants to get a quick takeout if someone was too sick or exhausted to cook, no community support, no school, no church, etc.

"If they can endure that, we can endure this with God's help," we often said when things didn't go well in Wamena, and we were tired, sick, or discouraged.

The local evangelists needed prayer support just as much as the western missionaries. Most didn't have large groups of people overseas praying for them, but often only small local churches. Their communication was done by HF radio (provided they had one) and they couldn't broadcast all their troubles over the island. Not many people would find out about their struggles, hardships, and medical problems, so we included these evangelists in our prayers—even though we only met a few of them.

Friends, Fun, and Fuel

"Anke!"

I looked over to the road. A smiling Papuan person waved from an angkot. Anke smiled and waved back.

"I can't believe it. Wherever we go, people know you," I said to my Dutch friend. We were on a motorbike tour and had stopped to give our bottoms a break from the bumpy ride on the rough road. I took a deep breath of the fresh air—slightly tainted by a faint hint of pig droppings—and looked around taking in the views and observing the people. I took a photo of water lilies on a pond.

These trips out of Wamena (even if it was just for half an hour) were invaluable for my mental well-being. It was good to leave the bustling town with people everywhere, including the glue-sniffing street kids and people in rags looking for money, which made my heart ache every time. Out here, I enjoyed looking at the neat little hamlets and produce gardens. There was no rubbish, the fences and grass-thatched wooden huts were mostly in good repair, and trees and bushes provided shade. On the outside, dark, red plants lined many of the fences which added a lovely touch. When people here wore their traditional attire it looked natural and dignified, and they didn't look poor amongst their beautiful gardens and livestock.

Anke worked for a Dutch organization and was mostly involved in community development projects. While most westerners living in towns like Wamena or Sentani had their own sub-culture, most single missionaries who worked mainly in the villages, were a lot more adapted to the Papuan lifestyle. They all went to local churches, ate the food the villagers cooked, and had much closer friendships with the Papuans than most other westerners. I admired the way they adapted and related to the people in a much deeper way than most foreigners—apart from those living with a tribe. Many single missionaries were highly trained and had left sophisticated lifestyles in their home countries, but here they adjusted to simple living conditions which took strength and courage.

"Anke, I can't believe you're taking the motorbike up those steep, muddy roads to the mountain villages while I almost chicken out on a flat, dirt road!"

Anke had learned to ride motorcycles in Papua. When one of her projects had road access, she would go by motorbike instead of an airplane. While I had ten thousands of kilometers of motorbike experience—all on good European roads—I didn't dare go where she went. The only place I dared to go to and Anke didn't, was the gas station. It never ceased to amaze me, this fearless and confident go-getter had some type of "fuel-drum-o-phobia." I must admit, the gas station didn't give me a reassuring feeling either. Usually, when I arrived at the site, cars, trucks, and motorbikes were filled from cut open fuel drums sitting in the sun next to a little shed. A bald, beefy, betel nut-chewing Papuan man with sunglasses would dip a handled tin into the fuel drum. He'd then pour the fuel into the tank through a funnel covered with a filthy cloth. Gasoline often spilled over the motorbike and onto the already drenched ground, while someone sat in a nearby corner smoking!

Apart from our joint trips out of town, we also enjoyed the fellowship of the single missionaries and aid workers at our homes over meals. They were wonderful, inspirational, and courageous people who enriched our lives with their help, friendship, stories, and humor.

We had ridden our motorbikes up a steep dirt road with rough rocks which sometimes made the wheels veer off track. We had parked the bikes and looked around the hydropower plant area at Walesi which supplied Wamena with electricity. I would have enjoyed much more our little walk and the view from the large bridge over the rushing Oue River, if I hadn't dreaded the return trip so much. The view over Wamena and the Baliem Valley was spectacular. Dark cumulonimbus clouds were building up all around, and beautiful rainbows appeared. It was time to get home before the weather would reach us, so we got back onto our motorbikes.

"Phew." *Well, I'm not going to get any points for grace and style. The objective is to get down in one piece.*

I took a deep breath, sent up a quick prayer, and released the clutch. With one foot on the back brake, one foot on the ground, and my heart pounding, I slowly made my way down the steep, dirt road and was able to keep the motorbike on its wheels. This was no problem for Anke who even had a passenger.

Whether it was cooking with ingredients I had never heard of, speaking in a new language, or riding a motorbike on rough, steep roads, this place was stretching me every day. Every little accomplishment felt good and made me more confident and happy.

My newfound confidence of that day went right down the drain when Jan, Anke, and I visited a cave at Kurulu a few months later. We rode our motorbikes across the large Pikhe Bridge over the Baliem River and around the long, flat White Sands hill. To do our backs and motorbikes a favor, we navigated around the potholes which obliterated the unpaved road. On our left side, the vast Baliem Valley stretched out with clusters of flat-topped trees, little islands of rock and sand protruding from the flat fertile plain, and the tall gray mountains looming on the far side. We passed by grassy plains with grazing cows; gardens full of sweet potatoes, cassava, corn, and sugarcane as well as square fishponds covered in water lilies. To the right, we saw steep rocks and hills covered with grass, shrubs, and forest. I gasped when I saw the vertical limestone rock cliffs on the Baliem Valley's northeastern side rising right next to the road.

Our destination was a limestone cave with stalagmites and stalactites. We parked our motorcycles and found a Papuan man who agreed to let us in and show us around. The cave was cool and spacious and had openings in several places letting in light.

"Oh, my goodness, I can barely stay on my feet, it's so slippery."

When a short, young Papuan lady carrying a toddler on her shoulders saw me struggling, she gave me her hand and helped me get up a little slope. I felt like an elephant compared to her. She was so sure-footed with her bare feet, while I could barely walk here with my sturdy shoes. I felt even worse when on the way down our guide told me to use the side of his bare foot as a steppingstone. I probably felt more pain than he did when I reluctantly agreed because I knew I wouldn't go anywhere if I refused his help (unless I'd slide down on my backside which I needed intact for the ride back).

We were sad when Anke finished her contract, and she left Papua. Before leaving, Anke trained her successors in the organization to work on the water projects, bridges, and other jobs. She also taught our friend, Robin, to ride a motorbike so she could go on "real-girls-motorbike-trips" with me now.

"Ugh! It takes so much energy to get to know people, become friends, and then see them leave," I lamented to Hans after Anke had returned to the Netherlands. She had been an inspiration to us with her down-to-earth, confident, outgoing, and positive attitude. I missed her, our meals together, our motorbike trips, her hair-raising stories, and her courage that often blew me away.

"I'm not even keen on making friends with the newcomers. They're short-termers, so we'll lose them again."

We had to decide: would we withdraw and choose not to get too close to people who would leave again, or would we instead make the most of the time we had together? The answer was clear; although the separation was painful, I wouldn't have wanted to miss out on Anke's friendship for anything. Even though Anke was one of a kind, the new people would all enrich our lives in their own way—and we hoped we'd do the same for them.

"So, Robin, have you ever been in a helicopter before?" Hans asked our new American friend. She was a single teacher who had come to Papua to teach missionary children at the small international school in Wamena.

"As a matter-of-fact, I have," Robin replied. "Just once in Albania and it was even owned by Helimission as well."

"No way!" Hans exclaimed. "That would have been this one then."

The helicopter, as well as Hans and Robin, had been sent to Papua after a time in Albania. What a small world! Robin joined us for brunch most Sunday mornings and often had us over for meals at her house. After realizing how overworked Hans was, she helped him update maintenance manuals in her spare time. Now when the men did a maintenance flight to measure vibrations, she rode on the same helicopter she had been in on the other side of the globe. Robin and I became good friends. We went on walks and motorbike trips, shared many meals, and talked about everything important to us. I loved her sharp wit and fantastic cooking, but I especially loved the depth of her faith in Jesus. Having a friend like her was a real gift from God.

"What? You've lived in Papua for a year and have never been to the beach? That has to change," Robin decided during one of our shared meals.

"You tell me when you'll go to Sentani next and I'll come too. I'll arrange a place for you to stay, a car, and a boat and we'll go snorkeling together." This woman was amazing.

Eventually, the trip happened after being postponed because of complications of crucial helicopter parts being lost and delayed and my back going out (I won't bore you with the details of either). Suffice to say taking time off never came easy for anyone on our team! As promised, Robin organized a car and the three of us, along with another couple, drove to Depapre where we showed our Surat Jalan at the police station before hiring an outrigger boat with an engine to take us to a beach, only accessible by boat.

"Wow! So far I've only seen a beach like this on posters," I said to the others. "If it weren't for the tiny creepy crawlies, I would think I was dreaming!"

We enjoyed a few hours at this beautiful, lonely, tropical beach and after having mostly practiced snorkeling in a pool before, it was fantastic to experience the real deal. I had always enjoyed underwater documentaries on TV, but I had never expected to see this much color and biodiversity in such a small area. There were all kinds of corals; fish in all shapes, colors, and sizes; and even large, blue starfish. Occasionally, I had to lift my head above the surface to assure myself I hadn't slipped off into another world. (A nasty sunburn on a few square inches of exposed skin reassured me for a long time it had been the real world).

The island of New Guinea was an extraordinary part of creation with all its different landscapes between the Coral Sea and the snowcapped, mountain peaks. The island boasted a rich, diverse flora and fauna including marsupials, reptiles, and the magnificent birds of paradise. Geologically, it had an incredible wealth of minerals. Both sides of the island combined, boasted well over a thousand different tongues, the highest concentration of distinct languages anywhere on earth—and so many different cultures and customs. A lifetime would be too short to explore it all.

If only this were an ideal world without malaria, other deadly diseases, and bloody, tribal wars. Or without people coming from all around the world and destroying so much of the island for material gain through mining and cutting down parts of the virgin forests. We later heard many of the corals were destroyed by fishing with explosives extracted from unexploded bombs and ammunition from World War II, which hadn't spared this remote place. Although parts of the island could appear like paradise, the evidence of a fallen world was obvious everywhere.

The Cool, Spacious Fruit of our Labor

Early May 2001

"Flight follower, Papa Victor on the water."

"What?" My head shot up from the accounting book. "Water?"

I was working in the office of our brand new hangar, listening to the flight-following channel on the HF radio with half an ear.

Oh, that's right, Tom is flying the floatplane in the southern lowlands.

I continued adding the payments at the clean, large desk in our spacious, quiet, and comfortably cool office with white tiled floors and big windows. These let in lots of light, but rarely any dust and little sound from the noisy airport. What a change from the tiny, overcrowded cabin which got baked in the midday sun and let in the dust and the infernal noise of the F-27 and Hercules airplanes!

The two-way HF (high frequency) radio for flight-following and contacting jungle villages sat on the L-shaped main desk in the finance office which ran along a big part of the room. A counter window faced the foyer featuring a bench. From there, people could put in flight requests or wait to talk to the pilots. In addition to Jan's front desk, there was now enough space for the small photocopying machine, the phone/fax machine, an accounting desk, a safe for money and important documents, a filing cabinet, shelves for the books and folders, and locked cupboards.

"Hotel Mike Echo landing Tokuni," Brian reported to the flight follower on the coast who monitored all the movements of mission aircraft via radio.

"Hotel Mike Echo landing Tokuni," the flight follower confirmed.

"Mike Echo," Brian replied to confirm he had been understood correctly by the flight follower and to conclude that communication. It was good for us as well to know where our helicopters were and to communicate directly if need be. Apart from landings and take-offs, the pilots reported their positions every twenty minutes. All those communications were recorded on paper with their exact time by the flight follower. In the case of an accident, the aircraft's approximate location would be known, narrowing the search area. In addition, civilian aircraft also were equipped with an ELT (emergency location transmitter). It would automatically transmit a homing signal in case of a substantial impact.

"Mike Echo on the ground," Brian reported.

Thank you, God, for another safe landing!

By listening to the radio traffic, I learned how it was done. Sometimes emergency medevacs came up on Sundays when no flight following was done by the mission aviation organization on the coast, so we team members needed to do it.

"Hotel Mike Echo leaving Tokuni, six POB," Brian called a few minutes later, letting the flight follower know how many persons were on board. In the next transmission, he reported his estimated time of arrival: "Hotel Mike Echo, ETA Wamena ten twenty-five."

Brian would soon have to change to another radio and contact the Wamena air traffic controller. Since air transport was the only way to reach most places in Papua—apart from walking—air traffic could get heavy especially in the narrow mountain passes. It was vital to receive and transmit information about the aircraft's position and altitude and to exchange weather reports.

On the secondary flight-following channels, the more extroverted pilots sometimes enjoyed private conversations as well.

"Hey Bob, how are you?" Brian one day addressed my new best friend. "I've just picked up a patient with a nasty injury. He wanted to kill a pig, but it charged at him and ripped a chunk out of his private parts."

Short silence on the air.

"Another good reason to be a vegetarian."

The lack of airwave privacy was a problem for the missionaries on the remote stations who also relied on HF radios to stay in contact with their mission agencies, friends, and medical personnel in the towns. When they told a close friend they were pregnant, or talked to the doctor on the coast about a medical issue, most likely the whole island would know about it. I'm sure everybody welcomed the arrival of satellite phones no matter what the expense.

A few minutes before the helicopter was due to arrive, I walked over to the little kitchenette in the pilots' office. I filled the water heater with filtered water, in case Brian or his passengers were interested in a hot drink or instant noodles. On my way back, I avoided looking at the extensive aviation chart of Papua covering almost the entire wall. I knew I would lose track of time, poring over it instead of getting my work done. I was fascinated by the fact there were still large white spots on the map reading, "Relief data incomplete" or "Elevation is not believed to exceed five thousand feet." (This was before satellite maps were available on the Internet). Papua was one of the last frontiers.

Jan walked into the office singing and whistling along with the praise music playing. We all enjoyed the new building which allowed everyone to work efficiently.

"Hotel Mike Echo landing Wamena."

I walked through the corridor and the spacious hangar to watch the helicopter land on one of the two helipads behind the building and to greet our friends. I closed my ears with my fingers and turned my face from the dust beaten up by the rotor wind. A large sliding door to close off the hangar and protect it from the strong afternoon winds and powerful rotor downwash was another important project, which gave Hans something to think about. But the main part was done. The hangar protected the helicopters and the mechanics from the extreme UV light and the tropical downpours. There was a clean, even floor, electricity, air compressors, proper storage for equipment, tools, spare parts, and paperwork.

Hans set up the working areas in the hangar and workshops with the help of Alex and Victor. "Ah, I love the *clean-shop*," Hans said to me when he came into the office for a drink of water. "Now I can open the gearbox and turbine without worrying about dust getting in."

The clean-shop had easy-closing windows, keeping the dust out, cabinets to store parts in, and other practical features like a large magnifying glass, a parts washer, and an ultrasonic cleaner. This area was designated for working with dynamic components which needed to be kept clean when they were opened up. The room outside the clean-shop was the workshop for cutting, drilling, spraying paint, and every other work requiring cleanup afterward. Regular helicopter inspections and maintenance work were done in the hangar area where Hans and Alex built an A-frame crane structure with a chain hoist. This could be wheeled over to the helicopters to remove the rotor and the engine.

A wide door connected the clean shop and the workshop. A sturdy hook in the ceiling could hold the entire main rotor of a helicopter, which fit inside the two workshops when the connecting door was open. The men could now balance the rotor in broad daylight—even on windy days as the workshops were closed off and draft free. What an improvement! There would be no more working night shifts in someone else's storage shed in between rice bags and rats.

Hans also set up the parts room with the rows of shelves, holding the multitude of big and small spare parts, screws, bolts, nuts, gaskets, etc. all in little bins and labeled for easy access—much unlike their previous life in plastic trunks.

One wall of Hans' maintenance office was mainly taken up by bookshelves filled with maintenance records and manuals. I was always amazed at the amount of paperwork involved in aviation. A frequent quote by aviation people was: "An aircraft is legally airworthy when the weight of the paperwork equals the weight of the aircraft."

Looking at the maintenance office, this didn't seem far from the truth.

The room treasured by everyone (also by mission pilots stopping in Wamena, who were only up for a chat after a visit there) was the bathroom. It had a sink, a toilet, and shower. The latter would come in handy if anyone accidentally got showered with jet fuel again or when we would run out of water at home.

A Momentous Event

"It can't be done."
"Too expensive!"
"Mr. Tanner, you'll never be a pilot."

Those were some reactions by people from other mission organizations, and of Ernst Tanner's flight instructor when he first contemplated becoming a pilot and using helicopters for mission work in the late nineteen-sixties. Even though the mission aviation people assured Ernst that helicopters would be fantastic tools for mission work, nobody thought they would be affordable.

June 2001

And yet, here we were traveling to Switzerland to celebrate the thirtieth anniversary of Helimission, which was officially founded in 1971! Against all the odds, Ernst and Hedi Tanner stepped out in faith and started the adventure. After all, if God was for helicopters in mission work (and for an artist and preacher flying one) who could be against it? It had been a rough, bumpy road until the Helimission organization was born and it cost much more than money to begin and keep operations going. With the Lord's help, in three decades countless people's lives in different parts of the globe were touched, changed, or saved. Previously unreached people had heard the gospel, seen the *JESUS* film, or had received life-saving medical help or food aid after natural disasters, etc. Only God knows how many tribes and individuals Helimission operations had touched since 1971.

A Momentous Event

After three days of traveling, Hans and I arrived at Helimission headquarters in Trogen, jet-lagged and tired. We had gone ahead of Brian and Andy, who kept the flight program in Papua going as long as possible and would arrive in time for the celebrations. Hans was scheduled to perform a helicopter inspection at the headquarters. Since hordes of guests were expected to eat and stay at headquarters, I had been invited to come to Switzerland too. I would help Simon's lovely, intelligent, and hard-working wife, Brikena, with cooking and housework. Besides, there was plenty of work preparing for the big event. I had devoured Hedi Tanner's book, *More Than an Adventure*, and always enjoyed coming to Trogen and spending time with the Tanner family and office staff.

"Wow, who would have thought?" I said to Hans fighting back the tears. "When we left Germany last year, I thought we wouldn't see our families and friends again for three years. Now, I see some for the second time in a little over a year!"

My brother and his family came from Germany to see us before things became too busy. Little Daniel was one-year-old by now and as cute as a button with his snub nose and big, brown eyes.

Soon, the pilots and mechanics from the different Helimission bases in Africa arrived.

"Haha, it almost feels like meeting celebrities," I said to Hans. "Many of them I've only seen in Helimission newsletters and films."

The house was buzzing with people who needed a place to sleep, something to eat, or clothes washed. Brikena hauled carloads of groceries to the kitchen. Everybody worked from morning until late at night to prepare for the monumental event. A group of Papuan singers and dancers came to perform at the anniversary.

"Look at them," I said to Hans one night, pointing at the lively Papuan group. They were posing for photos in front of the sunset, holding up a clock showing it was nine thirty at night.

"Our friends in Papua won't believe it's still light at this hour," they explained. All year round the sun went down at six p.m. in Indonesia, and we had missed balmy summer evenings.

After the sun had long gone down and our work was finished, we would often end up having midnight yogurt in Brikena's kitchen and catch up with the people from the different bases.

On Saturday night before the anniversary celebration, the town square of the over eight-hundred-year-old Trogen community was turned into an open-air cinema. The weather forecast was less than promising, so we all prayed for good weather. We watched the thunderclouds building up all around and were amazed to see them circling Trogen, causing thunderstorms and heavy rain, but never reaching the town. Many people came to watch the film *China Cry* and enjoyed the perfectly dry evening.

On Sunday morning, coffee and *Zuepfe* (Swiss plaited bread) were served on the town square under the bright, blue sky and people streamed into the historic church building for a Thanksgiving service. Many needed to sit on benches outside—including Hans' and my parents who had traveled to Trogen. A Swiss group and the Papuan group each performed traditional singing and dancing, and the day continued with a bazaar, food stalls, and helicopter flights which kept us hopping before the main celebratory service.

This Helimission celebration was a rare opportunity for the faithful prayer warriors, donors, volunteers, board members, office staff, leadership, pilots, and mechanics to mingle and corporately praise God and celebrate what He had done.

"This is the steering wheel of Helimission," Ernst said and presented his son, Simon, with a car steering wheel made of chocolate during the festivities up on the stage.

"But I'll keep the gas and the brake pedal for the remainder of the year," he teased.

From then on, Simon would be the head of Helimission with Ernst at his side as an adviser. Ernst would also continue Helimission film showings and preaching at churches.

When the sites had been cleaned up after the grand event, we were all exhausted. Before going back to the respective bases in Africa and Indonesia, the international Helimission team got to wind down during a retreat at headquarters. After a few days of devotions, prayer, and singing, we all afforded our last bit of strength to walk up one of Switzerland's beautiful mountains.

Before starting our three-day journey back to Wamena, our small Papua delegation drove to another part of Switzerland to visit Thomas, a pilot friend of Brian's. We were so tired we only marginally appreciated the beautiful scenery. When we got to the helicopter company where Thomas worked, we weren't overly excited when he announced: "In a moment, I'll show you the area."

We had already endured a two-hour drive. Couldn't we chill out a little, maybe have a coffee before going for another drive?

"Let me push the heli out the hangar real quick." We were instantly wide-awake!

Thomas put supplies for a mountain cabin into a special basket on the helicopter skids and we all got into the chopper. We comfortably enjoyed the splendor of the majestic snow-covered Swiss Alps, waving at mountain climbers who were making the exhausting trip to the summit by their sweat. After flying past peaks and glaciers, we arrived at the mountain cabin where a lady came out to receive the supplies.

We swapped lives in our home countries for those on the mission field, entailing hardships of many sorts, but God knew how to give us rich rewards along the way!

"I can't wait to see Freckles," I said to Hans, while we were packing our suitcases to travel back to Papua. "Isn't it amazing how attached we got to this cute, misbehaving dog with an attitude?"

At one point, we considered borrowing a friend's gun with anesthesia shots to be able to give her a bath, put the flea collar back on and clip her toenails. We weren't sure how to convince her that scaring people on the road wasn't a splendid form of entertainment, but extremely impolite and unacceptable. However, she was an excellent watchdog and had clearly wrapped us around her paw.

Jan had emailed us that each time he came home with our motorbike, Freckles was jumping up and down, but as soon as she'd see it wasn't us on the motorbike, her ears and tail would slump. When he opened the house door, she'd go and check every room to see if we were there and scratch on the bathroom door. She seemed to miss us as much as we missed her (although she'd have never admitted it). It was time to go home.

The Ton of Bricks

July 2000

"I'm sorry. Freckles didn't make it," Brian said after getting off the phone. We gave him a blank stare while his words sank in. We were breaking our trip to Papua at Jakarta for a few days so the men could attend to business there. We had already heard that people had tried to kill Freckles two nights earlier. They trapped the dog with a snare when she got out through a fence hole under the thick hedge. Jan, who stayed at our house, ran outside when he heard the commotion when the people beat the dog. He managed to scare them away but found Freckles more dead than alive. The vet and Luana tried to save her with injections and an IV drip. No success.

We were so sad and angry.

"Let's get a huge, scary dog, that nobody will dare to kill," Hans defiantly suggested. We were in Jakarta for another two days, and there were no pet shops or breeders in Papua. Most mongrels found in Wamena weren't trainable watchdogs. We had to act quickly. We went to a mall and looked at dogs in a pet shop. There was a large scary-looking black dog, but it was ugly and scared even us. The next big dog was a beautiful oversized Golden Retriever. It was love at first sight.

"Hmmm, Golden Retrievers aren't exactly renowned for being fierce, scary guard dogs." I contemplated.

"No, you're right," Hans retorted, "but the people in Wamena don't know that. They'll be scared by his sheer size and the big dog's voice."

"You've got a point there." Any excuse would have done for me at that moment, but this one even seemed plausible. "Let's buy him and get the poor thing out of this tiny cage."

The dog's name was Aldo. When the shop attendant let him out of the cage, he knocked things over in the pet shop with his fluffy tail and put his large paws on the countertops with ease. He loved to be out of the cage and around people. The bark echoed through the mall. Yes, he would impress the people in Wamena. We made all the arrangements and a Swiss helicopter business partner of Hans' in Jakarta even gave us a cage we could use for the transport. We made a down payment at the pet shop and bought a collar and a chain leash.

Later in the day, Jan called to tell us, "Whatever you do don't bring the dog! The quarantine officials will kill him as soon as he gets to Sentani."

Our hearts sank. That couldn't be. Why in the world couldn't we bring such a beautiful, healthy dog? We then learned that unlike Java, New Guinea was rabies-free with strict quarantine rules. None of the documented vaccines in Aldo's paperwork would make a difference. Disappointed and sad, we went back to the pet shop, canceled the deal, and said good-bye to Aldo before returning to Papua. We couldn't return the collar and chain leash so we took them along hoping we'd find a good dog in Wamena after all.

Jan met us on the coast to work on our visa paperwork. We could tell he'd had a few rough days. When the visa business and more shopping were taken care of, we flew home to Wamena. Jan had already told us that the killing of Freckles hadn't been the only trouble. There had been problems with our house helper, and she hadn't come in for a while.

The dog food Jan cooked several days ago while the people tried to kill Freckles was still in the pot, burned to a crisp. Having to bury the dog and preparing to go to the coast for our visa paperwork, Jan hadn't had a chance to clean the house or wash the dishes. Here we were, the house was a mess, and the three of us had suitcases full of dirty laundry. There had been problems with the house helper before, and now I needed to dismiss her. I had to shop and cook for the three of us plus Brian and Andy, because their families were away for a week, cooking at a retreat of another mission. I was close to collapsing.

Where do I even start?

Jan and Hans got onto the dishes while I tried to clean the house and sort through the laundry.

What would I cook for the five of us? Right, I still had two large chickens in the freezer which Luana had procured from the coast. I put one of them in the microwave to thaw and then changed the setting to the convection oven for roasting. That would be a great lunch for the men.

What's that smell? I looked around the kitchen and noticed the electricity had gone off. It turned out the extension cord of the microwave oven was melting, and a circuit breaker had flipped. I moved the chicken to the gas oven and checked on it a while later.

Yikes! What in the world is that now?

Dark fluid oozed from the roasting chicken. Upon further investigation, it turned out the bird still had a little plastic bag with the heart and liver inside. I had never seen that before in Wamena, but this chicken came from a different supplier. I cut up the chicken to salvage some of the meat, making a huge mess in the process. I returned the chicken breast, thighs, and wings to the oven washed off the carcass and put it into a stockpot. Chicken saved. Next, I tried to clean up the gooey mess with lots of bleach. The kitchen disaster was under control.

The phone rang. "Brian and Andy just called on the radio. They're still flying and won't make it for lunch."

Aargh!

In between the work, I often sniffled and teared up. I missed Freckles so much. Why was it that after each time away, things back in Papua seemed to hit us like a ton of bricks? It felt like starting out the ride from a standstill in the highest gear until things ran somewhat smoothly again.

I was halfway finished cleaning the house and wondering when I'd have time to go to the office to sort out our travel expense reports. To my surprise, Hans and Jan were coming home in the middle of the work day.

"Hey, Elke. We brought you a handful of Aldo!"

Here they were, both with a big grin and holding out a tiny puppy to me which would have fit into the first Aldo's mouth. It was gray-brown and looked at me cross-eyed. When Hans put it into my hand, it didn't weigh more than a small kitten. Oh, how cute! But I just didn't have any energy or nerves left to care for a three-week-old dog.

"It's too young! Take it back to its mom for another few weeks."

"No, no! The people who sold him to us said he could already eat by himself," Hans and Jan protested.

"If you are not going to return it, at least get one of its brothers or sisters to keep it company and warm at night."

They wouldn't, so I prepared a small box with an old towel in it for the puppy. We didn't think long about a name. He was called Aldo. Unfortunately, the little fellow was far from house-trained. So apart from all the housework, not having a helper, and cooking for two extra people, I had a little puppy which very vocally missed its mom, made a mess in the house, and demanded constant attention. I remembered a conversation with my mother in my childhood:

"Mom, why are little animals and little children so cute?"

"So you don't throw them against the wall."

I hadn't asked any more questions. Aldo was cute enough to be safe.

I soon admitted that even though the puppy was giving me additional work and wanted my constant attention, I enjoyed caring for him. After a while, he stopped shivering and didn't fall over as often while running. He was still plump and uncoordinated, and when he occasionally fell over while scratching or eating, he rolled all the way onto his back because he was getting so round. Every week he doubled in size and weight and got stronger and more rascally. Soon he could spend the days outside, which made for a lot less cleaning, and only came in at night. He had to sit and wait for us to clap our hands before he could eat. It was priceless to watch the little bottom go down while he looked up at us cross-eyed. He was so cute. But we still missed Freckles.

Without a house helper, I became so exhausted; I often didn't even know how to find the energy to cook dinner. One thing was clear: if I wanted to survive and do anything else besides housework, I needed to find a new helper. Luana's house help knew a young lady who was looking for work, so I decided to give her a try. All I knew so far was that Agustina was a young Western Dani lady, married to a Bible school teacher.

"Hello, welcome," I greeted Agustina when Luana brought her to our house. After looking into her shy, honest-looking face, I noticed a bump a bit lower.

"You're pregnant. Are you sure you want to start working just now?"

"Yes, I'm four months pregnant, but it doesn't matter, I really want to work," Agustina insisted. "When the time comes for me to give birth, I'll take a little time off and then bring the baby to work."

Well, it would surely be nice to have a baby in the house. Why not give her a try?

"Can you start tomorrow?"

Agustina had never worked for westerners before. I started showing her where to wash her hands when she came in and how to do the dishes and clean the floors. Most times, I washed the laundry myself. Since the hangar building was finished, I also worked at the office fewer hours. Agustina wasn't fast, but she was honest, kind, and respectful. Our previous house helper called me *nyonya*, the most respectful way of addressing a woman, but I hadn't felt she respected me in her heart and actions. Agustina called me *kakak* (older sibling), and I knew this relationship would be honest and warm.

In the morning, Agustina walked to work and afterward I would take her home to the Bible school complex where she lived just outside Wamena. While I would never have given a pregnant lady a ride on my motorbike in Germany, here it was the best option. While riding downhill back toward the town, I took a deep breath and looked at the beautiful scenery. I enjoyed Agustina's company and help, and now I also had a reason and the time to go out of town by motorbike. What a breath of fresh air after feeling overworked and overwhelmed. I thought of my large motorbike in Germany that I could only ride when I found the time. Here in Papua, I could use most things I enjoyed for ministry. My little motorbike got me around for shopping, transporting people, getting to the hangar fast, but also to get out of town to clear my head, even if it was only for a few minutes. I loved photography, and here it was part of my job to take photos for newsletters and presentations. I could sometimes sing and play the guitar at our Sunday fellowship as well. It felt like all my former hobbies suddenly were useful. (Well, sailing wasn't in up here in the mountains, but sometimes sailors' knots came in handy).

The Flight That Wouldn't End

"Hey, Hans and Elke, can you join me on a medevac?" Brian, who had just returned from a flight, asked us while the helicopter was refueled and the stretcher put in.

We looked at each other. "Sure."

The emergency call came from Benawa, a village in the northern foothills of the mountain range. The flight time would be about half an hour. Now that the hangar building was finished, Hans could spare a little time for going on a flight for a change. I had already experienced how much a helicopter trip through the Papuan mountains did for my mental well-being, so I always tried to make the time. However, I was always nervous about the patient's condition.

"Elke, I think it's a pregnant lady. Maybe you can sit in the back with her on the return flight, so why don't you sit up front on the way out."

Fantastic! We strapped ourselves in and headed for the North Gap. When we arrived at Benawa, a health worker met us with the patient's paperwork for the hospital in Wamena.

"There she comes!"

A group of people headed toward the helicopter. It turned out the patient was not about to give birth, but still had several months to go. She was barely conscious and probably suffering from cerebral malaria, which could cause a coma and brain damage. The group of people tried to take the young woman to the helicopter, half carrying her and half helping her to walk. Oh dear! The woman was struggling in her delirium, and it took time and effort to strap her onto the helicopter's stretcher. This was not what we expected. Brian looked concerned.

"Okay, we need to pray for her to calm down. If she stays this agitated, we can't take her."

We prayed together, and she immediately calmed down. We quickly got into the helicopter and took off. Hans ended up sitting in the back again, along with two other men and the woman strapped to the stretcher.

The weather wasn't cooperating either, and Brian searched a way around the built-up clouds which added to the flight time. I kept looking over my shoulder to the back. We all prayed quietly, and the lady was calm—too calm in fact. Hans thought we might have lost her. But not for long. About fifteen minutes into the flight, she started struggling and raving and even grabbed the door handle. The three men leaned on her struggling to hold her down to prevent her from opening the helicopter door.

"Hans, you know what you have to do," Brian said over the intercom. "If it gets too dangerous, you'll have to knock her out."

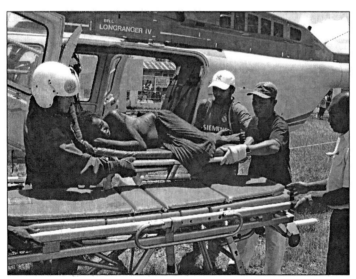

Delivering an injured woman to the hospital

What a thought. You pick up a sick woman for medical help, and have to beat her unconscious to make sure she doesn't fall out of a helicopter flying over forest-covered mountains! I was rarely glad when a helicopter flight ended, but this one seemed to take forever. We were all relieved when we landed at the Wamena hospital and turned the woman over to the medical staff.

(We later heard she left the hospital before finishing the treatment and we never knew what became of her).

Rich and Poor

*"The rich and the poor have this in common,
The LORD is the maker of them all."
Proverbs 22:2*

The issue of rich and poor was on my mind a lot. In Germany, we belonged to the middle class. My parents owned a shop, and I never experienced financial problems. While some people around us had been a bit less fortunate, everybody had good health care, a place to live with adequate heating, and more than enough to eat. The issue of classes had been on the back of my mind. All the children I knew went to the same school—no matter if their parents were tradesmen or doctors, owned a factory, or worked in it. In German schools, the topic of social justice was always present. With our history in World War II, schools taught that people of no race, religion, or skin color were better than another.

Like in every country I visited, most German people weren't fond of immigrants who didn't want to integrate or learn the local language. So the word foreigner had a slightly negative touch because of the black sheep among them. However, we all loved the Italian ice-cream parlor in the middle of our small town where people from all walks of life met. We found the Prego and other Italian words of the owner quite charming. Other immigrants who integrated themselves into the German community were well accepted too.

In Wamena, everything was different from what I was used to. We gave up our good jobs and were now living on donations. We relied entirely on God's provision which mainly came through the financial support of friends, family, and other mission-minded people. We never knew how much money would come in each month. When we stepped off the plane in Indonesia, all of a sudden we had become foreigners, but at the same time we were regarded as "rich westerners." While we had come down a huge step in our living conditions, we now belonged to the upper class of Wamena, by living in a house with running water, owning a motorcycle, and wearing shoes. (During our years in Papua, that situation changed drastically with fancy stores and houses going up all around, dwarfing ours, and many people becoming wealthy and owning cars.)

The question was how we would deal with it all. I observed what some other foreigners around me did, and I wasn't always impressed. Regarding my house helper, I came to the conclusion I needed to pay at least as much as was right by government regulations and considering her family situation. If I couldn't pay that, I couldn't have a house helper. It was also common to provide meals, so I gave Agustina breakfast when she came in and then she had lunch with us. Healthcare was also our responsibility.

"How do you manage to get your helper to eat with you?" a friend asked. "When we were in Bandung, it was impossible to get the Javanese ladies to eat with us, and so we haven't even tried here."

Most of the missionaries had studied the Indonesian language on the island of Java where the culture was very different from the Melanesian cultures here in Papua. There the house helpers wouldn't eat with their employers because the class hierarchy was very distinct. My grandmother had told me how during the Nazi regime in Germany, the government had forbidden them to eat at the same table as their Polish farm helper. Some people found ways around these regulations—like pushing two tables close together to obey the rule, but not exclude their valued helpers. The ones who had been caught disobeying had been in serious trouble. Thank God, those times were over!

"Agustina was a bit shy at first. I think she wasn't used to eating at a table and using a knife and fork, but she got over it," I answered my friend's question.

It turned out that in the Papuan culture, eating together had great significance. It also was a good way to get to know each other, talk about our daily lives or different worldviews in a relaxed atmosphere (once the atmosphere became relaxed, that was!).

"Oh, you're still on the dishes," I said to Agustina as I came into the kitchen.
"I'm sorry, but I'm so afraid of breaking something."
"Right, that's good, but don't worry too much, it's just stuff!"
That was easy for me to say. It took me a while to accept the fact the lady I worked with every day lived in a crude shack without running water and minimal belongings, while we had it so much better. I had never been in a place before with such a huge difference in living conditions. It was a painful reality to face. Our part was to give our employees an adequate salary, making sure their health care was paid for, showing our appreciation, and treating them with love and respect as brothers and sisters in Christ. Sometimes, over the years, I responded to situations inappropriately and treated my helper unfairly, which I regret.

In the Bible, we read over and over how God wants us to care for the poor, the sick, the lonely, the widows and orphans, and to treat everyone fairly—subordinates or superiors. We came here to serve the people of Papua and wrote about it in the newsletters. At the same time, we found ourselves fighting against being put into the position of a master, just because of our skin color. We all depended on each other. I saw the toll it had taken on me not to have a house helper, so I really appreciated the help.

We felt God wanted us to appreciate and respect everybody we met and not judge them by their education, living standard, or skin color. We found that a person's contribution depended much more on their attitude than on their origin, education, or position.

However, at times, it was a big stretch for us when we had to keep functioning like clockwork in our type of work, while people around us were a lot more laid-back. Clocks and calendars hadn't been part of the Melanesian culture before outsiders came in. Saving and storing food for winter also hadn't been part of their lifestyle. Crops grew all year round, there were always animals to hunt in the forest, and people didn't rely on the ability to preserve food. However, our ancestors wouldn't have survived the first winter without strategic planning and preserving food for themselves and their livestock. Although God had made people different, He had made us all and valued and loved us all the same.

Often, we were humbled by the faithfulness and attitude of the local workers. While some only worked with us for a short time and couldn't get used to the discipline needed to run an aviation operation, others stayed on for many years—often much longer than any western co-workers and became the backbone of the operations. Pak Teben, for example, had worked for Helimission for many years, and every day he did his work faithfully with a gentle, quiet spirit, keeping the hangar grounds mowed and maintained. It warmed my heart how he always kept the welfare of Archie, the hangar dog, in mind making sure the guard on duty would not forget to feed him. He also cared for his family in a responsible way. I respected this humble and hard-working man more than many well-educated westerners I met over the years.

Sometimes, when donations came in slow but we still needed to pay the bills, we sure didn't feel wealthy, even though many people assumed our resources were limitless. After all, we still wore shoes and lived in a house with running water. Thankfully, after years in missions, while trusting God for our income, I can't remember when we ever had to leave a bill unpaid. To God be the glory!

"I know how to be abased, and I know how to abound. Everywhere and in all things I have learned both to be full and to be hungry, both to abound and to suffer need."
Philippians 4:12

Point of No Return

The new Western Dani version of the *JESUS* film had been completed, and now it needed to get to the people.

"What do you think about going on a road trip to show the *JESUS* film?" Hans and I asked Tom.

"Sure! Let's do it," Tom said so we planned a trip to Makki in the Western Dani territory in the North Baliem area for August 25. How exciting, I couldn't wait!

August 20, 2001

I was surprised to hear the phone ringing before seven in the morning. It was Tammy.

"Elke, do you have the phone number of MSF or of a nurse who could come along on a flight? Tom's airplane is overdue, and we presume he might have crashed."

My heart fell to the bottom of my stomach. *Oh no, not Tom! Oh Lord, let him be alive, let him be okay.* I silently prayed over and over while I looked up the phone numbers for a nurse and Doctors Without Borders.

I hurried to the office to help and to listen to the HF radio for more news. By now, the villagers confirmed Tom crashed near the Korupun airstrip, and he and his passengers were alive, although injured.

"Thank you, Lord!" I sighed with relief but still worried about their condition. Andy prepared the helicopter and flew to Korupun. Tom's wife, Rosa, arrived at the office as well as other friends from the mission community for her support. We all prayed and shared the little bits of information we had. Rosa seemed composed, but I couldn't imagine how she must be feeling. She had already been at school, preparing for the day of teaching when she had received the phone call about the accident.

More and more news came in by radio. None of the three passengers were critically injured, and one walked away from the wreckage unharmed. Tom's injuries were the most severe. We learned that Korupun is one of the most challenging airstrips in the Papuan mountains (and there are hardly any easy ones). To turn left from a bigger valley into the side valley where Korupun is located, the airplane pilots have to fly closely along the mountainside on the right. Once the pilots turn into the narrow side valley, there is not enough width to turn the plane around and the valley is closed off by a mountain. When they commence the approach to Korupun—a steep airstrip between the mountains—they can't abort and are committed to land.

Since the crash site was away from the runway, another airplane was able to land at Korupun and take Tom to Wamena. Brian was away on Helimission business, but Andy was able to assist. He evacuated two injured passengers by helicopter and took them to the Wamena hospital where Hans was already standing by to help unload. After what seemed like an eternity, the airplane landed in Wamena, and we all ran over to see Tom. Since ambulances weren't always available in Wamena, he was put on a stretcher in the "red rocket," an enclosed, boxy, old Indonesian-made Toyota pickup with benches. Since Tom was tall, his feet stuck out the back of the car. I got a glimpse of his face. Seeing our friend in this condition was hard to bear.

Tom's leadership wanted to send him to a different hospital at the coast, but he refused. "If the Wamena hospital is good enough for the patients I fly, then it's good enough for me." (The average patient's size was about two feet shorter than he was, so two chairs were put behind Tom's bed to make it long enough.) After the medical staff assessed Tom's injuries and administered medical care at the hospital, his colleagues began to interview him by his bedside for the accident investigation.

We were relieved to hear a surgeon was available at the hospital (which wasn't always the case). He was even able to make twenty-two cosmetic stitches preventing noticeable scars in Tom's face which had been lacerated by the helmet's visor. The deep cut in his thigh was a different story, and Tom would need a wheelchair and crutches for a while.

"Tom looked as if he was dead when they brought him into the hospital," Hans told me when we were both home that night. Hans didn't look too good either. We were still shaken up by the day's events.

Two days later, Tom was released from the hospital and we went to visit him at home.

"Yeah, that's going to help," Rosa said when I sheepishly gave Tom a bar of Swiss chocolate. She entirely lacked a sweet tooth — much unlike Tom. I felt helpless and silly about the chocolate too, but it didn't feel right to come with empty hands either. What could we bring, do, or say to cheer up our friend in this situation?

"Sorry, Hans and Elke, I can't go to Makki with you on the weekend for the *JESUS* film showing."

I couldn't believe Tom even thought of this, after just surviving a plane crash! He filled us in on what had happened and later we heard more from the accident investigators. On the morning of the crash, the sunlight had come over the mountain ridge and caused a so-called *sunshadow* or *black hole effect*, blackening out the mountain side. When the plane had come out of these lighting conditions and Tom had seen clearly again, he realized he had entered the valley too high for a safe landing at Korupun and had already passed the *point of no return*. Trying to land wouldn't only have put the peoples' lives on board at risk, but also the villagers' waiting at the end of the airstrip since the plane would unavoidably overshoot the runway. So Tom had decided against attempting the landing.

What had happened next amazed the accident investigators. Tom had managed to turn the plane around in the narrow side valley against all the odds but lost too much altitude in the process. A crash in the rugged terrain was unavoidable. (A similar crash in the past had resulted in the airplane cartwheeling and bursting into flames, killing the pilot and a missionary family.) During the sharp turn, the horizontal stabilizer (tail feathers) of Tom's airplane clipped a banana tree. Because the plane was already close to stall speed this was all it took for the plane to stop climbing. It was miraculous how it settled between two sharp rock outcrops, ripping off both wings, but allowing the plane to slowly settle to the ground. It turned out, not only were the wings ripped off, but the empennage (tail assembly of the aircraft, including stabilizers, elevators, and rudder) was twisted upside down and the whole engine compartment was separated from the plane. Only the main cabin area, where the four occupants were, remained intact. Before passing out, Tom had managed to switch off power and fuel to prevent a fire—and even apologized to his passengers.

The villagers at the airstrip had immediately started running toward the wreck but stopped in their tracks. "Let's pray first that we won't find any dead bodies," someone suggested. Sadly, airplane crashes were all too common in the Papuan mountains and everyone knew most were fatal. Miraculously, their prayer was answered.

After getting out of the plane, one passenger had bumped his head on a tree so hard he needed stitches. Bad luck after just surviving a plane crash! Another passenger was later seen sitting above the crash site eating a sweet potato which he had recovered from the wreckage. The third one had sustained worse injuries from the crash.

Since Tom was loved and respected, people in the local churches all over Wamena prayed for him.

Dirt Roads, Rats, and the *JESUS* Film

Early September 2001

"Good news," Tom told us the following week. "The doctor says I'm good to go. We can show the *JESUS* film in Makki this weekend. I'll still need my crutches, though."

None of us would have believed that Tom would be able to go on a trip so soon after his crash. God had answered the multitude of prayers for Tom, and the leg wound hadn't become infected. Nius, our guard from Makki, offered to come along and arrange everything via HF radio, including accommodation for us at the old mission house there.

"No need to bring anything," he said. "The house has all the bedding."

Kees, a Dutch civil engineer involved in a building project, was able to come along. He was happy for this opportunity to see the way people lived in the mountain villages. Saturday came, we loaded up the Daihatsu, and off we went. I was so excited finally to see what lay beyond Pyramid! This was my type of fun: beautiful landscapes, good company, and most of all; it was not just for our enjoyment but for ministry.

The weather was "fine as frog hairs" as Tom would say. After leaving the Grand Valley, the road became rough, steep, and winding in parts. After yet another bend, the view opened up, and before us lay the beautiful North Baliem area. Deep down below the road, the

Baliem River wound its way toward its Grand Valley. The hillsides were full of hamlets and gardens and were only forest-covered in the higher regions. The scenery was not as open as the Grand Valley nor as steep as the regions Southeast of Wamena. After driving for three and a half hours, we arrived at Makki in the afternoon. Nius showed us the way to the unoccupied mission house.

"What, you didn't bring the keys?" Nius asked in disbelief.

"What keys? Doesn't the church here have the keys?"

What would we do now? In Wamena, we lived in a house of the same mission that owned this compound, but nobody had ever mentioned keys to the Makki house. Nius took us to the church compound and the house of Pak Willem, the District Superintendent. He didn't have a key either.

Bummer!

Pak Willem and his wife, Wellena, welcomed us into their home instead. If only we had brought sleeping bags and mats. I felt for Tom, with his injuries and crutches, who wouldn't have a bed or western bathroom now.

We set up the generator outside, and the other equipment inside the church and children appeared in the building. One child started to sing and soon all the others joined in with their loud, cheerful voices. "*Dalam nama Yesus ...*" (In the name of Jesus) they started singing in Indonesian and then sang one song after another in Indonesian and their own tribal language, Western Dani.

When the cicadas' sounds ceased echoing from the mountains and darkness fell, the adults also poured into the church. We had expected people to flock to the church as soon as we arrived, but they had still been busy working in their gardens, washing their clothes and sweet potatoes, and preparing for Sunday. Young and old people congregated in the church and sat on the floor. There were men of all ages, petite elderly ladies with canes, and young mothers with their babies in the net bags on their backs. (You could always tell when there was a baby in a net bag because they were additionally covered in an Indonesian sarong or a blanket to keep them warm).

The film started and people chattered about the amazing things they saw on the screen. For many of the attendees, it was the first film they ever saw, and for all of them, it would have been the first film ever in their heart language. We could see the emotion reflected on their faces, body language, and sounds. When baby Jesus was first shown, the people clapped and cheered. When a donkey pulling a cart with wheels walked by, people would bite their knuckles and utter sounds of amazement. "Ayeeee!"

They murmured when they saw the big herd of pigs. I was glad the film didn't show them going over the cliff and into the lake which might have caused a riot in this culture. When Jesus was beaten and crucified, tears streamed down the peoples' faces, and when He appeared resurrected, they again clapped and cheered.

I was affected myself, but one thought really hit me while watching the film: it was set two thousand years ago and yet, some aspects of it appeared modern in this setting. There were houses with windows and white walls, a donkey cart, soldiers in armor, and the like. In contrast, the people surrounding me only knew steel, paint, and woven clothes since the missionaries had arrived in airplanes less than fifty years ago. Up until then, they hadn't invented the wheel; didn't know paper, fabric, or shoes; and the thatched houses were made of boards hewn with stone axes and tied together with vines. Over the mountains, there were people still living in such conditions today.

After the movie was finished and people had gone home, we went back to Pak Willem's house for a candlelight dinner as there was no electricity at Makki. Some church elders joined us for the meal. Earlier, I had seen Ibu Wellena walking behind the house, holding two rabbits by their ears. There hadn't been a happy ending for the rabbits, but we had a fantastic meal way beyond our expectations. Ibu Wellena had cooked up a storm. There was rice, sweet potatoes, rabbit meat, and a vegetable I had never tasted before. It was so delicious I couldn't stop eating. It turned out to be *Labu Siam*—chayote, choco, or Caribbean squash—finely cut and prepared with shallots, garlic, and fresh herbs from the forest.

"That film was wonderful," Ibu Wellena said. "Most elderly people don't speak Indonesian, and they said the Bible stories really came alive to them tonight when they saw them acted out in their language."

I felt so blessed and privileged to be here. Just over a year ago, we had gone to Pyramid with Brent, who had worked on producing the Western Dani version of the *JESUS* film, and now we were here showing it to Western Dani people.

The evening ended, and we turned into our rooms where we stretched out on mattresses on the bare floor. Since we didn't have sleeping bags with us and our gracious hosts didn't have spare blankets, we used the crude dirty blankets the speakers had been wrapped in for the transport. We soon discovered fleas inhabited them. While we were still thinking of the fleabites, we heard a high-pitched sound: approaching mosquitoes. There was nothing we could do about them, but at least we didn't need to worry about malaria. The Anopheles mosquitoes that carried the disease couldn't stand the low temperatures at this altitude.

Finally, I fell asleep. Soon, I was woken up again by the sound of something messing with the plastic wrappers of our instant noodles and chocolate bars. I lit my flashlight and saw a rat going after our provisions. I threw a shoe and watched the rat running up the wooden boards and disappearing through a gap under the corrugated steel roof. By now Hans was sitting upright too. *Good night!* I tried to go back to sleep. A minute later, I heard the rat again; this time it had brought a friend. I threw more things, fought off more mosquitoes, and now needed to go to the toilet. I didn't want to wake anybody by trying to find my way to the other side of the house in the dark, so I decided to go outside. I finished my "business" in the moonlight and returned to the house.

Oh no!

The door had fallen shut. I would have to either sleep outside or wake up someone after all. Kees slept in the room closest to the door, so I knocked on his window until he woke up and let me back into the house.

In the morning, we found holes in almost all our food items and were thankful to our hosts for their wonderful hospitality once again.

"That's why I have to keep all my food in a closed wooden cupboard overnight," Ibu Wellena told me. I made a mental note to put our food in tin cans on our next trip.

Many people hadn't been able to attend on the previous night and requested we show the *JESUS* film again during the Sunday morning church service. It was a bit too bright for people to see clearly, but they didn't mind. In each of the two showings, more than five hundred people watched the *JESUS* film—although many of them had come twice. Despite the uncomfortable night with fleas, rats, and mosquitoes, this had been one of the best weekend trips I had ever experienced.

An Unexpected Threat

Although the construction workers had finished the hangar, it seemed like the project would never stop. The big sliding doors still needed to be built. Building those would be a daunting task on a twenty-meter-wide building, in a valley which got hit by strong winds nearly every afternoon and also by the strong helicopter rotor downwash. This project gave Hans headaches. What was worthy of a full-blown migraine, however, was when he one day measured the open front of the hangar to design the sliding doors and found distorted steel roof trusses!

Thankfully, Kees, the Dutch civil engineer who had joined us on the trip to Makki, was still in Wamena. Every year Kees volunteered several weeks for a Christian nonprofit organization needing to build. He had impressed us with his dedication to giving part of his work time to the Lord and with his commitment. "No matter if I work for a paying customer or I volunteer, I always put in the same effort."

Kees looked at the roof construction with Hans and made some calculations. The result was devastating.

"I'm sorry, Hans, I've calculated the pressure that hits each square meter of the roof during the tropical downpours. These trusses are too weak to sustain the construction in an intense rain."

If the weak trusses weren't bad enough, some wood purlins had shrunk and now twisted the trusses, weakening them even further. The same afternoon, we learned the shocking news a building on the coast had just collapsed during construction, injuring workers. It was built in a similar fashion to our hangar but with a wider span. We also heard a worker suggested chickens must be sacrificed in a ritual to make sure nothing like that would happen again. We preferred the more scientific approach the civil engineer suggested.

Kees made more calculations, and we prayed. Each time the rains pelted our roof in the middle of the night, Brian and Hans lay awake wondering if they should go down to the hangar and push out the helicopters. The very building erected to protect the helicopters from the elements was now threatening to destroy them.

There was nothing Hans could do other than to get to work again with the workers, adding reinforcements to the roof, while the needed hangar door had to wait. Kees helped design an improvement and our team prepared hydraulic supports to lift the trusses to preload the new reinforcement. Hans and Jan bought the materials for the roof reinforcement on the coast, but no one could fly the steel to Wamena because of a severe airplane shortage. Getting supplies for this landlocked town had become so precarious that rice was the only thing flown into Wamena and all other materials had to wait. We were stuck between a rock and a hard place.

September 12, 2001 (September 11, US time)

Ring, ring, ring!

It was six o'clock in the morning. I was always uneasy when the phone rang before seven a.m. because it usually wasn't good news. This call was no exception. Luana called to inform us about the planes crashing into the twin towers of the World Trade Center in New York City. I could hardly believe what I heard. We knew this would have big consequences.

"Well, I guess we all know, this means war," Brian stated, and we all nodded.

We had bought a used TV to watch the international news in English, which by now had been discontinued on the Indonesian channel. In the following weeks, Brian obtained a satellite dish and receiver and set it up at our house. We would meet and watch the "war on terrorism" of the USA unfold in Afghanistan. This war caused an uproar in the Muslim world. Hans noticed people on the street looking at him with contempt and hate. Most people here didn't know which countries we came from. Our skin color branded us as *orang barat* (westerners). The climate for missionaries and western aid workers sometimes changed dramatically with the world news.

The Lord Gives, and the Lord Takes Away

October 2001

Ring, ring, ring!
The rain pelted the roof, and it was still pitch black around me. It was four thirty in the morning, and I scrambled out of bed to the phone. Pak Hengki was on the other end. Three days earlier his wife, Agustina, my dear house helper, had delivered a baby. As it was the custom in most highland tribes, the parents hadn't given the child a name yet.

Not everything was well with the baby girl. I had looked at her through the incubator glass. She weighed about two kilograms. Most babies born to my friends in Germany weighed twice as much, but that wasn't the biggest problem. A ball was protruding from her tiny forehead. The doctor said surgery would only be possible from the age of three months on. Until then, he was unable to determine what was causing the ball, either fluid, some sort of tissue, or a tumor.

I tried to understand what Pak Hengki was saying, but the rain was incessantly pelting the metal roof, making it almost impossible to hear. I understood they wanted to go home from the hospital now and something about the baby. When I asked again what the problem was, he cried: "*Mati! Mati! Mati!*" My heart sank: the baby had died.

This phone call had been the third one before seven in the morning within three months, and each message had been worse than the previous one. Later in the day, I went to Agustina's place to be with her and offer help. It was so sad. While there was supposed to be joy for a new life which the parents eagerly anticipated for nine months, now there was only emptiness, grief, and pain.

Before the graveyard funeral, a mourning ceremony with a meal was held at a house close to ours. I had never attended a Papuan funeral before and didn't know what to expect. Men were walking around the yard, setting up for a bakar batu feast. I arrived at the simple wooden house, took off my shoes, and entered. Women of all ages, who sat on the floor along the walls weeping, filled the semi-dark room. An old lady led the younger ones in a time of collective wailing, sounding like a chant. I gave Agustina a hug, sat down on the floor, and couldn't hold back the tears myself. The baby girl was lying on the floor, wrapped in a cute, padded baby blanket and looked as if she was sleeping. Agustina sat on the floor in front of her lifeless firstborn child—slumped and motionless. I couldn't imagine Agustina and Hengki's pain.

Although I must have stuck out like a sore thumb with my white skin amongst the Papuan people of all ages, I felt my visit was appreciated. A man opened the door and asked me to come out, so they could accept my offer to drive them to the market with the Helimission car to buy vegetables and other food. I stepped outside the dark house and squinted in the bright sunlight, struggling to see through my tears. The men looked at me astonished when they saw my red eyes. I later learned, some people were given the job to lead the wailing, even if they weren't affected by the death. They trained and practiced for it, preferably by a noisy river where people didn't hear them. Even though some crying and wailings might not have been genuine in my western understanding, it showed the family the support and care of the community, which had come together from within Wamena and from Hengki and Agustina's villages.

I felt so helpless trying to comfort Agustina and was glad to help in a practical way by driving people and contributing money. When wealthier people died, they would slaughter a pig and have a traditional pig feast, but this time the meal was simpler, and there were fish and tofu besides the rice, vegetables, and sweet potatoes. The food supply in Wamena was severely limited by now because of the cargo airplane shortage. I hadn't been able to find flour and some other food items in a while, but we could still come by the food we needed even if it was costly and inconvenient. The local population was hit a lot harder. Rice prices quadrupled, but salaries were still the same. Cooking kerosene was unavailable, and wood was expensive.

The afternoon funeral was at the cemetery outside Wamena, close to Agustina's home. After the local pastors held a moving ceremony and read some Bible verses, we watched as the tiny black coffin was lowered into the ground. My heart ached as I tried to process this unreal sight. A small cross was ready to mark the grave and now I read the girl's name for the first time: Alesina.

The funeral and time of collective grieving took three days, according to Agustina's culture and soon after, she came back to work.

With my limited language skills and busy life supporting Helimission, I had few opportunities to reach out to people in the community. I was thankful God had brought Agustina to us when she was still pregnant so we could give her support in this difficult time of grief and pain.

Just over a year later, Agustina became pregnant again. I made sure she received enough vitamins and protein, and we were all overjoyed when the baby was born healthy and weighed in at (in this part of the world a near record-breaking) seven pounds (thirty-two hundred grams).

Trouble, Joy, Sadness, and Kindness at Tiom

October 2001

"How about another trip to show the *JESUS* film?" I suggested to Hans and Tom.

"Sure, what do you have in mind?"

"How about Tiom? That's reachable by car, and there should be a good turnout."

Tom no longer needed crutches which would make things a lot easier for him. Tiom was reachable by the same road as Makki in about five hours and also lay in the Western Dani territory. We could use the new version of the *JESUS* film again. We set a date, and I called Tiom on the office radio during the daily morning radio schedule. The person at the other end liked the idea and promised to make the arrangements. He asked how many people would come so that they could have accommodation ready for us. Great!

Pak Dissen, a native of Tiom, came along and so did Victor, our friend and co-worker. Although it had been another busy week, we got off on Friday afternoon. We would stay at Makki for the first night so we could spend the whole next day at Tiom. By now, we had obtained the keys to the mission house at Makki from an office on the coast and had been given official permission to use it.

It was pitch black when we arrived at Makki since there was no electricity. We were glad when Ibu Wellena and some other people came to greet us. With our flashlights, we made it into the wooden house and lit candles. What a lovely, cozy place. The house was still fully equipped with cutlery, crockery, and firewood. There were books and magazines.

"This would be a perfect holiday house," I said to Hans.

This time, we had brought sleeping bags, found beds with mattresses for everybody, and got a good night's sleep—undisturbed by rats. In the morning, we looked around the compound, ate breakfast, and then drove on towards Tiom. We crossed the Baliem via a long bridge and made it across a section of the road, which had been washed out by a stream. The road condition was terrible with either jagged rocks or deep mud. In this part of the North Baliem area, grass covered most of the steep hillsides and signs of civilization were visible everywhere, unlike most other places in the mountains I had seen. Only the mountaintops were still covered in virgin forest.

When our shaken-up bones got too achy, we took short breaks, stretched our legs, enjoyed the scenery, and greeted people along the way. Tom, who was unusually quiet and deep in thought this time, still had a friendly word and a handshake for everyone he met. At lunchtime, we had a picnic on the shady bank of the Baliem River and then drove into Tiom. The village was much more open with broader views than Makki, a lovely, shady place tucked in between the mountains.

Since I had made the arrangements by radio, I was glad Pak Dissen was with us and knew who we needed to talk to. The mission house next to the airstrip was opened for us, and we found rooms with beds for everybody. Although it was quite clean, this house looked like no one had lived in it for a while and most of the cupboards were empty. Some friendly people made a fire for us in the woodstove, so we could cook a meal and boil rainwater to drink. This time I had packed the food in tin cans but hoped we wouldn't have to worry about rats.

"Well, we should go report to the police station with our Surat Jalans," Tom suggested, and we pulled out our travel permits. I looked at it and felt sick to my stomach. "Oh my goodness, Tiom isn't on the list!"

Our travel permits were usually issued for three months, and most of the bigger places around Wamena were listed. For some reason, Tiom was not.

"What do we do now?" I looked at Hans.

"There's not much we can do. We'll have to go anyway."

We hoped and prayed we wouldn't get into trouble. Being a pilot who flew almost everywhere in these mountains, Tom had a travel permit for Tiom. He also knew Indonesian the best, so we let him go first and do all the talking. Besides, we had never met anybody who didn't like Tom, so this would be our best chance. Hans and I tagged along and smiled, trying to be as polite and friendly as we could. The police officers were friendly, stamped and signed our papers, and everything went well. What a relief!

Next, we found out the military wouldn't be happy if we reported to the police but not to them, so we went to the military post. There we got into trouble because I didn't know which pastor was responsible for the *JESUS* film showing. After a while, they let us off the hook, and I made a new list of mental notes: *remember to check everybody's Surat Jalan, ask for a name of a pastor in charge, and report to all possible authorities right away.*

With all formalities finished, we went for a walk through the village and enjoyed the afternoon sun and chats with the people of Tiom. I especially enjoyed being out of trouble. We found a kiosk made of crude wooden boards with a mesh wire window where canned sardines, candles, matches, soap, colored string for net bags, cooking oil, sugar, sweets, and cans of soft drinks were sold for outrageous prices.

"Unbelievable in which corners of the world Coca-Cola is sold," Hans said.

We set up the equipment at the Baptist church, and people came streaming in. I was tired and knew I wouldn't be able to stay awake during the movie, so I went back to the house where I lit candles and checked out the books the missionaries had left behind. My heart pounded when I heard somebody approaching the house. I was on my own and probably every God-fearing person of the area was at the church watching the film. Who could this be? I saw a light and heard a hissing noise before the knock on the door. It turned out to be a friendly, elderly Papuan man who had noticed I had returned to the house by myself and thought I might need some light. He wanted to bring me a kerosene lamp which was the source of the hissing sound. How nice and thoughtful!

The next morning, we all went to the church service. We hadn't been to many local church services yet. It would have been good to join an Indonesian church to learn the language quicker and to build relationships, but with the heavy workload for Hans Monday through Saturday nights, it had been more important for us to get rest on Sundays, hear sermons we understood, and to spend time with our single friends.

Like at Makki, most people in the spacious, light, wooden building were Papuan with only a few transmigrants among them. The people sang Indonesian and Western Dani songs. Even though I felt out of place, I enjoyed the service. When the offering was taken, some ladies in neat, pretty dresses performed a special song while making rhythmic swaying moves with their arms in front of them. I didn't understand the words but enjoyed the harmony and peace of the music, which sounded different from anything I had heard before.

A young, and much-overdressed, pastor held the sermon.

"I hope they won't ask us to say something," I said to Hans. Of course, they did. To our relief, Tom, who was used to this kind of thing, got up. Tom, who still walked with a limp, shared about his present situation. He wasn't sure what the future held for him and his family after the airplane accident. He had come face-to-face with the possibility of having to leave Papua—which was part of why he had been so quiet on this trip. I'm sure his testimony that day touched the hearts of every person in the church.

Over the years, I found one of the only ways for us westerners to deeply connect with the local people was in suffering and vulnerability. Because we had white skin and appeared to be rich in their eyes, most Papuans seemed to believe we had no problems. We wore shoes and clothes without holes, owned a motorcycle, and always had plenty of food. Like with my toothache, we could fly to places with better medical care. What worries could we possibly have? This thinking often resulted in shallow relationships. Jesus, however, had come to earth as a baby born in a stable, eaten with people on the fringes of society, and suffered and died for us.

When the people saw Tom limping and heard about his crash, God's miraculous protection of him and his passengers, and his worries, they realized westerners suffered and feared uncertainty as well.

When we talked about our faith in God, people often seemed to think: "That might work for you, but my circumstances are different." But in fact, we all needed God's protection and help, and friends who'd encourage us, no matter what our—or their—circumstances were.

I heard of a missionary in Africa who asked persecuted Christians what a good western missionary should be like in their eyes. None of them seemed to know a good answer but wherever he went people said there was one missionary they loved. They wouldn't go into detail. At one point, the man said he wouldn't leave before they told him what it was about the man they loved. Finally, they answered: "He needs us." When he had been at a point of need, he had turned to the locals who had helped him out. That had made him one of them.

What a revelation. We, westerners, are at great risk of appearing in a position of strength, giving out good things which are satisfying to ourselves, but often less so to the locals who may feel powerless and needy. True change often starts with sharing in sickness and weakness.

We were all hurting for Tom and the family and couldn't bear the thought of them possibly leaving Papua.

Welcome to the Jungle

October 2001

After the long weekend in Tiom, I launched into house and office work again. In the evening, we went to Brian and Luana's house for a meal and to catch up.

"We have to add another flight to Moi to the schedule," Brian filled us in. "Tim needs to go to the coast for meetings."

Tim's wife, Kathy, and their three young kids would be by themselves for ten days. Luana turned to me: "I think Kathy would do well with you there for company."

Wow, now there was a thought! We had followed the news of the events around the surveys in the Point X-Ray area, even when we were still in Germany. We regularly prayed for the families who worked at this new mission station in the Moi tribe. However, because the helicopter was usually filled to the weight limit with supplies, there was rarely an opportunity for anybody to go along and visit the station. There was only one day to prepare. My mind raced: what about Hans? What would he eat? A helicopter ride. Ten days in the jungle. Would I survive that? I sure hoped I would be able to help Kathy and not get sick and cause even more trouble.

"Don't worry, Tammy and I will feed Hans," Luana assured me.

"No problem, then I can work late and catch up on things," Hans tried to encourage me (I wasn't so sure that would be a good thing).

Visiting this jungle area was a great opportunity, which might not come again. Even if I hated it there (which was unlikely), I would still get two long helicopter flights over one of the most beautiful and untouched areas of the world, which would make up for a lot of trouble. The next day I packed my duffel bag with all the things I might need at a jungle station. I prepared myself for ten steaming hot days and nights in the middle of nowhere. I packed insect repellent and ammonia solution to treat insect bites, and high, sturdy shoes to hopefully protect me from snakebites.

I asked Ibu Agustina to bake lots of bread and cinnamon rolls for Hans. Then I went shopping for fresh vegetables, frozen chickens, and sweets for the seven children of the three pioneer missionary families. After all, I had to make sure they'd like me. Otherwise, they might make life miserable for me (not that I was too worried about that).

Andy was the pilot this time. I was excited to sit up front because the unobstructed views of mountains, swamps, forests, and waterfalls through the huge windscreen and the chin bubble window on the bottom would be spectacular. We flew over Tiom where the road ended. While the car trip had taken us five hours on the terrible road, it only took us about half an hour by helicopter.

After roughly another hour of flying over steep forest-covered mountain ranges and my first attempt at steering a helicopter for a few minutes, Andy descended toward a mountainside with a small clearing. The area looked uninhabited as far as I could see, but soon I noticed a few metal roofs on the clearing and a thin plume of smoke rising from below. The smoke came from a garden near a few tribal huts. The tin roofs covered the three missionary houses surrounding a cleared helipad—the new Moi mission station in the Point X-Ray area.

The three families welcomed us when we landed on the helipad. Some tribesmen looked on from a distance. By now, I had seen many people in traditional Papuan clothing of gourds and hair nets carrying bows and arrows, but these people looked different. They weren't dressed up in feathers and painted with pig grease for a demonstration or feast, but rather looked matte from dirt and at ease with their weapons like on any normal day.

A few minutes ago I had looked at another world from a bird's-eye view; now I landed in it for real.

Andy took off and flew to the coastal town of Nabire where he would spend the night and refuel before doing more flights and picking up Tim the following morning. Tim and Kathy and their three children took me in and showed me around the house. So far I had only met Tim, but all five family members turned out to be amiable, and I was looking forward to spending time with Kathy and her three kids Brand, Tyler, and Alyssa—aged five, four, and two years.

The simple, wooden house with a corrugated steel roof was built on a hillside. I looked around.

Wow, everything that hasn't grown here was flown in on our helicopters!

The main floor housed an open kitchen and dining area. There were two small children's rooms with a loft-space on top, a tiny living room, the master bedroom, a small utility niche with the electricity boards and the radio connections, and a bathroom containing a sit-down toilet (yes!), a sink, and a shower. The entrance area where the shoes were kept under a rough wooden bench (ready for the kids to run out into the mud), led to a big porch with another bench to hang out with the tribal people. A lot of work had been done since the final surveys in June 2000 and since the families had moved in about a year ago!

"Your room is down here," Kathy said, leading the way down the wooden stairs.

The basement floors were made of beautiful natural rocks. Apart from the guestroom, there was a little workshop and another tiny room.

Solar panels provided the electricity during the day, and a little gasoline-powered generator was used at night if needed. Outside, there was a small newly-established vegetable garden and chickens and rabbits in cages.

Although the house was made of simple plain wooden boards, it felt cozy and homey the way it was furnished. As was to be expected in the rainforest, the room in the basement was damp. A mushroom growing out of a wooden beam testified to that. I made myself at home and put books on a shelf, which I planned to read by candle-light during the long, dark evenings.

The weather turned out to be not nearly as hot and steamy as I had feared and at night it got so cool that I was thankful for the quilt Kathy put on the bed for me. I went to sleep in the rustic, wide, wooden built-in berth with a mosquito net. I remembered Brian talking about sleeping there and worrying about snakes coming in at night through cracks in the walls. All the cracks between the wooden boards had been closed up by now, so I decided not to worry and went to sleep.

The next morning, Andy returned with the helicopter from Nabire and picked up Tim. I watched the helicopter take off and disappear behind the forest-covered mountains and swallowed hard. I had never felt this landlocked before in my life. From all the stories I had heard about this place, I knew I would never make it out of here in my strength. Experienced jungle survivors could make it to the next grass airstrip for little mission airplanes by hiking for two weeks—provided they wouldn't break a leg on a steep, slippery trail, fall into a white-water river, get bitten by poisonous snakes or scorpions, or fall into the hands of hostile tribal warriors. There was no way for this office girl to get out alive. I could now understand why missionaries sometimes had panic attacks after the helicopter left.

Kathy's words brought me out of these gloomy thoughts and back to realizing this was a beautiful day on a well-established and well-stocked mission station with three families including their lively children.

"Heli-days are always exciting and different from ordinary days. Good thing they usually only come up once in a few months, otherwise, we'd never get much done," she said with a laugh.

The three families went back to their houses and resumed their business.

"Okay, Kathy, put me to work."

With the kids playing in the mud and water, there were clothes to wash and fold every day and Kathy showed me how to use the washing machine with the generator. She also explained how to hang the laundry on her Canadian-style clothesline with guide wheels allowing for the clothes to be wheeled out over the steep, rugged yard and reeled in quickly when the almost daily tropical downpours arrived.

Unfortunately, I wasn't alone with my task. Insects surrounded me which I couldn't ignore. When it was a bee, I'd better not beat it, otherwise, it would sting me. If it was a mosquito, I had to kill it before it could bite me; and if it was another bug, I could relax. (On one of the following days, a bee made it into my pants and stung me on my leg. Thankfully, the ammonia solution brought instant relief after I skipped into my bedroom and applied it).

While the helicopter was still en route to Wamena, we kept the radio on to listen to the flight-following traffic. Then Kathy turned the radio off to conserve the solar-powered battery. I secretly wished it could have stayed on. Now there was nothing left connecting me to the outside world. It was time to immerse myself into this world. While I washed the dishes with cold water coming from an uphill spring, I looked at the beautiful scenery through the mosquito screen. There were no glass windows anywhere in the house and the fog at night was kept out by curtains. Even though every window had a screen, there was a constant battle with insects, which somehow found their way into the house. I looked up to the roof rafters and wondered, how in the world these could be kept clean from cobwebs.

"You are so busy caring for the children and all the housework, and did you say four hours of culture and language study on top of that?" I asked Kathy.

"That's right. Four hours for the women and eight hours for the men."

"Couldn't you get a house helper?"

"Well, we've thought about it, but it doesn't seem possible at this point. The tribal ladies have their gardens and children to take care of, and they can't grasp the concept of hygiene just yet. And if we bring a lady in from Wamena or Sentani, she wouldn't have her family here, and in this culture, there are no single women."

"Oh, yes, that would make it difficult."

At least for these ten days, I would hopefully give Kathy a break from much of the housework so she could keep up the language and culture study. She also wanted to write to her supporters back home, so the thank-you notes could go out on the helicopter when it returned with Tim. There were so many things to think of in a place like this. Apart from no shops and pharmacies, there were no mailboxes either. If the pilot forgot the mailbag, there wouldn't be any letters from loved ones in months, and the only connection to the outside world would be the brief emails sent over the HF radio.

"Kathy, how does that work with no single women?" I couldn't grasp this strange concept. I was shocked to learn that girls between eight and twelve years of age were given to men in marriage. If a husband died, the wife would get passed on to a brother or other relative because the family had paid the bride price. Often men had several wives. However strange this concept seemed, widows were taken care of with this practice.

Kathy had the fabulous ability to cook a tasty meal with the ingredients she had available in her pantry or tiny garden. Whatever didn't grow here or hadn't come on the helicopter, she simply didn't have. Sometimes the tribal ladies brought leaves or tubers from their gardens to trade for instant noodles, rice, salt, or the like. When Kathy occasionally gave the ladies fruit from the coast, they would keep the seeds to plant in their gardens. Kathy included the fresh local produce into the diet. I watched in awe and copied several recipes.

Besides the eight hours of culture and language study, communication with the mission, etc., the men had to care for the houses and yards and keep the tropical plants from reclaiming the area. The biggest job besides the language study was getting the airstrip project underway. This project was a daunting task on this steep, forest-covered mountainside.

On some afternoons, the whole team gathered to compare notes and exchange new words and phrases they had learned in the Moi language. While I folded the laundry, I listened to the conversations. Since nobody from the outside world had ever studied this language or reduced it to writing before, there were no dictionaries, and every word, expression, and verb form, etc. had to be researched and recorded. Stephen put all the words into a database on the computer accessible to the whole team. I was impressed with the team's diligence and work ethic. The team members always greeted me warmly, but never stopped for a longer chat during work hours.

I was so glad I had come here. I enjoyed spending time with the missionary families as well as some tribal people and getting to know life and work on a jungle mission station. I hadn't seen a single snake yet (and I wouldn't throughout my entire stay).

The team would get together to wind down, relax, and socialize over games and snacks on Friday nights. Kathy and I made pizza and watched a movie with the three children on Saturday night. On Sundays, the team got together for church services they held amongst themselves, followed by cooking, eating, and fellowship. The mission station had only been open for about a year. It would take years for the team to learn enough of the tribe's culture and language to communicate the gospel clearly. Everybody longed for the day when the tribe could join in the church services.

With the growing knowledge of the language, combined with observations of daily life, the team had already gained much insight into the worldview of the Moi people. Some of their findings were mind-boggling. The people wouldn't go out at night because they were afraid of evil spirits and believed the moon was a bad man. Once during a walk with the missionaries, a Moi man had stopped in his tracks at the sight of a bird.

"We can't continue on this path," he stated. "The bird has warned me that somebody is trying to ambush and kill me." He insisted they'd take a different—much longer—route. It turned out every family had a totem bird they weren't allowed to hunt or eat which would give them signs and guidance.

Another time, one of the Moi men wanted to borrow Tim's sandals.

"Why would you want to do that?" Tim had asked, "You can walk so much better on these slippery paths with your bare feet."

As a matter-of-fact, missionaries sometimes debated which shoes would be best in this terrain, because they hadn't found any in which they could keep up with the barefooted locals and not get foot rot (athlete's foot) during long survey trips.

"No, no, that's not it," the tribal man had explained. "If my enemies see me walk past, they can use my footprint to put a curse on me. But they can't do that if I wear sandals."

Another time, a man had come up from the river distressed, out of breath, and pale (well, as pale as a Melanesian man can get). He had felt forced to walk a long detour because apparently, a ghost had blocked his path down at the river.

Like in the Eastern highlands, people here also killed one of two twins after birthçin this case the stronger one, because they believed it was a spirit eating the weaker one. I had already heard of the gruesome practice of slashing and cutting people all over their bodies after a centipede or other poisonous animal bit them. I couldn't imagine how hard it must be for my new friends to witness all the harrowing practices for a long time without being able to intervene. Some of their tribal friends died needlessly of dehydration or blood loss. Suggesting to the people there were no spirits (like most westerners believed) and that bloodletting and water deprivation were harmful practices wouldn't have helped either. The people believed that doing anything else would lead to the certain death of the patient while angering the spirits, which would cause further problems to the community. It was good the missionaries had come to this tribe when they did. With the extremely high child mortality rate, no healthcare, and frequent revenge killings (even for natural deaths which they didn't believe in), a few years later the small tribe might have vanished forever.

"I'm going over to Carolyn's to talk to the ladies," Kathy said. "Are you coming?"

"Sure!"

The housework and homeschooling were done, and now it was time for the daily culture and language study. Chieftain Tokomadi's wife—affectionately dubbed "Grandma" by the missionaries—and her daughter-in-law, Weiwa, were finished with most of their day's work as well and sat down on Carolyn's porch. Weiwa's son was running around and playing. Weiwa was heavily pregnant, but that didn't stop her from smoking a huge bamboo pipe.

I guess she won't be getting a brochure from a health insurance company about the dangers of smoking during pregnancy.

Carolyn brought out a photo album decorated with pictures of people from around the world, houses, towns, the sea, and other things the tribal ladies had never seen.

While a lot of the information was hard for the tribal people to comprehend, they caught onto other concepts surprisingly quick. Earlier on, the team had asked the people to show them where the sun rises in the morning and where it goes down. Of course, the locals could point it out. When the outsiders had asked how the sun gets back to the East overnight, the Moi people could only guess. The team had then used a ball and a flashlight to explain how the earth is a ball and rotates around the sun. They had also told them that one family was on furlough on the other side of the world.

"Oh, then it's nighttime now where they are," one lady had commented.

Lack of intelligence was not why these people still lived in Stone Age conditions. More likely the causes were the fears and taboos which were always present in their minds, inhibiting any advancements.

Often, the villagers came to the porch or into the house. I was amazed at how dirty they were. It had been hard to believe at first, but they never washed from birth to death. They were afraid of ponds and rivers and believed evil spirits lived in the water. The women's only attire were short plant-fiber skirts and colorful necklaces, and the men wore their traditional gourds like the men in the Wamena area. Unlike those, they carried their bows and arrows around all the time. Some were wearing head nets as well. The people loved to hang out and to trade. They often exchanged their produce for rice, noodles, or peanuts. When they worked on the airstrip, they would also be paid in food items, tools, clothes, cooking utensils, or other things they asked for.

It wasn't only the adults who looked for a good opportunity. Two-year-old Alyssa hadn't eaten up her sandwich during breakfast and was supposed to finish it later. When "Grandma" came to the porch for a visit, Alyssa ran for her half-eaten sandwich and offered it to her. The "First Lady" accepted, wrapped it in a banana leaf, and put it into her net bag for later.

During our short time of rest after lunch and in the evenings, I often read. The book *Torches of Joy* by John Dekker—a missionary to the Western Dani tribe—was quite revealing. A Dani man had put on a pig feast for Dekker once. A while later, that man had returned and demanded a machete. When John countered that the man hadn't worked for it first, the Dani had replied, "But I gave you a pig. Remember?" In this man's culture, a gift could be regarded as an advance payment.

When a man came to the house and brought me a bunch of bananas, I immediately went down to my room and brought him a chocolate bar in return.

"The chocolate was worth way more than the bananas, which grow here in abundance," Kathy commented afterward.

"I don't care. Just making sure he doesn't come back later for my flashlight or something like that!"

I enjoyed spending time with Kathy and the kids and there was always something for me to do. I tried to learn as much as I could, watching how Kathy made do with whatever food she had in the pantry, the garden, or had traded with the local ladies. Time and time again, Kathy cooked tasty, nutritious food despite the limited choices. At least she had a refrigerator which ran with solar energy and helped keep the food fresh. Kathy made bread, cinnamon rolls, and granola. I copied some of her wonderful recipes to try at home.

"That's a good idea to make your own pancake mix," I said to Kathy.

"Yeah, there are several mixes like that in my cookbooks. You prepare the dry ingredients in bulk. Then you can just scoop out a few cups as needed and mix it with the liquid ingredients and cook much faster."

"Right, and you don't have all the preservatives and other food additives, like in the industrial mixes."

The pancake mix would become the all-time favorite of my brunch guests. The homemade granola would make great food for hikes, for breakfast, or a snack in between.

I tried to get breakfast ready before the radio schedule in the morning. Every morning at seven o'clock, Kathy had to radio the mission leadership on the coast. (When more mission stations opened over the years, they all had to do the same, and if one of them didn't report for three days, our helicopter would be sent there to check if something was wrong). At six o'clock in the evening, there was another radio check in, and after all the business was taken care of, the children talked to their dad on the coast.

The children were great. They showed me their treasures, explained things to me, and we played together. However, they were no angels, and I was impressed how well Kathy disciplined them. She always did it in a calm, fair manner and the children accepted her authority.

"Elke, would you like to see the airstrip site?" Kathy's five-year-old son, Brandt asked.

"Sure!"

We went out from between the houses and up the hill into the forest. Apparently, we were walking on a trail, but I would have never guessed. We walked up a steep slope through tall grass and ferns, climbed over fallen trees, half-rotten tree trunks, and little streamlets. I breathed heavily walking uphill in the humid warmth and was drenched in perspiration. When we got to the site, all there was to see was a wide, long-sloped forest clearing full of charred tree stumps, with several streamlets running through it and bees buzzing around. I couldn't imagine this would one day become a runway. One thing was clear: Helimission wouldn't run out of work here anytime soon. (It would take another five years of work plus a year to get all the permits before small planes could land there).

This time we were going down to Grandma and Weiwa's hamlet. The older children came along, while Alyssa stayed behind with the Indonesian family. I couldn't believe how steep and slippery the trail was. Kathy and Carolyn nonchalantly walked down the jungle path as if they were walking along a paved sidewalk. They talked about the

Moi language grammar, while I tried to keep up without slipping on the wet rocks or tripping over roots. I was quite pleased that I only fell once. After a while, we reached two huts in a tiny forest clearing and had to slide down the last drop.

Nobody was home, so we walked downhill a bit further. We crossed a fallen tree over a stream and got to a large garden, surrounded by a log fence. Trees with their limbs cut off were still standing in the garden because the stone-axes weren't suitable to cut through the thick tree trunks. Grandma and Weiwa were still working. The little boy was with them, and the children ran about the garden. Grandma, fearing for her precious produce, commanded us all to go ahead to the huts together with Weiwa. This time we walked up a large fallen tree. I gracelessly inched my way up the log. Weiwa walked up the same log sure-footed with her round baby belly and a load of firewood. I felt like an elephant once more.

We sat down in the open front area of the ladies' hut and the kids lit a small cooking fire before running off to play with Weiwa's little son. We all held our breath when we saw Grandma slowly coming up the trail with a heavy load of garden produce and more firewood. When she finally dropped the heavy load next to the hut, we all exhaled with a sigh. Even if I had wanted to, I couldn't have helped her carry her heavy load. It had been a challenge for me to balance my body weight up that steep path and fallen tree trunk. These were tough women who led a hard life.

Grandma gave us cooking bananas and sugarcane. We put the bananas into the fire and took them back out when the outsides were charred and black. Weiwa and Grandma got out their large bamboo pipes, stuffed them with tobacco, and lit them with a piece of flint. I couldn't believe how easy that looked. It took no longer than it would have with a lighter. When I looked up, I saw a young Moi man appearing out of the forest. He stopped in his tracks and stared at us. We must have been a strange sight to him—all these colorfully dressed pale people and blond kids. He continued on his path.

While I munched on my cooking banana, which tasted more like a potato than fruit, I looked around and couldn't help but feel like I was inside a TV documentary. This experience was so surreal. I had just walked into the Stone Age! Before I could ask anyone to pinch me, a big horsefly obliged to assure me I wasn't dreaming. When we finished our bananas, we ate the sugarcane. I pulled my Swiss pocketknife out of my backpack and started peeling off the outer skin. Soon I noticed two pairs of brown eyes staring at my very sharp knife. Sorry, there would be no trading deal possible because this was an engraved wedding gift.

The sky was dark gray and the air hot and humid. A thunderstorm was imminent. Kathy and Carolyn completed putting all the new Moi expressions they had learned in their notebooks, we finished our food, thanked the ladies, and headed home. I looked at the incredibly steep ascent. Had we really come down this way in one piece? The walk uphill was more exhausting, but also easier because this way around I could find solid footholds with the front of my feet instead of the heels.

Halfway up the hill, four-year-old Tyler got tired and grumpy. He had buzzed around the place uphill and downhill with the other kids and used all his energy. When we got to the house, he didn't even want to take part in the mud bath the others were enjoying. Living in Moi was no walk in the park and even visiting the neighbors was a strenuous effort. Carolyn's two blond girls, seven-year-old Ashley and nearly six-year-old Mariah were real jungle bunnies who often ran around muddy and barefoot. Here I saw real MK's (missionary kids) in their natural habitat. I had already learned from them that you didn't need hot water and a bowl to eat *Super Mie* (Indonesian instant noodles), but you could just sprinkle the seasoning over the dry noodles and eat them with your fingers out of the pack. They were really crunchy that way!

On Friday night, we all headed over to Stephen and Carolyn's house for another game night which was great fun. I got to know the nice Indonesian family better. Pak Andersen, Ibu Lieke, and their two girls, Noel (five years old) and Tyana (two years old) were from Manado in North Sulawesi. They loved the Moi people. I was sad when I thought of the contrast this relationship was to the ones I observed in the towns where these two ethnic groups often seemed antagonistic.

I walked home on the footpath connecting the houses, balancing on the walking planks which covered the muddy parts. What a place to live. There was not a level or dry spot anywhere around apart from the helipad, which had been specifically created—probably by moving a lot of dirt. It rained most afternoons and nights, which made the paths soggy. The pigs used the paths as well to walk on and as a toilet. I'm sure the team must have dreamed of walking along broad esplanades and riding bicycles on asphalt roads, not having to look down in front of their feet for every step. I stopped and looked over the moonlit valley. I couldn't imagine a more beautiful, peaceful sight. And yet a few months back, we had prayed hard for this place because of the spiritual battle raging over it. I had never really felt the spiritual darkness Ernst Tanner had talked about several years earlier in Germany, but I knew now how real it was.

The best description I can think of for these lonely missionary outposts in a cruel, dark world full of tribal wars, fear, and spirit worship was "Embassies of Heaven." The days of the undisturbed reign of the evil one in these places were numbered.

"Elke, would you like to share with us how you became a believer and how you came to be a missionary to Papua?" Stephen asked during another Sunday service the team celebrated together. "I can translate to Indonesian for Andersen and the family."

I hadn't often put that into words before and needed a moment to think. I had always believed in God and gone through Christian children's and youth groups growing up. I had asked Jesus into my life as a teenager and from the age of twenty-four, I had hoped to go to the mission field. However, I had deviated from the path toward it. Only when I had felt completely helpless and stuck in the situation I was in, did I surrender my life, my dreams, and my belongings to God. That's when my life of joy and fulfillment had begun and had continued ever since. Hans had also come to the end of his rope before asking the Lord to take total control of his life. If we both hadn't done that, we would have never gotten married nor been part of this exciting work.

After my testimony, we had a Bible reading and sang songs. Then we all cooked and ate together. What a great team and what a privilege for me to spend time with these dedicated, hardworking people in the middle of the Papuan jungle.

How wonderful would it be when one day the Moi people would join in the worship of our Creator. Only God knew how many more years of hard work, blood, sweat, and tears it would take until that day would come. The team was dedicated to continuing learning the language to the extent that it would enable them to clearly share the gospel for the first time in the history of the tribe and to translate the Bible.

"Good news," Hans told me on the radio one night after the regular traffic was over. It was so good to hear his voice—seemingly coming from a different planet. "The 'good man' has applied with Helimission."

My heart leaped. Of course, Hans was referring to Tom but didn't want to let the whole island know. Tom had actually come to Papua to fly helicopters, but his organization had discontinued using them. Tom was no longer allowed to fly airplanes for his organization in Papua after the crash, even though he had over twenty-eight years of accident-free flying under his belt. Brian had asked him if he wanted to join our team. Since he felt confirmed to continue serving the Lord in the area he was best qualified in and loved, Helimission was the perfect match. Tom's heart's desire—as Helimission's—was to reach the last tribes and people groups with the gospel. Helicopters were vital for that endeavor in this land of thousands of square miles of trackless jungle and rugged mountains where it took an average of eight years to build an airstrip.

"I'm definitely ready to have Tim back," Kathy said.

"I know. I love it here, but I can't wait to see Hans either," I replied. I had been away from home for nine days now. We could tell the children were ready for their dad to come home too. We were all disappointed when we heard Tim wouldn't arrive on Friday as planned. First, he had encountered trouble in getting from the coast up to Wamena. Now, one of our helicopters was out of hours and due for inspection, while the maintenance work on the second one hadn't been finished yet.

Alyssa had come down with bloody diarrhea. Kathy, who was a nurse, treated her with medicine and tried to keep her hydrated as well as she could, but the poor little girl didn't get better and kept losing weight. Both Pak Andersen's wife, Ibu Lieke, and their older daughter, Noel, suffered from toothaches. They were planning on going to the dentist in December when the next helicopter flight was scheduled. Every day, five-year-old Noel cried because of the pain.

Now, I got a little glimpse of what it meant to live on an isolated jungle station without access to medical facilities when things weren't going according to plan. I knew the helicopter would pick me up after two weeks, but these folks usually had stretches of several months before the next opportunity came to leave their tiny station in the vast jungle. It was a major effort to venture out from the houses, so they were mostly confined to this tiny spot on a mountainside. In a few years, when the airstrip would be finished, they would have a stretch of sloped, open ground where they could exercise and walk without constantly having to watch where they stepped and worry about getting stuck in mud or slipping. While for me, this was an exciting opportunity and adventure, for them it was a reality of life for years to come.

Everybody was glad when the Long Ranger was back in the air on Monday since now the Jet Ranger was grounded for an inspection. Hans had finished maintenance and modifications on Mike Echo, the Long Ranger and Tim had helped him all Saturday. Brian had a busy flight schedule on Monday, and the chances of getting through the weather were too slim in the afternoons, so Tim's return flight was scheduled for Tuesday morning.

Alyssa's health wasn't improving. Despite all the efforts, she had lost ten percent of her body weight, and we were worried. When Brian finished his flights and returned to the base early Monday afternoon, Luana and the men discussed the situation with Kathy on the radio. They concluded Alyssa needed help fast. Brian and Tim took their chances with the weather and took off with medicine and a malaria test kit. At least, this would bring them closer to take Alyssa to the hospital at Nabire first thing on Tuesday morning.

We all hoped and prayed the men wouldn't have to turn back because of the weather or land somewhere on the way and spend the night. Kathy turned on the radio and soon we heard Brian's voice over the crackling static calling the mission station.

"Hi, Kathy. How is the weather at your end?"

"It's overcast, and the clouds are getting lower. Over."

"Are the clouds already covering Andersen's house or are the trees overhead the house still visible?" Andersen's house was the one furthest up the mountain.

"Andersen's house is still clear. Over," Kathy reported after a quick look out the window. It was drizzling, and we worried the helicopter wouldn't make it through.

"I think our best option is to fly into the lowlands and follow the river. This way we can stay below the clouds."

This sounded like a good plan, but we had observed the fog coming up from the river many times. All we could do was pray and wait.

After what felt like an eternity, we heard the faint chopping sound of a two-bladed helicopter rotor coming up the valley. For a long time now, I thought this was one of the coolest sounds on earth, but this time it sounded even sweeter to me. Now we could see our beautiful "Mike Echo" appear between the dark mountain walls accompanied by the sound of its jet engine. The Long Ranger with the green and red position lights and the flashing strobe lights looked magnificent in front of the gray backdrop of the mountains in the dreary weather. The noise became ear-battering, and we had to turn our faces away as they were hit by the powerful rotor wind, but it felt like a weight dropped off our shoulders when the skids touched down on the helipad.

Thank you, Lord!

After some bear hugs, we all got together at Tim and Kathy's house where we celebrated the safe trip with afternoon tea while the daylight faded away completely. The medicines and malaria test kit were brought out, and Alyssa was tested, but it turned out negative. It had been so sad to see the quiet, blond, blue-eyed girl so sick and we were relieved she would soon get the help she needed. Kathy radioed Luana in Wamena who gave her more medical advice.

It was decided that Alyssa should go to the hospital on the coast in the morning. Since Ibu Lieke and Noel had a toothache, Brian would take them along as well to get their teeth fixed. However, we all felt it would be best not to tell Ibu Lieke about it that night because we knew she would not sleep. Ibu Lieke had lived in the jungle for over a year and hadn't left the jungle station for the last nine months, so this was a big event for her. Since the Long Ranger had seven seats, Brian invited all the women, including me, along to Nabire for shopping and a change of scenery.

We had guessed right—Ibu Lieke was extremely excited. "What am I going to wear?"

The tropical waterfront town of Nabire was a stark contrast to the mountain jungle we had just come from. There were busy roads, houses, shops, and people everywhere. On the side of the road, we saw market stalls with an abundance of tropical fruits on display.

Whenever our pilots had to go to Nabire, Debbie and Eko, who were working there with another mission aviation organization, would either host them or help them in any other way they could. Apparently, they did the same for the Moi team and this time was no exception. Debbie drove us to the hospital and would take care of us all day. All the medical and dental issues were taken care of, and Alyssa had more tests done and received the right medication which would help her recover quickly.

Now, we all went shopping. Since Nabire had a seaport, all the shops were well-stocked—unlike Wamena, which was still in a supply crisis due to the lack of cargo planes. Brian's last stop before heading back to Wamena would be Nabire for refueling. Since the helicopter was going back to Wamena empty, I used the opportunity to buy supplies for our team in Wamena, including cement, sacks of flour, and rice.

We were sad to hear Debbie and her family would leave soon. However, this presented the opportunity to buy some of their household goods and other things that would be useful in Moi. So I stayed behind with the kind family in Nabire to make more room in the helicopter. My time in the jungle had come to an abrupt end.

When Brian got back to Nabire to refuel, he brought along my bag (which Kathy had packed and put on the helicopter within twelve minutes of their landing), and we loaded up the supplies for our team in Wamena. The vast, blue ocean was an immensely different sight compared to the green mountain slopes I had been looking at for two weeks.

"We'll have to stop at Pogapa for fuel," Brian said after trying to find his way around the thick clouds. With the added flight time, we'd need more jet fuel to reach Wamena. We landed at the Pogapa airstrip where another mission aviation organization had positioned fuel drums for cases like that on Helimission's request. Immediately, villagers who wanted a ride, a letter delivered, or just a look (I would have done the same if a helicopter had landed close to my house) surrounded us. We couldn't fulfill any of their requests. The weather looked so ominous that I wasn't even sure if we could make it out of Pogapa at all. However, Brian was more optimistic. After the fuel had been topped up from a drum with a pump and filter, we were on our way again.

"You can help me here," Brian said pulling out small laminated aviation maps, "Look out for good ways through the clouds, like the definition of the ridges, and hold these maps for me please."

While I did, he compared the lines on the map—which didn't look much thicker than a hair—to the rivers they symbolized and identified the villages we saw. I was impressed. I could see now why pilots had to have hundreds of hours of experience before even being considered for flying in this territory. While controlling the aircraft, the pilot had to navigate and keep an eye on the weather, altitude, air speed, fuel, and other gauges. He also had to remain in contact with the air traffic controller and the flight follower, reporting the position and flight path and then correct it again if the weather didn't allow for it. Besides that, he would have to be prepared to find a spot for an emergency landing in case something should be wrong with the helicopter. I gained a whole new level of respect and admiration for the pilots who flew out here.

We finally made it out of the rain. The sun came out, and I could hardly believe what I saw: a brilliantly bright and sparkling completely circular rainbow! I had occasionally seen faint round little rainbows on clouds below with the helicopter's shadow inside them, but I had seen nothing like this before. With the rugged, gray rocks towering next to us, and the lush, green rainforest below, it was like a sight straight out of a fairy tale.

We saw several more rainbows in the clouds and beautiful waterfalls. I marveled at the changing scenery and vegetation that differed at the various altitudes. On higher plains, low shrubs grew on turf. Here and there we saw white sand, dark brown ponds, and even a few footpaths. In the lower regions, we would see gardens and villages, and when we got closer to Wamena, there were a few roads. We were glad the weather was good enough to get through the clouds, and we wouldn't have to stay overnight in a mountain village.

As usual, when I entered the Baliem Valley returning from the mountains, the sight of the wide-open expanse and the total flatness of the valley blew me away. In a few minutes, this wonderful flight—and my two weeks in another world—would be over. Because of the difficult weather, the flight had taken nearly three hours. I really felt my bottom now and wasn't heartbroken when we arrived, and I could get out of my seat. And of course, there was my dear husband to greet me!

Search and Rescue

November 12, 2001

"I just received a phone call from Paul at TMF," Brian announced during our weekly fellowship meeting at his house a few days after I returned from Moi. "We need to be on high alert over the next few days."

A high-profile Papuan leader had been murdered at the North coast. In the following days, we paid close attention to the situation and limited our movements. Thousands of people on the coast took to the streets to pay last respects to their leader. A procession of about five thousand people accompanied the coffin on the forty-five-kilometer trip from where the chief's body was found, back to his home and tribal land at Sentani. About ten thousand people joined the funeral which was followed by protests and rampaging. Some of our favorite shops in Sentani were destroyed, but tribalism was in our favor for a change, and things stayed quiet in Wamena.

"If he had been from our tribe, we wouldn't only have burned down a few shops and houses," a Dani man scoffed at hearing the news. I didn't want to give anyone ideas, so I stopped short of remarking that I thought the crime victim had been a leader of all Papuans.

Life went on between the excitement and distractions. Lots of work needed catching up after my return from Moi. I was going through receipts and adding numbers in the accounting book when Hans rushed into the office.

"Mausi, a mission plane is missing near Nabire, and we have to go immediately!"

"Oh, my goodness!" I jumped up. "Do you have any more information? Did people die?"

"No idea, the plane hasn't been found yet," Hans said already halfway down the corridor.

"Can I get you a change of clothes and toiletries from home?"

"No time, we have to leave when the helicopter is fueled, and the SAR equipment is loaded."

It was already three o'clock in the afternoon. The flight to Nabire in perfect conditions took about two hours, and there were only three hours of daylight left. No time to lose. A few minutes later, the turbine started, and the rotor blades beat the air faster and faster. I covered my ears and turned my face from the dust, whipped up by the forceful rotor wind. The helicopter with Brian, Andy, and Hans was on its way.

Jan and I went inside and tuned into the radio flight-following channel. Now that the activity and excitement had left with the helicopter, feelings of sadness and loneliness crept up inside me. I wasn't looking forward to an unexpected night without Hans. I prayed, hoping for the best.

Maybe the pilot made an emergency landing? How must the families of the missing people be feeling now? Oh, I hope they find them alive!

About an hour into our team's flight, news about the missing airplane came in. A spotter on a search plane saw it for a split second. It had crashed into a mountain and was hidden in a ravine by trees and the steep terrain. Our hopes sank. This was the worst case scenario with little hope of survivors. Since it would get dark soon, the airplane had to return to its base at Nabire, and our helicopter also needed to get fuel there.

"Oh, these poor people," I said to Jan. "In case someone is still alive, they must wait through the night in the wreckage for help."

"That's right, but we have a GPS position, and the guys can get there first thing in the morning."

"Hotel Mike Echo landing Nabire," Brian finally reported. We were relieved our team had made it to Nabire before sundown.

After a restless night's sleep, I was back at the hangar in the early morning, waiting for news. I continued praying for a good outcome. With the first light of day, our helicopter crew took off from Nabire, heading for the crash site. Even though our team received an approximate GPS position from the pilot who had spotted the wreck the previous afternoon, it took another twenty minutes of circling over treetops until they sighted the wreckage in the rugged terrain.

"The airplane is lying upside down, and there is no sign of life," Brian reported on the radio.

Jan and I tried to concentrate on work, but we jumped each time we heard a radio transmission from Brian. We could piece together that there was no place to put down the helicopter anywhere near the crash site. Andy and Hans seemed to be clearing a landing zone nearby to start the recovery operation. The helicopter had to make several flights between Nabire and the landing zone to transport people and equipment. It was 9:55 a.m. by now and Brian's fourth time over the crash site. His next radio transmission made our jaws drop. "A man is sitting outside the wreckage. I repeat: a man is sitting outside the wreckage."

When Hans returned after three days, he filled in the gaps between the brief radio transmissions.

"When we first got to the crash site, Brian honked the air horn while hovering above it. I looked down with binoculars for signs of life in the cabin. Nothing. It looked bad. The wreckage lay in a steep ravine on a mountain slope and was surrounded by tall trees. We couldn't find a spot to land. The terrain was too steep and covered in forest."

"So, what did you do?" I asked.

"About seven kilometers away there was a creek with an opening in the forest canopy. It was large enough to fit through with the spinning rotor. I hung out the side and made sure the tail wasn't catching anything, while we slowly eased our way down. The shrubs on the creek bank were too tall to land in, but we were prepared and ready to jump from the hovering helicopter. Andy jumped out first, and I handed him the chainsaw, ax, and some other tools. Then I carefully stepped on the skid and jumped too."

"Wow! So far we have only seen stuff like that on TV," I interrupted.

"Yeah, not your typical work day, for sure! Anyway, we cleared the landing zone while Brian flew back to Nabire to refuel. When he came back, we had the spot ready. We held our breath as he came in with Mike Echo. Man, it was a tight squeeze between the trees."

"Even for a helicopter, huh?"

"Yeah. These machines are amazing! Brian brought a SAR team of the Indonesian police along. He showed them the crash site from the air for orientation, and they immediately set off into the jungle toward the crash site. Some hike that was!"

"I wonder if they knew what they were getting into. Did they have any mountain jungle training?"

"Apparently, they had been specially trained after the CASA crash in January, but that terrain was crazy!"

While sipping my coffee, I tried to imagine the four miles of steep terrain in the thick, trackless jungle.

"Then we flew back to Nabire to pick up two guys who had just arrived," Hans continued. "They were trained in rappelling and ready to go down to the wreck. We brought them to the crash site to decide whether it was worth the risk to go down, because so far, we had seen no sign of life."

"And that's when you saw the guy?"

"Yes, we couldn't believe it! And he didn't even seem to notice us! You've been next to a heli with the strong rotor wind. Add the violently swaying vegetation and imagine the infernal noise echoing from the mountain. You can't miss that! Brian even honked the horn, but no reaction."

"He must have suffered a bad shock." I remembered praying that whoever might be alive would be asleep and not aware of the thunderstorm and any dead bodies around.

"We then flew back to the landing zone and prepared everything for the rappelling operation."

"What a job, going down there looking for dead bodies!" I shuddered.

"Yeah, not for the fainthearted.

Since we had to hover out of ground effect for the rappelling, we needed every bit of engine power to stay out of trouble."

(To hover a helicopter high above the ground, thus "out of ground effect," requires extraordinary engine power. Power reserves are vital to minimize the accident risk, especially while flying above and between treetops with little room to maneuver. A change in wind direction or sudden gusts, which will sway the aircraft, requires extra power to counter the action).

"So apart from preparing and securing the ropes, we removed the doors and other non-essentials like unused seats and took the "down-the-rope-men" one at a time. We returned to the crash site to let the first guy rappel down. The area was so confined by the mountain and trees that the three of us worked together to get the heli positioned over the tiny clearing. Brian controlled the hovering helicopter; Andy kept an eye on the instruments, radios, and clearance to the treetops; and I hung out the side of the heli, guiding Brian into position with commands over the intercom."

"That sounds tricky enough even with no one rappelling down!"

"Sure was. I kept calling out: 'Straight ahead. Turn right. Stop! Two forward!'"

"Two what?"

"Meters," Hans explained. "Left one. Steady! Left one. Forward one. Back two. Right one."

"Were you secured by a safety belt or something?"

"Yes, of course, I had a harness on." Hans sipped his coffee and continued.

"When we reached a suitable hole in the tree canopy, the first rescuer stepped out of the heli. I had to keep giving commands: 'Rope is outside. Steady! Man on the skids. Left one. Man on the rope. Right one—steady! Halfway down. Forward one—steady. One off the ground. Man above ground. Man on the ground! Aft one. Man free of rope. Steady.' I was sure glad I wasn't the one dangling on the rope between the trees under the ear-bashing noise and rotor wind!"

"No kidding! You must have been relieved when he was safely on the ground."

"I wish that had been it! When I wanted to pull in, the rope got tangled in some bushes."

"Oh no!" I gasped. "That could have brought the heli down on top of them all."

"Yeah, but you always have to anticipate stuff like that," Hans reassured me. "The rescuer tried to free the rope from the ground, and I tried from the top, but no luck."

"And then?" I was glad I only heard about this when everybody was safe on the ground.

"I kept trying, all the while calling out commands to Brian to maintain the position. The pilots couldn't see the spot from the cockpit. Just as I was getting the cutter ready to sever the rope, the guy on the ground got it loose."

"Praise the Lord; you guys were safe!"

I hadn't realized before how dangerous these search and rescue operations could be for the rescuers.

"I kept calling commands to keep the heli in position while I pulled in the rope," Hans continued. "When that was done, I finally gave the all clear and Brian pulled upward. After a turn, we repeated the same thing with the other rescuer before we headed back to Nabire."

"Enough excitement for one day," I said but learned the day had been far from over.

"After turning away from the crash site, we received a radio call from the SAR team in the jungle below. They were fighting their way to the crash site up the steep slopes in the jungle. Through the thick tree canopy, they couldn't get a GPS signal nor see far enough. By now they had lost orientation and asked us to fly overhead toward the crash site to show them the direction."

"Oh dear, the poor guys!" I was itching to go into the jungle some time, but I knew it would be difficult walking in any case. A steep trackless slope on an isolated mountain at high altitude sounded impossible.

"Even though I leaned out the doorframe, I couldn't see the men through the vegetation. But they radioed they saw us right overhead. So we pointed them in the right direction and headed back to Nabire."

"Finally, to get some rest?"

"Not much. By now it was clear the larger helicopter with the winch from the gold mine near Timika wasn't making it through the cloudy weather that day. Even if it had, the turbulences picked up and would get too strong for a winching operation to extract the men that afternoon. So we refueled the heli in Nabire and loaded up supplies for the guys to spend the night. We also got medicines and food, took it all to the crash site, and dropped it in for the guys."

"My goodness, unbelievable that the poor survivor spent another night in the jungle with the dead bodies!"

We later found out that even though the rescuers were lowered next to the accident scene, the one who reached the ground first needed over an hour to climb to the wreckage, because of the forbidding terrain. Then they examined and treated the survivor as well as they could and splintered his broken arm. They made him as comfortable as they could on the upside-down airplane wing which was the most level and dry spot for miles around. They did their best to keep the patient hydrated and nourished and from falling off the sloping airplane wing into the stream below.

"We talked to the guys on the ground by radio one last time," Hans continued. "They confirmed the other people on the plane were dead. There was nothing left we could do at the scene, so we returned to the landing zone, picked up the seats, doors, and the gear we left there and flew back to Nabire. We were exhausted."

The heli had been in the air for six hours that day. Our team's last duty in this matter had been to deliver the tragic news that the other four men, including the mission pilot, would not return home to their families.

The following morning the helicopter from the gold mine made it across the mountain ranges and took over the rescue. Our helicopter finally returned to Wamena after helping to save a man's life. On the way home, the helicopter flew past the crash site once more, showing the SAR team on the ground the way to the Cessna 185 wreckage again. Because of the extremely rugged terrain, the brave men needed two days to overcome the four miles/seven kilometers distance between the landing zone and the crash site. But in the end, they recovered the bodies. Another sad story, which showed how difficult and dangerous flying was in this part of the world. This was only one of many crashes our helicopter team responded to. Later, we heard the injured survivor recovered well.

There was no wracking my mind over a Christmas present that year: I would give Hans a backpack with toiletries, socks, underwear, a T-shirt, flashlight, candles, matches, ready-to-eat food, bottled water, etc. to keep at the office. If you think that's not a romantic Christmas gift, neither do I, but at the time it was hard to find nice gifts in Wamena. (Once, I resorted to renting a small, yellow dump truck for Hans, who loves trucks so that he could go for a drive). At least this one was useful to have at the office for responding to emergencies at a moment's notice.

Flying the Extra Mile

Brian was a man of many talents, but one, in particular, impressed me: He was a world class encourager. He didn't just keep our team pumped through the hardest times, but he also always thought of ways to brighten up the lives of the missionaries on their stations.

When the helicopter was scheduled to fly toward the South Gap with only a little cargo one day, Brian dropped me off at Polimo on the way to spend time with Kaethe who rarely had the opportunity to speak German. While this was intended for Kaethe's encouragement, I'm not sure who enjoyed the time more, Kaethe or me.

While Brian, Luana, and the kids were in the USA on home assignment, Jan, Hans, and I went through a difficult time. So the family sent a care package for the three of us with just the right things, words, and cards which hit the nerve of our situation in a good, funny way. There's nothing like encouragement from people who know how you feel, and have "been there and done that."

For a long time, the Moi team talked about the little food packages we women had prepared for them on Brian's request and which they had found on their seats after the final survey. Shortly after that event, Brian had dropped off the guys in the tribe for two weeks to start building the mission station from scratch. When he returned with supplies, the two men had seemed overwhelmed by the mammoth task ahead. He had invited them to get back into the helicopter to come along for a short supply run to another location. Upon entering their area on the return flight, he gave them a good pep-talk: "God has given you this valley; the angels of heaven are surrounding it, eagerly watching to see what will happen next. Now, go and be faithful to the task God has given you and work at it with all your heart."

Shifting the focus from the material world with all the dangers, threats, and hardships to an eternal point of view often did wonders for all of us.

The biggest ever operation brighten-up-a-missionary-family's-day happened during American Thanksgiving 2001. We noticed a family who did excellent work among a lowland tribe was often discouraged. Brian thought they were beyond a quick pep talk and came up with a more drastic solution. He got the whole team and some other friends involved. Luana managed to get a turkey from the coast and got up in the middle of the night to roast it and make her fabulous gravy. Some other ladies and I made side dishes and Brian loaded the bird with all the fixings along with some lucky ladies (including me) to deliver this "meal on skids." After being speechless at first, the family excitedly showed us around their cabin-style home with minimal plumbing (they bathed in the river next to the house), the little tribal village and their tiny school building where the four children were homeschooled. Then we left them to their turkey dinner and flew home. From that day on, the family was cheerful each time we saw them, even though their situation remained challenging.

Genuine encouragement is an immensely underrated spiritual gift.

Flowers, Faith, and Thankfulness

December 2001

How are we supposed to land here?
I looked out the helicopter and then at the pilot. Brian didn't seem the least bit concerned and circled down in the narrow valley.

Well, it looks like he's done that before.

I tried to relax, even though it looked as if the tail rotor was about to hit one side of the valley and the nose the opposite one (which, of course, wasn't the case). We circled down in tight turns and landed on the spot prepared as a helipad. Even after being around helicopters for a year and a half, I didn't fully appreciate their versatility.

A few minutes earlier we had picked up Trijntje at Polimo. We had followed the Baliem and then the smaller Mugwi River and landed at the village of Yuarima a few miles up the valley.

A group of young ladies with feather headdresses and painted faces came to greet us by singing, dancing, and handing us daisies. What a welcome! We unloaded the generator and other equipment for the *JESUS* film showing and walked down to the church building. The neat little church with a metal roof was made of black wooden boards, like our house, and surrounded by a low stone wall, lined with flowers and bushes. The Mugwi River flowed right next to the yard.

"Looks like Switzerland," I said to Brian.

Sweet potato vines (also part of the people's diet) were growing on stakes in a garden behind the church, reminding me of a vineyard.

We set up the equipment for the film showing at the church and placed an umbrella over the generator when it rained. The church filled up with women who sat down on the dirt floor. Men and children were turned away since this was part of a ladies' conference, and the church was packed full as it was. People positioned themselves at the windows to watch from the outside. The film was not available in the local language, only in Indonesian. Ibu Katharina, a bright young lady, basically knew the Gospel of Luke by heart and narrated the whole film. Brian and I waited outside and looked around. Several men crossed a traditional suspension bridge, made of sticks and vines. They were carrying bags of rice, a wok, and other supplies. We shook hands and found they were on their way home to the mountain village of Angguruk after a shopping trip in Wamena. Walking and running several days in this forbidding terrain was part of life for the people living in these mountains.

"Please, come eat with us," the pastor invited us after the film.

"Thank you so much," Trijntje replied for the three of us. "Unfortunately, we have to leave now, so we don't get weathered in." She noticed Brian looking at the clouds. Besides many warm smiles and handshakes, we were given handmade net bags and a live chicken. Raindrops covered the windshield when we took off. We flew down the narrow valley and back to Polimo. Here, we received two cabbages as a gift.

The people here were more thankful and appreciative compared to the Moi people. Here, people had been affected by the gospel for nearly five decades. Many chose the gospel and forgiveness over the unending cycle of war, spirit worship, and taboos. They could now accept that hygiene, better nutrition, and health care—which had changed their lives for the better—were possible without the age-old fears and taboos.

The small, lightweight equipment Brian bought with the help of USA donors had now been used by various teams to show the *JESUS* film to approximately sixteen thousand persons. People had carried the film by helicopter, airplane, car, motorcycle, and on foot. I hoped each time the film was shown that it brought the Bible stories to life for the people as Ibu Wellena had said at Makki, or it presented the gospel for the first time to those who wouldn't normally attend church.

The Desire of the Heart

December 2001

I opened the guitar case covered in stickers. The guitar wasn't the most beautiful one I had ever seen. However, when I took it out of the case, I saw the wood and the craftsmanship were exquisite. I played a few chords which sounded clean, clear, and beautiful. It was almost effortless to play. The label said: Handmade in Canada.

Oh, why did I look at the guitar?

I knew we could never afford it. There had been just enough donations to keep us going, and there was no thought of buying an outstanding musical instrument like this.

It had all started a few weeks earlier. Johannes and his wife had moved to another island to open a new Helimission base and I had returned the beautiful guitar they had graciously allowed me to use for so long. After a few weeks without a guitar, I felt the tension rising. It was interesting to see how much playing the guitar did for my mental balance. I had been desperate enough to buy a guitar at a local store for the equivalent of fifteen dollars. It sounded accordingly and was next to impossible to tune.

"When the American students who came to teach English at EduVenture arrived, I saw one of them carrying a guitar," Luana told me after hearing about my misery. "His time here will be up soon. Maybe he'll sell it to you."

I contacted the young man named Matt and asked if he might be interested in selling the guitar and if so, for what price.

"Well, I hadn't thought about selling it," Matt said, "but you can play it and see what you think."

My heart raced. Upon hearing what he had paid for the guitar and the case, all my hope vanished. I should have stopped the deal right then, but what do you do when the heart is longing? He sent the guitar for me to try out. When Hans, Brian, and Luana saw I was positively lovestruck, they all encouraged me to buy it.

"I can write Matt a check in US dollars, and you can pay us back in Rupiah in installments," Luana offered. I still believed there was no way to justify having such an exceptional instrument since I wasn't exactly a concert guitarist. Yet, the faintest glimmer of hope remained that somehow I had a chance to buy it. Time was running out, and Matt's departure date was approaching. When he came to town the next time, we talked.

"Well, I've thought about it, and I've prayed about it," Matt started out, and my mind raced ahead. Surely he would say: "… and I'd like to keep it in the family for the grandchildren." To my utter amazement, the sentence finished differently: "… and it's a gift."

I heard the blood rushing through my ears. Did he really say what I thought he did? I probably stared at him with my jaw dropped for a moment while trying to resume breathing. Although he hardly knew me, he was serious. I couldn't believe he did that. What an incredibly generous gift!

"But there is one condition," Matt added. "You can't take it away from Papua. So when you leave, you must pass it on to somebody."

Fair enough. Outside Papua, I could for sure buy a reasonable guitar. Since I felt so inadequate for this gift, this made me feel better. I would take care of this treasure for a while—a long while, I hoped. Over the following years, I would play Amber (Matt had even named the guitar) at the ladies' Bible study, at retreats, during church services, at home by myself to praise God, or just for relaxation and stress relief. I would never forget Matt's kindness and generosity and often prayed he would get a good guitar again in the USA or wherever he moved to. I trust he did because he serves the same amazing and loving God I do.

After I had passed on the guitar to my Papuan friend Paul years later, I was pleased to hear it was used in Papuan praise music CD's and even in a ministry film. I recently found out Paul's son now plays it in worship services as well. When I returned to Papua after turning over the instrument, good guitars had become available there too, so I was never without one.

You Can't Escape Your Fate

(Not for dog lovers)

"Elke, we have a problem," Tammy told me on the phone. "There is a dog in our yard and Archie has him cornered in the hedge."

Archie was the Helimission dog who patrolled the airport and had girlfriends all over town, but officially lived with whatever Helimission family occupied the house across from the airport.

"Oh dear. And how can I help you there?"

"I wondered if you'd want him. It's a nice looking dog. It seems like somebody put him in our yard on purpose since there is no way he could have gotten in by himself. He can't stay here. Otherwise, they'll keep fighting."

"Aldo is still small and won't be a real watchdog for a while yet," I thought out loud. "He'll probably love to have a friend, so why not?"

We picked up the tame, friendly dog and named him Billy. He became friends with Aldo, and the night guard got along with him too. Billy looked clean and healthy with a nice, shiny coat, much unlike the usual street mutts. Our only reasonably plausible theory about his appearance was somebody had bonded with the dog and couldn't stand the thought of him becoming "RW" (dog meat) in a restaurant. Westerners were known to treat their animals well and not eat RW, so leaving a dog with them would drastically raise its chance of survival. (This idea was not so far-fetched, thinking of the people who asked if we could take in their children, hoping we would turn them into doctors.)

Aldo enjoyed having a playmate, and we liked Billy as well. One day, Agustina pointed at him, "I think he is fat enough for butchering now."

She blew up her cheeks to further explain her meaning.

Yikes!

Billy wasn't safe after all! I didn't elaborate our culture believed it was unthinkable to eat a dog but explained we kept them as pets and watchdogs.

Every morning at four thirty the call to prayer rung out from the mosque. We were so used to the sound; it no longer woke us up. However, this morning there was another sound which roused us: "Ouhooooowouwouwooo!"

From now on, our dog would take it upon himself to lead all the dogs up and down the street howling along with the Morning Prayer from the mosque. Hans would complain to his friends he didn't mind his dog having a different faith—but he also didn't pray so loudly inside, that the dog couldn't sleep outside.

When it was time to give the dogs a bath we found Billy had a dark side. He hated soap and water and bit the guard who tried to wash him. A couple of weeks and biting attempts later, we decided enough was enough. I called the guard.

"We need to get rid of Billy before he bites again. Could you please go around to the restaurants and ask how much they pay for a dog and how they kill it." (I wanted to give the proceeds to him as amends for the bite).

I couldn't believe I had sunk this low. A few weeks earlier I found it barbaric to eat a dog, and now I was well on the way to having *my* pooch butchered! But what else could we do? Apparently, the local vet had once tried to put a dog to sleep by injection but gotten the dose wrong and the owner had to finish it off.

When the guard came back from his restaurant survey he reported, "At most restaurants, they put the dogs into an old rice bag and club them to death. At others, they burn them alive."

I felt nauseated and told him I might reconsider. The only ways of killing I would tolerate would have been a clean shot between the eyes or a quick ax to the neck, but not this. No dog in my care should suffer like that. We were at a loss. Billy couldn't go on biting people. Would we have to kill him ourselves?

Luana called: "Are you sure you want to have Billy killed or can somebody else have a chance?"

It turned out that one of the Papuan men who worked with our Irish friend, Sue, needed a watchdog because he kept having trouble with people breaking in. I must admit, I was glad somebody wanted to give Billy another chance because apart from his nipping habits he was a nice dog. I told Sue they could try it as long as they were aware they might get bitten. A little later Billy got picked up. The man wasn't ready for the dog yet, so he asked if Billy could stay at Sue's house for three days while he prepared everything.

Soon I received another phone call from Luana: "Elke, Billy is causing problems already."

"Oh no, I knew it: He bit somebody!"

"That's not it. The girls who work at Sue's house have fallen in love with Billy and now they want to keep him."

"Oh!" I could see how that could happen. Billy could give you such a charming look out of his brown doggie eyes. That was probably what saved him from becoming a spicy meat dish all along.

Events turned out differently in the end. Thieves came during the night and stole Billy. A fate delayed but not avoided. Billy hadn't been able to charm his way out this time and most likely become RW after all. At least none of us had had to kill him, and Billy would bite people no more. We all have to face the consequences of our actions one day or another.

"At least the 'religious' dog has gone, and I can sleep again," Hans said.

The following morning at four thirty we heard: "Ouhoooooohwouwouwou!"

Hans jumped up and looked through the curtain. There was Aldo standing on his rear legs calling all his fellow tail-waggers in the neighborhood to worship. He had picked up a bad habit.

Emotional Roller-Coaster

Two large net bags full of vegetables were hanging down from my shoulders as I was riding the motorbike home from the market. I felt like a hunter who had made a great kill. I had never felt this way about groceries from a supermarket in Germany where everything I wanted was readily available. Here it wasn't guaranteed I'd find nice potatoes at the market or ripe tomatoes. (Getting kidney beans and beef had inspired me once to make Chili con Carne for our Helimission fellowship meal, but it took trips to all four markets around town to get enough ripe tomatoes to complete the meal.)

At home, I disinfected and prepared the vegetables before putting them into the refrigerator, ready to use. You never knew when a phone call would require going to the hangar immediately, making up beds for stranded pilots or a missionary family, putting together a meal for eight, or staying off the streets for a day due to riots and demonstrations. Everything needed to be ready.

Back in Germany, my life was stable with a steady income and always followed a schedule. Here I found myself always on my toes responding to unforeseen situations and trying to keep some sort of a routine despite it all. Another unknown factor was our financial situation. We never knew how many financial gifts from European supporters would come each month. While steadiness and reliability had been the major traits asked of me in Germany, now flexibility became the number one position.

"Stop it! What are you doing?" I yelled at some men who were about to beat a man lying on the street, next to his bicycle. "Check out if 'mama' here is okay before beating up the guy. It wasn't his fault!" Nobody paid the slightest attention to the old lady lying on the asphalt. I couldn't get my head around this Papuan cultural idiosyncrasy: No matter whose fault it was, the one inflicting an injury was held accountable. The man on the bicycle had clearly tried to avoid the two ladies, suddenly traversing to the side of the street without looking.

The angry men let the cyclist go. The old lady got up and was fine. The cyclist looked over to me with a relieved and thankful look. While I was relieved as well, I once again started the day with a bad taste in my mouth and a challenge before me. Would I judge the people for their worldview and habits which were so contradictory to mine, or would I accept them and treat them with love and respect anyway, trying to model the lifestyle Jesus was teaching me? Sure, in Germany I had occasionally gotten in a lather about something too, but not usually to this extent! Just leaving the house here was a physical and emotional hazard. However, life was also more rewarding, eventful, and full of life. Before breakfast today I had saved a man from losing some teeth. How's that? There was no doubt in my mind: I wouldn't want to live anywhere else, and I wouldn't trade this life for anything.

It was the same with my faith and seeing the Body of Christ at work. In Germany, I had read books about people relying on God, while I had relied on my income, doctors, insurances, and infrastructure. Here, most of the above had fallen away and God's provision was noticeable—sometimes at the last dramatic moment.

Playing a little part in bringing medical help and hope for today and eternity to isolated tribal communities was worth putting up with almost anything. Taking on and overcoming another challenge, or feeding a tasty meal to friends seemed like an accomplishment. The other rewards were countless as well: the joy about the first rain after our water supply had run dry, flying through one of the wildest and most beautiful places on earth in a helicopter, and meeting some of the finest and most interesting people alive. Nevertheless, the constant roller-coaster of emotions was tiring and draining.

"I wish just once I could finish at five p.m., come home, and wind down," Hans said when I dropped off his dinner at the hangar once again. This dream wasn't about to come true. Helimission was the only organization available to fly missionaries or local people to and from isolated places without an airstrip, so lives depended on Hans' work. It often took so much time, energy, and creativity to finish a job and he rarely came home before dark. As long as there weren't more people available to join the team, nobody would have a nine to five job. Far from it. Most days there were things to attend to at home as well, like negotiating with a neighbor whose chicken had flown into our yard and been killed by the dog, the lights going out because the guard tried a new cooking appliance from China which was too much for the circuit breaker, a computer crash wiping out all our contacts, etc. It saddened me that my beloved husband was constantly under so much pressure, but I also knew he was as fulfilled as I was.

It was the beginning of January 2002 and time to part with friends once more. Andy, Tammy, and the children were leaving Papua. We would miss them so much. Brian, Luana, Hans, and I accompanied the family to the coast, and we spent time together at a hotel before we were to say goodbye. Our roller-coaster ride had hit rock bottom, but now it was heading for the top again. Tom and Rosa, who we loved and appreciated, were joining Helimission. We were all of the same heart and mind in our desire to reach the last tribes for Christ and we were all overjoyed to have them on the team.

Breakdown in the Jungle

February 2002

"Helimission—Hotel Mike Foxtrot!"

"Go ahead, Brian," Hans replied on the HF (high frequency) radio.

"Hans, the engine oil temperature has gone way up, and I need to land as soon as possible."

These were words no mechanic likes to hear, especially when the aircraft was still midair over a vast area of the impenetrable jungle with no place to land. Seven minutes later, which felt like an eternity, everybody in the office breathed a sigh of relief.

"Hotel Mike Foxtrot on the ground Dekai."

The engine had held up, and the next clearing turned out to be the short grass strip of the jungle village of Dekai where small airplanes could land. (This was before Dekai became the capital of the new Yahukimo regency—a combination of the areas of the Yali, Hupla, Kimyal and Momuna tribes—and totally transformed by rapid development by the Indonesian government. If this had happened a few years later, there would have been roads, a port, government buildings, a hotel, a hospital, a bank, schools, restaurants, and even a mobile phone tower, but the moment Mike Fox's oil temperature went through the roof, there was only a sleepy jungle village with a little grass airstrip.)

Once safe on the ground, Brian called on the sat phone and informed Hans of the oil temperature's exceedance level and how long it had been high. There was more tech talk about gauges, symptoms, and indicators until Hans said: "Okay, Brian, give me twenty minutes to look into this."

Hans pulled out the aircraft manuals to find out which inspections needed to be done and to verify the safe limits. Then he contacted Brian again and gave him instructions to perform checks.

"Sorry, Brian, you won't be able to fly home today," Hans concluded. "We must do more engine checks on location in Dekai."

A fixed-wing mission pilot with a small Cessna picked up Brian and took him back to Wamena.

The next morning the men loaded the other helicopter with tools and spare parts. Brian dropped off Tom, Alex, and Hans at Dekai to work on the stranded Jet Ranger, before beginning his scheduled flights for the day. During the last ten months after moving into the new hangar, Hans had been spoiled working comfortably cool and dry under the high roof and on the clean, flat concrete floor. Now it was back to working outside on the grass. Hans looked around, and all he could see was trees. It felt like working in a pit. Although it was still early, the humidity and heat were hard to bear. Temperatures under the tropical sun soon reached 97°F/36°C in the shade.

Villagers crowded in at the scene and made themselves comfortable around the helicopter for the entertainment. Not much happened in Dekai in those days and they wouldn't miss this opportunity to see the white boys up close.

Sweat was pouring down Hans' forehead.

"I just burned my hand on a polished wrench that was lying in the sun. We could fry eggs on the cowlings," he said. The men strung a tarpaulin over the two-bladed rotor for shade, spreading it out like a tent. The friendly villagers thought this was a splendid idea and moved in closer around the helicopter to enjoy the shade. However, the Momuna people hadn't showered that morning so the air quality up the ladder under the rotor head drastically deteriorated. (By the way, the Papuans think white people smell bad.) Tom came to the rescue by fanning fresh air with a large banana leaf while Hans kept turning the wrenches. After assessing the situation, Hans made a few sat phone calls from the middle of the jungle to a Rolls-Royce service center in Australia.

"Sorry guys, we won't be able to finish today," Hans said to Tom, Alex, and Brian who had just returned from his flights. "We'll have to come back tomorrow with more tools and equipment."

The men returned to Wamena, and we were glad they didn't have to stay overnight in the malaria-infested jungle village.

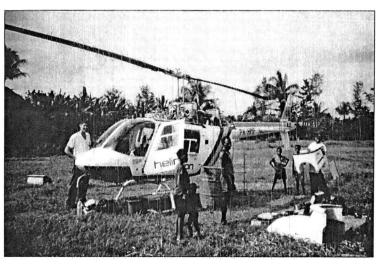

Tom (left) and Alex (far right) at work

The following morning Brian dropped off Hans and Tom in Dekai again before starting his busy flight program. Besides the tools and spare parts, Tom brought the generator, projector, and screen to make the most of this unplanned event. While the men worked on the helicopter, the villagers watched the *JESUS* film in the small wooden village church.

Around midday, Tom decided it was time to cool off. Along with all the other men and boys from the village, he skinny-dipped in the stream.

"Come on, Hans; the water is great!" Tom tried to entice him. No success.

(Hans has since often commented to Tom about the great experience of fixing that helicopter in Dekai, except for the recurring nightmares about him skinny-dipping.J)

On the third day in the jungle, the men resolved the problem, and the Jet Ranger was ready for the ferry flight back to the base. It was accompanied by a mission airplane. After a final test flight, Hans got out of the helicopter and said to the village people: "Thank you all for your help. The helicopter is now working well."

"That's right," the village chief replied with a reassuring expression. "I can hear the helicopter sounds better than when it came and is in good order."

Eastern Exposure

March 2002

"Welcome! It's so good to see you!"

We were picking up Elisabeth and Lita at the Wamena airport. Elisabeth was the kind secretary responsible for the Wamena base at Helimission headquarters in Switzerland. Lita was the friendly lady at the Jakarta office who was the first one to welcome us to Indonesia. Both ladies worked hard in their respective offices to make operations on the Wamena base possible, and now they would see the fruit of their labor.

I couldn't wait to show them around this beautiful place on the opposite side of the globe of Helimission headquarters—not just geographically, but in a thousand other ways. I had given the house and the office a good spring cleaning and hoped I had found all the cobwebs, cockroaches, and gecko droppings which quickly accumulated when one wasn't looking for a few hours. By now, we were used to our surroundings not being as clean as back home. Later on, I heard a wise lady say: "On the mission field you lower your standards one by one—with tears." I had already shed many of those tears but Elisabeth, who would stay with us, hadn't.

Elisabeth brought chocolate, cheese, and dried meat specialties from Switzerland—things we sometimes dreamt of at night. We put the delicacies on our tongues, closed our eyes, and savored the exquisite tastes. They tasted much better to us now than back home where they had been available anytime.

"Did you bring things for yourself in your suitcase as well?" I asked Elisabeth.

"Don't worry," she said with a laugh and continued unpacking all the items the team had ordered, including fire resistant fabric to cover the helicopter seats, technical equipment, and a pair of waterproof hiking boots for me.

"Thank you so much! I can't wait to try them out in the mud and water."

I wouldn't have to wait long. The other team members were too busy with their regular tasks, so I was assigned as the tour-guide. But business comes before pleasure, so Elisabeth accompanied me to the banks and offices where I paid the phone and electricity bills while Lita worked at the office with Jan.

"We took half the day, just to pay a few bills," Elisabeth commented when we were finished.

"I know. I'm so glad Luana told me to be glad when I get one thing ticked off my to-do list every day, instead of five, like back home."

After picking up Lita, we drove out of Wamena and up along the hillsides lining the valley. As usual, the magnificent view over the Baliem Valley made up for the uncomfortable ride. Now the unpaved, rocky, winding road was getting scarily steep, and I had already switched to the lower gear range in the four-wheel-drive car.

"I think this is as far as we should go today," I said to Lita and Elisabeth. "From here on it gets steeper and I'm not experienced yet with four-wheel driving. I better turn around."

This was easier said than done because the track was narrow with the steep hillside on the right and the drop into the valley on our left. The edge was hidden underneath tall grass and shrubs. I frowned.

"Ladies, could you please help me by keeping an eye on the front and back of the car, so I don't hit anything or go over the edge?" Elisabeth and Lita got out of the car.

"Come forward another meter." "Stop!"

The ladies' commands kept me out of trouble, and I got a good workout ranking the car backward and forward about eight times without power steering. When the car was finally facing the right direction (and my pulse had slowed down), we continued before stopping at a nice spot for a picnic—while waiting for the radiator to stop boiling over.

"Does this happen a lot?" Elisabeth inquired, looking at the steaming, battered, old Daihatsu.

"Yes, every time we drive uphill. The spare parts are already on the way from Jakarta and should be here in a few weeks."

Next, we went to a cave and waterfall, crossing a traditional Papuan vine bridge. I was so proud to show off my beautiful new home area. What a special place God had sent us to—even with the bad roads. How boring would it have been to get into an ordinary car, drive on a smooth road, and stop at a marked parking lot at a well-known lookout along with seventy-five tourists? Out here there was always a sense of adventure in the air—although sometimes more than I wished for.

Next, it was time to get my new hiking boots muddy, so we took an afternoon drive to the washout. This area, where a huge landslide covered a long stretch of the road to Kurima, was normally passable by cars. However, weeks of heavy rains had caused three new landslides. The fresh mud and silt were too soft for vehicles to pass. Even pedestrians sank into the mud up to their calves unless they jumped from rock to rock. After sinking into the mud a few times, my brand-new boots looked like the real deal.

We talked to a teenager living nearby and asked about the landslides.

"Oh, that was so scary. That night we woke up to a terrifying rumbling sound and wondered if our house would get buried under the mud and rocks."

I shuddered at the thought and was glad we lived in the middle of town and far away from the hill continuing to crumble away.

Lita, coming from the "concrete jungles" and traffic jams of Jakarta and Elisabeth from clean and organized Switzerland, seemed to enjoy their time thoroughly. The two women took in all the sights, sounds, and smells, and enjoyed the local fruit and other foods as well as a traditional bakar batu pig feast.

I marveled at how perfectly God had scheduled everything for this visit. While the mission stations only scheduled the helicopter to come in once every several months as needed (and then the weight limit was usually maxed out by supplies or passengers), Elisabeth visited all three stations that totally relied on the helicopter. She made friends with the missionaries, and from then on there were faces to the names she read in the monthly reports.

"This is a call for the prayer chain," Luana said on the phone a few days after Elisabeth's return from Moi. "Mee-ona has fallen gravely ill. Apparently, the people are already mourning for him."

This couldn't be! Mee-ona, this intelligent Moi teenager who had been dubbed "Bright Eyes" by the pilots, had lived long enough to get so close to hearing the gospel. He mustn't die before finding salvation in Christ! Besides, Mee-ona was a valuable language helper for the missionary team. He was delirious and in and out of consciousness. (When people in the tribe fell unconscious, they were often regarded as dead as without medical help this was usually the end.)

"That's not all," Luana continued. "Several more people in the tribe have fallen ill, and Mariah also has been sick with a high fever for a few days now."

This seemed to be an epidemic starting up. As the tribal tradition required, most sick people were given deep cuts and slashes to drain the "bad blood" and to appease the spirits. Mee-ona, however, became the first patient of this tribe whom the missionaries treated with modern medicines. None of the others had trusted these foreign ways yet. Also, we all fervently prayed for Mee-ona's life to be spared. About that time, the young man regained consciousness.

Just when we thought the worst was over, the next emergency call came in. Mariah's father, Stephen, severed a tendon in his finger and needed surgery. It was clear it was high time to go help, but there was not enough daylight left on this Saturday afternoon. On Sunday morning, Brian and Tom flew to Moi and took Stephen and seven-year-old Mariah to a hospital. God was clearly going before them. A surgeon was available and able to perform the complicated surgery on Stephen's hand. Mariah was checked as well, but no clear cause of the illness she and half the tribe had come down with was found. On the next day, Brian and Tom took the two patients back to their isolated jungle station. Over the following days, Mariah and the people of the tribe recovered and even Mee-ona's life was spared. What a relief!

Grounded

March 25, 2002

On the day the Long Ranger returned from Moi, Hans took it in for a needed inspection. Components of the smaller Jet Ranger had already been sent to Australia for repair after the problems at Dekai—which now left us without a helicopter. The recent events were a stark reminder of how urgent it was to have a helicopter running at all times. We hoped and prayed no more emergencies would come up during the inspection week. Life was so fragile.

"Bad news, Brian," Hans announced with a frown. "I found excessive corrosion on the gear shaft bearing housing in the transmission. It will take a while to get a replacement."

The missionaries, evangelists, and sick people in the jungles would be without helicopter service for much longer than a week. We prayed like never before for no emergencies to arise. The men made the best use of this calamity by fixing other issues, resealing the engine deck, and re-painting shabby or flaky parts. It made sense to prepare the helicopter for the work ahead while nothing else could be done.

A small oil leak on the turbine engine's compressor also needed to be sealed. This inadvertent downtime of the helicopter was a good opportunity to remove the engine. When Hans opened the bearing housing of the compressor, his heart sank. More components were faulty instead of just the seal. Now the engine needed to be disassembled, and the compressor module sent off to Australia for an unexpected warranty repair.

One problem after another was discovered and the situation deteriorated. Our hopes of having a machine in the air faded further. The worst part was that a conflict arose with assumptions and accusations as for the cause of the problems while not enough consideration was given to facts. We were all crushed. Morale was about the lowest it had ever been. It hurt me to see my dear husband so discouraged, and I didn't feel much better myself. Not only was hard work needed, but also determination to keep going day after day and continue the repairs and maintenance with poor logistical support in the remote location.

When the most important repairs were done, cosmetic work could be tackled to keep the helicopter in top shape. The tail boom and other helicopter parts looked rather shabby after being parked in the weather for the last few years before the hangar was built. This downtime was Hans' chance to respray them without causing further ground time. Hans had experience with paint jobs and got to work stripping the old paint first.

"I don't believe it," Hans said when he came into the office. "I just found a whole heap of corrosion pitting in the most critical area!"

"What does that mean?" I could tell from Hans' face this was serious.

"That's a dangerous form of corrosion which weakens the aluminum much like a crack. If we hadn't found this, the tail boom could have broken under stress." (The machine had been bought second-hand, and the problem had been previously painted over).

"Oh dear. At least you found it before something happened."

"I know, but this means another massive delay and a cost blowout. We can't fix that. We'll need a new tail boom!"

More misunderstandings and accusations arose. The situation became unbearable. The conflict escalated, and we expected the end of our career in Papua to be near. Everyone involved needed to stop doing what they were doing and to consider the facts. Thankfully, our leadership from the head office was coming for a visit, and together we sat down to clarify the situation. Hans, as the lead mechanic, explained what led to the situation. He took everyone on a tour of the hangar and workshops to show the wear, tear, corrosion, and applicable limits.

In the end, all agreed the unscheduled work being done was beneficial to turn this previously unreliable secondhand machine into a reliable, powerful workhorse for years to come (which it did). The helicopter was outgrowing its childhood diseases kicking and screaming. However, afterward, work could go on from a much stronger position. Looking at the facts and seeing the hard work and achievement already done to this aircraft while grounded, turned the conflict around. Grace was extended, forgiveness exchanged, and genuine appreciation for the hard and diligent work was expressed.

To our consolation, two of the families from the heli-access-only bases were in town, so at least we wouldn't have to worry about them. Or did we?

"If we don't go in now, we won't be able to talk to the people in the tribe before we go on furlough for a year," Kevin and Allyson explained to Brian who couldn't believe what he was hearing. "We need to tell them what's going on and that we'll be back."

After hearing the helicopter would be unable to take them to their jungle stations for an unknown period, both Kevin and Ed with their families decided to make their way into each of their lowland jungle mission stations without the helicopter's help. Along with the four adults, there would be seven young children fighting their way from the nearest airstrip to their stations through the jungle, swamps, and rivers, without the option of calling the helicopter in case of an emergency—and the potential causes for those were innumerable.

On the Sunday before their trip, we all prayed for the two families at the missionary fellowship. They would be traveling within a day of each other. The problem was one family needed enough water to navigate the rivers while the other family needed the rivers to be low enough to cross on foot. Both stations were only about thirty miles apart. We prayed hard.

Both families were taken to the jungle airstrip closest to their respective stations by mission airplane. Ed and his family were able to go by motorboat at first, then by dugout canoe, and made it to their station of Obukain after four days of near perfect travel conditions.

Kevin and his family set off on foot through the jungle and swamps and crossed several large and small rivers.

"To keep us entertained, we counted leeches we found on our bodies but stopped after one hundred eighty," Allyson wrote in a radio transmitted email after they reached their station of Tokuni within two days. Papuans carried the children part of the way. We all thanked God for the good news, but the worry wouldn't be over until they'd either be back in civilization or at least one helicopter would be airworthy again.

The safe trip to their stations was only the first obstacle. Now they needed supplies. Since the helicopter was not an option, this problem was taken care of the old-fashioned way: by airdrop. These drops from airplanes had been routine in the old days when missionaries still hiked into the area where they started their base and sometimes stayed put until they had built an airstrip. In this safety-conscious day and age, however, it was uncommon. The mission personnel in town bought the supplies and packed them as safely as they could, but the impact from an airplane drop was still hard.

"Next time just put all the ingredients for coleslaw into the vegetable bag," Allyson suggested over the radio after receiving the partly smashed supplies. Still, this was an emergency solution while the helicopter was unavailable.

"Overall, it went quite well," our friend Tom reported after the airdrops at several stations. "But there were some losses. Usually, you put the stuff for the drop into two bags, a tight fitting and a loose fitting one; so when the inner one breaks the stuff is contained in the bigger one. Apparently, this time they didn't find a large enough bag and put the sugar in three tight fitting ones, but they still broke. On the second attempt, the sugar hit the shed, which used to be their bathroom, but the third one made it intact."

Nobody was hurt and everybody got fed. Mission accomplished.

"Irresponsible!" People commented, "If they do that, that's their choice, but they shouldn't expose their children to such risks."

This event was only one part of the lives our friends had surrendered to the service of God and the Papuan people. And how about the children who lived in those tribes with no medical care? Was it better to keep children in a secure environment in their home countries where they could still have traffic accidents, get into drug addiction, or experience other problems, rather than to model courage, dedication, care for others, and trust in God?

The courage and faith of these families again spurred us on to give our utmost even in difficult situations and to trust God with the rest.

Allyson allowed me to share her account of the return trip from the jungle with you:

"It is with great joy and a sense of shock I sit in our Wamena house and write this e-mail. Are we REALLY here? It seemed a bit like a dream at first!

We just want to let you all know how God led us moment by moment through the jungle. We left Tokuni in the dugout canoe as planned on Thursday morning. Our colleague, Demet, and a Tokuni fellow were paddling and then a second, smaller canoe carried some of our things and four other guys. We got off before eight o'clock in the morning with tears in the eyes of the chief's wife as she had her baby sitting up on her shoulders, eating cooked sago. We didn't need to exchange words for knowing we were both still emotionally spent from the baby's sickness and the great relief we felt in seeing her come back to life and strength.

We barely rounded the first bend in the river when our canoe scraped bottom, and we all had to get out and lighten the load and push it along. We continued this routine for several hours, cringing every time we clashed with the rocks below. We decided it would now take three to four days to reach our float plane landing site and we weren't sure we would even reach our goal of getting to the Awbono village on that first day!

Next thing we knew, there was a gurgling sound and suddenly LOTS of water in the canoe. We ended up pulling off to the shore, and when we unloaded everything, we saw three to four MAJOR cracks in the boat! We tried packing mud into the cracks and hoped it would get us to the next village where we maybe could buy other canoes and carry on. Well, the mud trick didn't work well, so Kevin, Rachelle, and I were bailing out the boat at a rapid rate while Demet and Zakius kept paddling us downstream. To our amazement, we actually made it to the village of Awbono, but only to discover everyone had gone and there were no canoes for sale! Since there was still time before sundown, we paddled on (bailing all the while) so we could get as far as possible that day.

Not long afterward, we heard a distant sound. A plane? A motorboat? I know it wasn't a plane, but WHAT were the chances it was a motorboat? To our absolute surprise and amazement, we soon SAW the motorized canoe, loaded down with some of our Tokuni teenagers and Sam (a sandalwood trader who had been to Tokuni before and whom we had requested to come for us a month earlier and had never heard back from)! We all leaped out of our canoe onto the bank, and the kids were jumping up and down, completely ecstatic! We could hardly believe our eyes.

Once Sam arrived at our spot, we discovered the Tokuni boys had told him a certain heli was coming to get us and he knew the Army Special Forces heli wouldn't do that, so he wondered what was going on. He managed to turn on an HF radio and landed right on our regular scheduled radio time where he heard from our colleagues that we had already left Tokuni and he should head straight up to meet us! He tried to call another outpost on the radio right after that, but his battery was dead. Another small miracle that he connected with our coworkers at just the right moment and before the battery died! He headed right off, and that's when we met him at about four p.m. on the river. Everyone else got out of the boat, and we got loaded up and off we went! In the short time we spent out of our canoe to see Sam coming, our boat was filling with water so when we got our things out, the water was within a fraction of an inch of soaking everything! It was time for a new mode of transportation!

It was a huge relief to move faster, and despite the darkness coming on and the rain pouring down, we kept on going. We all ended up under a tarp, and Sam kept going, with a flashlight, searching the waters for logs and things that might get in our way. By eight o'clock p.m. we made it to a place called Binamzain where the mission floatplane can land. That was another story, as we had arrived unannounced, had nowhere to stay, and it was dark and raining. We ended up staying in a national pastor's house which required trekking in knee-deep clayish mud in the dark for what seemed like forever at that point. Almost all of us fell at some point as the stuff was slick but we eventually made it! We were exhausted and tried to get *the kids cleaned up and changed and off to sleep. No one got supper that night even though we brought rice to cook.*

On Friday morning, we woke to rainy, yucky weather and tried to see if the mission airplane pilots could work us into the schedule that day. The long and the short is the weather cleared; the floatplane came in, and after some plane detours, we arrived in Wamena at two o'clock p.m. We could hardly believe we had made it back in less than two days!

We've spent the last two days in a state of overflowing thankfulness to God and incredible joy at His goodness to us. We're exhausted as the adrenaline of the last weeks has worn off but we can't seem to thank God enough for the series of small miracles and faith-enriching experiences He has allowed us to live through.

So, thank you for your prayers on our behalf. God had a plan all along, and His timing is perfect. He heard and answered the prayers of His people. Let's thank Him together for His protection and care and the way He has shown His grace to us."

The trip back from the jungle station in Tokuni to Wamena would have taken forty-five minutes by helicopter. Less than an hour of sitting in comfortable chairs and admiring the views was definitely the easier and safer option. But when we could not provide that service, God still had our backs and was more than able to surprise us.

It was the longest time without a running helicopter in our entire time in Wamena and one of our worst times, due to misunderstandings between headquarters and us, communication breakdowns, and logistical nightmares. It took nearly four months for the first chopper to be airborne again, with missionaries down to their last meal in the jungle and starting to hunt for food.

Empty Shelves

April 2002

I looked around the grocery store. The shelves were even emptier than last time, and a few packages of noodles had been spread out on the shelves in a feeble attempt to make them look less empty. I had heard that gardens in and around Wamena had been looted. It was depressing.

The town and general region were totally reliant on air transportation for passengers and supplies, but some airplanes had been taken out of service because of their age and condition; some were sent to other parts of the archipelago and others crashed. The cost of rice soared to five times the usual price. Many other food items, like flour, were rarely available. It was hard to get tickets for flights to the coast and back. Many Papuan people who lived in Wamena and depended on rice, were forced to give up their studies or work in town and return to the villages where their families grew food. The children from the mountain villages who attended school in Wamena and stayed in simple boarding houses were the hardest hit. Many showed signs of malnutrition. Our team had rice flown in on a mission airplane and rationed it out for the Helimission employees daily.

"Have you seen the new Antonov cargo jet? It's enormous!" Hans announced. We nearly jumped for joy when the Antonov A-72 from Estonia arrived and brought relief of the supply shortage. This plane was extraordinary in many ways. It was much bigger than all the other planes coming into Wamena, yet it could cope with the short runway and climbed powerfully out of the valley. The airplane had strong jet engines with a wonderful modern sound which made for quick runs from the coast to Wamena and even managed up to eight flights per day, weather permitting. Other planes managed three flights. Slowly, the stores filled up again, and prices came down.

"Fantastic, now that there's enough food in town, we'll finally be able to get the steel flown in for the hangar roof reinforcement," Hans rejoiced.

April 21, 2002

Ring, ring, ring!

We were sitting around the brunch table with our friends as on most Sunday mornings. I picked up the phone. It was Jan.

"What happened, Jan, is everything all right?"

"Well, on the way to church I noticed the Antonov Jet coming in at a steep angle and knew this couldn't be good, so I stopped the motorbike and watched what would happen."

He witnessed the beautiful Antonov touch down on the runway nose first, bounce twice and sheer off its nose landing gear. Then it had slid along the runway, grating away the bottom of its front before catching fire. Hans phoned Brian, and the men immediately made their way to the airport while Jan rushed to the hospital to request an ambulance. He returned to the airport frustrated.

"They wouldn't send an ambulance. They said nobody had reported a plane crash. When I explained that that's what I had come for they said they still wouldn't know whether someone had actually been injured. They weren't going to send anyone just in case."

To everybody's relief, the Antonov's crew made it out of the cockpit with only minor injuries. Our team took them to the hospital with the Helimission car, and they reported what had happened: the fire truck hadn't appeared for a long time, and the onboard handheld fire extinguisher was useless against the blaze. The crew helplessly watched the destruction of their beautiful aircraft. (The official accident report reads that the firefighters hadn't been able to start the fire truck until they had charged the batteries for twenty minutes.)

While we were thankful nobody was seriously injured, we were horrified at the thought this could have been a passenger plane. Later, the aviation authorities asked Hans to climb into aircraft's charred, smoldering remains to recover the voice and flight data recorders.

This accident crushed our hopes of reinforcing the hangar roof in the near future. During the heavy tropical downpours, we prayed the roof wouldn't cave in on top of the helicopters.

A Visitor from Home

May 2002

"There he is," I said to Hans and pointed toward the Sentani airport tarmac. Bernd saw us waving from the gallery and looked as if the weight of the world was dropping off his slim shoulders. If we hadn't been there, he would have been in a world of trouble. After the stop at Bali, there was hardly anyone left who spoke English—not even taxi drivers. With his small frame, Bernd perfectly fit in with most Indonesians, but his beard, light skin, and hair color branded him as *orang barat* (westerner).

Bernd was the first ever—and only—friend who came to Papua specifically to visit us! (I still feel bad for asking the poor man to carry socks, elastic to mend underwear, cake ingredients, nuts, dental floss, medicine, and female sanitary products, but this opportunity was too good to pass up. Thanks, Bernd—and Mom, for doing all the shopping!) I would have loved to show our friends and family the beautiful place we called home now, but the two-and-a-half-day trip (one way) and the time and money involved did not make it become a reality.

After a joyful reunion, we took Bernd to the police station to report his coming and obtain his travel permit. Afterward, I went to the shops to stock up on supplies for the next few months before flying back to Wamena the following day.

"Do we really need that much stuff?" Hans asked, looking slightly annoyed while loading the car. Bernd's visit was the perfect opportunity to explore this beautiful area from the ground, after only seeing it from the air. So Hans was taking the Saturdays off.

"Absolutely. We need enough food, warm clothes, and rain jackets in case the car breaks down. I also packed the camera equipment, lots of drinking water, sunscreen lotion, toilet paper, hand sanitizer, the satellite phone in case something happens, and of course, a first-aid kit."

We were going on an adventure after all. This was the stuff I dreamed of at night *and* during the day so I'd had plenty of time to think about all we might need.

After fueling and loading the car with enough food for a small army, we were off. There was no way to wipe that grin off my face. Most days when riding around town, I looked at the battered Toyota Land Cruisers packed to their roof racks with net bags full of goods and produce, woks, pots and pans, jerry cans, and machetes, waiting for more passengers before heading into the mountains. How I wished I could hop on one and go along. Now it was my turn to go on a trip. The smell of adventure was in the air.

I didn't care that we were bounced around on the rough road full of rocks and potholes. Hans was a good mechanic and an experienced driver with good judgment, so I wasn't too worried about the car breaking down or getting in trouble with the dodgy bridges or shallow rivers we had to cross. Steep parts still freaked me out, but just like in the helicopter, I prayed and also trusted the judgment and skill of the man at the controls.

The first thing you learn when you drive in the mountains is that on steep or long downhill stretches, you put the car in a low gear to make use of the engine's braking effect. This way the brakes won't run hot which could cause them to fail and send you over a cliff. This was all well in theory. However, the green four-wheel-drive Daihatsu (which was as comfortable as an old farm tractor) seemed to have a mind of its own. It often gave us an adrenaline rush when at the worst possible moment the gear jumped out, allowing the whole weight of the car and contents to gain momentum and speed in an instant.

"Aaaaaah!"

These were occasions when Hans wished we had a Steyr/Puch Pinzgauer all-terrain vehicle, like the Swiss Army used, as a mission car instead of this.

"There is a stream," Hans pointed out. "Let's replenish the cooling water. It will get steep from here on."

The part for the cooler still hadn't arrived from Jakarta, and Hans already knew the road from a previous *JESUS* film trip. After refilling the water and letting the engine cool down, we started a long, steep climb. Hans hadn't exaggerated. When we got close to the mountain pass toward Karubaga, Bernd, Jan, and I had to get out of the car because of the lack of engine power and walk the last bit uphill. The naturally-aspirated (thanks for the term, Hans) diesel engine couldn't handle the thin mountain air at thirty-two hundred meters above sealevel. Black smoke billowed from the exhaust while the car inched its way upward in the first low gear with the last remaining horsepower. The three of us had the same problem with the thin air and were panting while following the car on foot.

We were about as high up as Lake Habbema now. When I got a glimpse through the trees, I gasped. I couldn't see our side of the mountain, only the one across the valley. This road had been graded off a steep ridge, and there was no telling how many hundred feet of steep cliff there were to the bottom of the valley. Other stretches of the road had been cut out of a steep mountain slope. The views over the forest-covered ranges were magnificent. I enjoyed the quietness, the fresh cool mountain air, and the exotic bird calls.

"I think we shouldn't drive any further," Hans said after we had gone over the top of the pass and started the descent on the other side. "It only gets steeper from now on, and we might not make it back up. The engine is simply not powerful enough."

I swallowed hard. Steeper yet? I hadn't ever seen a steeper road than the one we had just come on, so I didn't argue.

"When we went to Karubaga to show the *JESUS* film, I wasn't sure if we'd make it back up. We had to unload all the equipment because the engine was too weak. I don't think we should try it just for fun. And besides, we'll run out of daylight for the trip home as it is."

A cloud caught up with us and blue-winged swallows played in the fog. While we ate our lunch, we noticed people walking up the steep road. Where were they going? I hadn't noticed any larger settlements for many kilometers.

When we started the return trip, we caught up with one man who had passed us. Despite the cold, he only wore red shorts and a T-shirt. He carried a net bag over his shoulder and a machete in his hand. By now we were so used to the sight of people, even children, walking around with machetes we weren't afraid the man would use it as the deadly weapon it could be. We stopped and offered him a ride. He accepted and told us he had set out on the three-day walk from Karubaga to Wamena (with no jacket, food, or water) to sort out a matter. Apparently, a relative of his had killed a man on the coast, and now he needed to arrange for the obligatory payment of pigs. We had heard of many such cases by now. Still, having a guy with a machete in the car whose relative had just killed somebody didn't give me a warm, fuzzy feeling. However, the man was friendly and appreciative that we shortened his trip by two and a half days.

Finally, the next Saturday arrived. This time we were driving to Pass Valley. We had often seen the village from the air on the way to Sentani, flying through the North Gap.

"I can't believe Anke makes this trip by motorbike," I said while trying not to hit my head on the window when a wheel hit another pothole. "I wouldn't even dream of doing that with the road in this condition!"

The trip could take between one and three hours, depending on rainfall and how long ago the road had been repaired last. We drove past the mission station and airstrip of Pass Valley and continued along steep mountainsides and rivers rushing past large boulders. We passed traditional huts and gardens, beautiful ferns, orchids, and other vegetation typical of this mountain region.

After a picnic, we turned around so we'd make it back to the Baliem Valley before nightfall. Now something happened that I had observed on every weekend trip out of town and which always made me smile: after the week's work was done in these areas where the gospel had already taken hold, people would come from their homes and gardens to play volleyball or soccer together. Most of those groups waved at us and laughed, invited us to play along, or posed for a photo. What a contrast and a beautiful change from the people who wanted to press us for money or rides. I hoped these healthy and fun community activities would not be replaced by watching TV soon as they had in many other parts of the world—including mine.

I loved those peaceful afternoons in the Highlands: the spicy odor of molasses grass; the smell of wood fires and roasting sweet potatoes; the sound of games and laughter mixed with the streams babbling and rushing and the wind in the Casuarina pines. Just before dark, the long, high-pitched cicadas call told the children it was time to go home for dinner.

The view of the Baliem Valley never failed to fill me with awe after a trip to the mountains. The steep hillsides gave way to the flat wide-open expanse. We got to the valley with the paved roads just before dark.

"Someone's in trouble," Hans said and pointed to an angkot on the roadside. A group of people was standing around it, and Hans went to have a look. The driver tried to fix the damaged prop shaft with his limited tools. Hans got his tools from the car, crawled under the angkot, and helped the driver fix the problem. The daylight faded, and soon it was pitch black. Over an hour later, the broken car was on its way again and so were we. Hans had done his good deed for the day. A nice end to another beautiful trip.

It was Bernd's last Saturday with us, and we were on our way to Bokondini, a village with one of the oldest mission stations in the area.

"Not that again," Hans said, and I turned my eyes from the beautiful mountain view to the muddy road. Several men with shovels were standing in our way and motioned us to stop.

"You need to pay if you want to continue," they demanded.

We would have gladly given them money for their efforts of fixing the road, but they asked an outrageous amount. After unpleasant negotiations and leaving money, we drove on with a bitter taste in our mouths. After about three hours of driving, we got to Kelila where we talked to the soldiers stationed there.

"No, you can't cross the bridge, it's impassable by car," a soldier told us. The big bridge was still under construction and Bokondini was cut off.

"The materials to finish the bridge are still on the coast," some local people told us. It was supposed to come to the highlands on the Antonov plane which crashed and burned, along with their hopes to have the bridge ready in time for a big conference. We walked over an improvised footbridge and down to the river.

"Could you please give me a ride to the next village?" a friendly transmigrant builder and chainsaw operator asked us when we were getting ready to drive back. "There is no radio here, and I need to request more materials."

During the drive, we found out his wife and two children were still in his village in another part of Indonesia, and he missed them. However, he enjoyed the work here in Papua and seemed to have a good relationship with the locals. He got out at the next post.

(A few weeks later, we heard a transmigrant chainsaw operator was killed and mutilated with a chainsaw by locals at that location.)

"Oh look, there's an old man on the side of the road. Maybe he needs a ride."

We had plenty of space and why not do the old and tired looking man a favor? We stopped. The following scene you usually only see in TV commercials, but with a different set of characters. In the TV version, there would be a beautiful young woman in a short skirt standing next to the road with her thumb up and when the car would stop she would whistle for her three bearded unwashed friends with huge backpacks. In the Papuan version, it a was an old man getting the car to stop and then whistling for his grandson with a little pig in his arms. Well, we couldn't say no now so we hoped the pig wouldn't drop anything. We could definitely smell its presence.

When we got out of the mountains and into the Baliem Valley, we saw another group of people hoping for a car to stop. Among them was a blind old lady. It was getting dark, and I wondered if another angkot would come.

Where is she going at this time of day anyway? Well, to her the lighting doesn't make too much of a difference, now, does it?

How did she cope in this environment with rocks lying around and deep irrigation trenches with only single round logs as bridges to cross over? She seemed unbothered and just getting on with life and people around her helped her out. We dropped her and the other passengers off at their villages while passing. When we turned down their offer of money, a lady gave us some sweet potatoes out of her net bag.

Sometimes I wondered if it would be easier just to drive past all these people and not hear their stories and be saddened by their problems and tough circumstances. We wouldn't worry about a widow and two orphans on another island whose husband and father had gone far to find a job to provide for his family but would never return. Still, I wouldn't have wanted to miss these encounters for anything.

Thank you, Bernd, for coming to visit and for giving us a reason to do something special!

"We usually fly to the coast two days before taking connecting flights away from the island," we told Bernd when it was time to start his return trip. "This way we have an extra day in case the airplane can't make it out because of the weather." Weather challenges were likely occurrences, and there weren't many flights between Sentani and Jakarta. It wasn't worth risking missing the flights on to Europe.

It was just as well that Bernd agreed. On the day of the planned departure, no airplane made it in or out of Wamena because people were burning tires on the runway. The rumor was that a commercial airline pilot had angered a man from the local parliament. After delaying the departure of the fifty-passenger plane to wait for the politician, the pilot eventually left without him. Otherwise, the crew and passengers might have gotten weathered in overnight. The furious politician had then called on his clan and made sure no airplane could take off or land in Wamena the next day. Because of allowing an extra day, Bernd made all his connections and got back to Germany as planned.

Differences

Why did she say that?

I was riding my motorbike down the busy road to the hangar with that question going round and round in my head.

"Aduh!" I braked hard and narrowly escaped a collision with a bicycle taxi. This was getting dangerous. I was so upset I could hardly concentrate on traffic. I could no longer ignore that something was wrong and something needed to be done.

During the last two years, we had gone through many struggles and problems which drained us of energy and often stole our joy. What kept us going was God's grace and love, the distinct calling we had for this work, the prayers of our families and friends back home, and to a huge extent the common goal and unity we had in the team. While we did our part of the work in town, we loved to hear the pilots' stories of what was going on in the jungle and the different mission stations. The pioneer missionaries' reports of success or setback spurred us on to give our best. We faced problems and challenges together as a team with our different unique gifts and a good leader who knew how to put them all to use. The team was like our new family where we felt secure, loved, appreciated, and valued despite our many shortcomings.

When things within the team weren't going well, it affected everything, including our well-being, productivity, and joy. No riot, earthquake, or empty water tank could compare with that. Even though we all loved each other, once in a while our personalities, stubbornness, different cultures, and negative experiences from the past would play their tricks on us and threaten the unity. Nothing hurt as badly and preoccupied our thoughts as much as a disturbed relationship within the team.

But, if she has something against me, can't she just tell me? Do I really have to take the initiative? I debated with myself and with God.

I hated conflict and confrontation, but if I wanted us all to continue to live in peace and harmony—and in one piece in traffic for that matter—something needed to happen. Over the past few weeks, I had sensed a wall going up between a friend and me, and I didn't know what to do about it. Then, a remark she made had clearly shown me things weren't right between us; there was no denying it. I knew, if I didn't want this to continue or to get worse, I had to do something. And besides, the Lord gently reminded me of what I had read in the Bible.

"Therefore if you bring your gift to the altar, and there remember that your brother has something against you, leave your gift there before the altar, and go your way. First be reconciled to your brother, and then come and offer your gift."
Matthew 5:23-24

Well, it was a sister, not a brother, but clearly, the ball was in my court.

Our friendship needed surgery—and there was no anesthesia for this one. This would be one of the hardest things I had ever done, so I prayed and thought and prayed and thought some more and then asked for a meeting. We sat down and had a long talk—with a tissue box on the table. Although it was painful, we brought one thing after the other out into the open and talked it through. I had so much to learn. I realized I sometimes had stubbornly behaved like a total idiot in her eyes, so I asked her for forgiveness which she granted me. She also asked me for forgiveness and this scary, painful situation ended with a big hug and a renewed relationship.

What a wonderful Master we serve. Our Lord Jesus Christ is a God of second chances who in the world full of pride, hate, condemnation, retaliation, and un-forgiveness has modeled meekness, humility, and reconciliation.

Differences

"If it is possible, as much as depends on you, live peaceably with all men" (Romans 12:18).

As our team grew over the years, so did the potential for conflict. A few years later, during a seminar on stress and trauma processing, we learned some astonishing things which we wished we had learned before going to the mission field. One of them was that it is not recommended to put people from more than three different cultures into one team. Otherwise, the team might use up more energy merely to get along and to resolve differences between the cultures than it gained with no increase in output. It appeared we hadn't done so badly, considering our team had Americans—two of which had some Mexican background—Swiss, Germans, Austronesian Indonesians from other islands, and local Melanesians from different Papuan tribes (some being traditional enemies). Throw in all our quirks, stubbornness, and idiosyncrasies along with all the pressure we were under and you have a recipe for disaster. It was only by God's grace we got along reasonably well and usually enjoyed working together.

This became clear when people from a secular aid organization visited us to get away from their colleagues to share their tears and heartache. At one point, Hans had listened to a group crying at the hangar because of their problems and then found someone else of the same struggling team in our living room in tears as well.

"I can't believe how big the difference is even between the Swiss and the German cultures," I told a friend. "In our first year of marriage, Hans and I were in for a big surprise. Amazing, how quickly a misunderstanding could put either one of us in the doghouse. We hadn't anticipated that."

One thing was for sure; we needed to give each other lots of grace or the benefit of the doubt if a team member did or said something that made the hair stand up on our necks. Verbal and non-verbal communication in different cultures was a minefield. (Let's not get started on table manners.) A polite meet and greet, meant to make someone feel welcome and accepted in one culture, could be interpreted as outright lying or at least a gross insincerity in another. An exclamation of an unpleasant surprise after receiving bad news could be regarded as killing the messenger. A polite way of greeting somebody in one culture could be regarded as cold and rejecting in another, and then again a warm welcome or heartfelt birthday greeting could be regarded as an invitation to commit adultery by some. Oh my!

No debate, discussion, or argument could overcome our human nature, pride, selfishness, hurt, and insecurity. Only love could.

"We need to speak the truth in love," Luana often said. That made sense.

We sometimes got a feel of what God's Word used without love could do when people tried to straighten us out with Bible verses. It didn't work.

I often wondered why God chose us humans to work on His Great Commission (Matthew 28:18-20) to make disciples of all the nations. Our limitations were probably part of God's plan too and He was trying to tell us: "Give up trying in your strength. Without asking for My help every day, it's hopeless."

Could it be then, that God did us a favor by letting us be a part of it?

"And above all things have fervent love for one another, for love will cover a multitude of sins." 1. Peter 4:8

"Owe no one anything except to love one another, for he who loves another has fulfilled the law." Romans 13:8

Truth and love—what a divine combination!

The Beginning of a Wonderful Friendship

Late June 2002

As I looked through the car windshield, I gasped when I saw the mountain dirt road in front of me had broken away in a landslide.

"Oh my goodness! What do we do now?"

The first hour and a half of the trip had gone well, and I enjoyed driving the four-wheel-drive Daihatsu. So far, I had always been a passenger on our trips further into the mountains, but it would be good to learn how to drive on rough tracks in this terrain myself. Hans was by my side, giving me advice on the more difficult sections. To make sure I didn't get anybody carsick (or scare the living daylights out of them), I did this without passengers.

We hadn't expected a landslide. Hans and I got out of the car to look at the damage. The gap in the road was more than a car length wide, and there was no way around it. On our left side, there was the steep hillside and on our right a steep drop into the North Baliem Valley.

"How in the world will Kaye and Joe get back to Wamena now? How can we even let them know we can't come to pick them up?" I said, looking down the landslide helplessly.

We were on the way to Makki to pick up our new friends, Joe and his daughter, Kaye, from Australia. The two were visiting their old mission station where Kaye had been born. Since we rented the house from their mission, we were asked to help them get around. Veteran missionaries were a great source of amazing stories, and as I suspected, I had been in for a field day when they stayed with us before this trip. Hans had taken them to Makki a week earlier and now their time in Papua was coming to an end.

"We'll have to change their flights," I kept rattling on while wracking my brain about what could be done. "I hope their connecting flights to Bali and Australia aren't booked for Tuesday already. Or maybe there are cars stuck on the other side of the landslide between Tiom and here which could give them a ride. But how do we contact ...?"

"Just shut up for a moment, I have to think!"

Hans was inspecting the broken off part of the road, walking across the section, and testing the yellow soil with his boots and his weight. There was still a tiny remnant of the road left.

"No way. You aren't seriously thinking of trying to cross this!" I swallowed hard and looked down into the valley. The car could fall in there and roll over several times before landing about a hundred meters below. My stomach wanted to turn. So far there had been no doubt in my mind that this would be as far as we'd go today.

Meanwhile, two Papuan men had appeared at the scene, and Hans came up with a plan.

"If we can find logs to stabilize the valley side and dig out a little channel to guide the wheels on the mountain side, we can make it," Hans said.

He sounded serious. Now, I really got worried.

"We can help," the men offered.

"Are you sure?" Hans asked.

"Let's get to work," they said.

One man had a spade. Others carried logs to the site and laid them down so they could stack rocks as a foundation. Meanwhile, Hans scraped a bit of the escarpment off and dug a little trench to guide the wheels and keep the car from slipping into the valley. Some children appeared and tried to lend a helping hand as well. Together they all dug and filled until there was a scary-looking passage along the deep drop with just enough width for the car to cross—maybe.

Hans, who had seen worse in his time in Albania, was determined to try to cross the landslide.

"Let's go!"

"A-hem, I think I should take some photos. I'll walk across."

Apart from always needing newsletter photos, I used that as an excuse not to have to be in the car. Along with the camera, I took the satellite phone, the first-aid kit, and the house keys out of the car. (This didn't boost Hans' confidence, but I had to think practical. I wanted to be able to call for help and bandage Hans in case the vehicle ended up down in the valley and get back into the house after dropping him off at the hospital.)

Hans slowly drove while I prayed at a hundred miles an hour. The wheels were following the little trench nicely, and a few photos later Hans safely arrived at the other side.

"*Puji Tuhan!*" (Praise the Lord!) The men and we said before we laughed with relief. We thanked the men for their help, and I took over the wheel again.

"But hurry and turn around quickly," the men urged us. "Look, the clouds are already coming."

Good point. A tropical downpour could send our repair job downhill with the rest.

We had driven to Makki twice before, so I knew there were steep, rocky, and muddy stretches yet to come. With Hans' good and calm advice, I felt safe and learned a lot.

"Always make sure you stay away from the edge. Sometimes a piece of the road has dropped off, and the edge is overgrown with grass, like over there," Hans pointed out.

"Okay." I avoided the edge on the valley side.

"I'm so glad Grandma doesn't see me right now," I said to Hans and shook my head with a grin. "When I was still sitting at my desk at the town council, I would never have dreamed of doing this kind of driving!"

After approximately another hour and a half, we arrived at the Makki mission house.

"Welcome! Come in and have a cold drink."

Kaye and Joe invited us into the cozy house where we had stayed on the way to Tiom. I was so thankful for this opportunity to visit this lovely house and beautiful area again. I only wished we could stay longer.

"Thank you. Did you have a good time?" we asked while taking off our muddy shoes and entering the house.

"Yes, it was great," Kaye replied. "But to be honest, quite emotional as well. So many memories came back, and I kept thinking: this tree was only so little when I looked out this window last."

Joe had apparently been as happy as a pig in the mud here in his old stomping grounds. Kaye offered us a drink made of *jeruk nipis* citrus fruit from the backyard. It was cold and refreshing, coming out of the the kerosene refrigerator they had revived.

"So, how was your trip?" the two inquired of us.

"Well, since you're asking ..." We explained the situation.

"So, we shouldn't stick around here for too much longer," I added, looking out the window at the overcast sky.

A group of Papuan friends was there to spend the last precious moments with Joe and Kaye. The time of separation hadn't quenched the affection for their old friends. We loaded the car, they said teary goodbyes, and off we went along the North Baliem Valley toward the Grand Valley and Wamena. This time Hans drove.

"Did I really drive through that?" I exclaimed when we drove through the first deep, muddy dip in the road and climbed the other side. Well, there was only one road. Apparently, this office girl had come a long way.

While being knocked around in the car on the bumpy road, we quietly prayed for the rain to hold off until we crossed the landslide. It did. We passengers got out again and held our breath while Hans crossed the dangerous section. The wood stayed in place, and we all cheered and thanked the Lord when the car was safely on the other side. (Soon after, the landslide worsened, and the road to Makki and Tiom was cut off for a long time until it was fixed with heavy equipment.)

We were sad when Joe and Kaye left the following day. We didn't suspect then that this new friendship would play a big part in our lives in future years to come.

Shock Waves

We were driving down the road with a friend. We had just heard that a well-known and respected expat family in the Papuan mission community had suddenly left.

"Do you have any idea why they left literally overnight after years in ministry?" I asked our friend.

"I don't know, but when it happens this quickly, it may be because of adultery."

My chin dropped.

How can he say something like that? This can't be it—surely not!

A few days later it was confirmed. The family's organization had indeed sent them back to their home country because the husband had been committing adultery. This news shook the whole mission community to the core.

"How terrible his wife and children must be feeling now," I said to Hans burying my face in my hands. "Can you imagine finding out something like that and then being sent home overnight, uprooted from your ministry, your house, your friends, your school—your whole life? I just cannot imagine!"

A difficult part of life on the mission field was that we constantly had to say good-bye—either to our families back in Europe or to friends from the mission community who were leaving. Normally, we had the opportunity to spend time with people before parting ways, even when we lived in different parts of the island. While we didn't have the same level of closeness with everyone who left, it was always emotional. The expat community consisted of people from different organizations and countries and everyone contributed in their own way.

Only a few weeks after the first family had left, we received more bad news. Another expat family was about to leave the country. Their organization told us to respect the family's privacy and not to visit them. We could see them off at the airport, instead. We couldn't make sense of the situation but complied with the request of the family's mission leadership.

"What's wrong?" we asked some friends. "Do you think they're sick or has someone in their family died back home?" None of them could tell us.

We went to the airport. People from the mission community congregated for the farewell, as usual, to send the family off. While we were all sad to see them go, the atmosphere was still cheery, and we tried not to make it harder than it was. We all surrounded the family holding hands, praying for them, and sending them off with our best wishes, hugs, and blessings. Local passers-by on the street watched on over the fence while we stood there waving until the plane disappeared.

Afterward, it was hard to concentrate and get things done. I felt emotionally drained. These goodbyes seemed to zap all my energy. One question kept going around in my mind.

Why did they have to leave? Are they okay?

A few hours later, a leader of that family's organization called a meeting with the whole mission community to address those questions.

"Oh good, maybe they'll tell us what happened," I said to Hans. "I can't stop worrying about them."

We attended the meeting, and everybody in the room expectantly looked at the man, hoping for answers. Nobody was prepared for what was coming. The man told us the cause for the sudden departure had been "moral failure."

The blood seemed to drain from my head. "Moral failure"—this expression had been used in the case of the other family who had left several weeks earlier. After a few seconds of stunned silence, people who were visibly upset asked questions. What did moral failure mean? This abstract expression left much to the imagination, and some were not willing to part with that simple explanation.

"Do I have to talk to my children?" one of my friends asked, demanding more answers from the leader. It was obvious the man felt terrible himself, but he hesitantly gave more explanations. To say the least, it was disturbing and didn't sound like an isolated affair, but rather like a deliberate act of deception and betrayal, harming people in the process.

I slumped in my chair.

"Haven't we just sent him off with a hero's farewell?" I asked Hans.

"If only we had been informed beforehand," Hans replied. "Now the local people who watched the sendoff might think that I applaud the man's indecency toward women."

We went home, unable to work for the rest of the day. I felt defeated, deceived, betrayed, and angry. I was at a total loss.

"As strange as that may sound," Hans said. "It does make sense to me now."

"What? How do you mean that?"

"There have sometimes been significant irregularities when I dealt with him, and I just couldn't understand how a fellow missionary could act the way he did. Each time I raised the issues, he'd cut me down and blame me instead, making it look like I was wrong for questioning his integrity. Now I realize the manipulations and cover-ups where only a part of bigger underlying secrets. Now I understand where the mess came from."

Over the coming days, local people told Hans they knew about these inappropriate sexual acts and it was no news to them that missionaries were "fooling around." When Hans told me, I felt sick to my stomach.

"So that means the local people knew about this all along and think many of us western missionaries behave in this way?" I said to Hans and other friends. "So what do they think when we say we've come in the name of Jesus?"

It felt like a rug had been pulled out from under my feet. What was the point in continuing to work here if people thought of us and our work that way?

"That explains why the daughters were always sent to the back of the house as soon as we arrived," an expat friend said, referring to an Indonesian family. We had observed the same. When we had gone to the house, we had seen through the windows that the daughters were sitting at the dining table, but when we entered, they were out of sight.

"Ugh, they felt like they had to protect them from us," we realized.

I could imagine people working for foreign companies were looking for companionship in the local population. But were we missionaries viewed in the same way? I remembered a midnight phone call I had received while staying at a coastal hotel with Hans. A man had asked in Indonesian if I was "looking for a friend." Annoyed and disgusted, I had hung up—twice.

"I wonder if the people who see me walking down the street think I want to take advantage of their daughters," Hans told me later.

It felt like innocence had been lost for all of us. The men's actions didn't only have consequences for themselves, their families, the women and girls they had been involved with, their co-workers, and supporters, but also for each one of us. Like an earthquake sends seismic shock waves for many miles around, the effects of these men's actions were radiating far and wide. The testimony of us missionaries seemed shattered.

As Iron Sharpens Iron

Our work had to go on, but it was hard to return to normal in the midst of turmoil. As during other hard times, we asked ourselves the all deciding question: was what we're doing still achieving our ultimate goal of reaching unreached tribes with the gospel? The answer was yes, so we needed to continue—no matter how we felt.

The local personnel of our organization was informed about the matter, and the situation was openly discussed with them. Openness was the only way to resolve a matter of any kind. Our response to issues like these mattered. Cover-up was the devil's strategy. We were to walk in the light. By being transparent and taking a stand against the misconduct, there was hope the reputation of us missionaries across various organizations wasn't utterly destroyed. Otherwise, not even the fact that the men had been sent away would have prevented that. Many local people seemed to think a crime or sin only became a problem when it was discovered. Getting caught was considered as the main problem and some people regarded getting away with something like a victory. The concept that integrity is what you do when nobody is looking wasn't widely embraced.

I still couldn't shake off the feelings of defeat, disgust, and anger. A good place for me to process things was our weekly ladies' Bible study. When we had our first session after the events, it felt like we were trying to dig ourselves out of the rubble from a collapsed building.

"One thing is for sure," a lady said. "None of us would just wake up one morning thinking 'I'll cheat on my spouse today.'"

"That's right," another added. "Sin is a slippery downhill slope, and it starts with one seemingly harmless small step."

"Yes, it all starts with a little lie, like there's no harm in a little flirting or just looking."

"So, what can we do to avoid taking such a first wrong step?"

We looked at each other. We all recognized we were humans, saved by grace, and not because of our righteousness.

"We need a strategy for purity, to prevent us from believing the lie of temptation!"

I remembered how Luana often prayed that we wouldn't disqualify ourselves from the work. That was definitely a prayer to echo. What we were doing here in Papua was a thorn in the devil's eye. While many unresolved issues and sin could make our work ineffective, we had just seen that adultery could be the "ejection seat" of the mission field.

Most aircraft accidents are the result of a chain of events which often started with a small problem. The same seemed to be the case in our lives; so we needed to nip sin in the bud. A small crack in a helicopter's acrylic windshield could spread because of strain and vibrations and lead to the whole window breaking. When a mechanic discovered a tiny crack, the procedure was to stop drill (making a small hole at the end of the crack to stop it from growing). The deceptive tempting thoughts would come, no doubt. They would always seem innocent, pleasant, and beautiful at first, but ultimately, they would lead to our downfall and terrible damage to others if left unchecked.

A prime example for this was porn. While it might look desirable and pleasant at first, it creates a negative effect on intimate marital relationships. It is addictive and often the problem keeps growing into infidelity, affairs, prostitution, and even child sex abuse. One little "pet sin" would grow into a monster, swallowing us and hurting others—especially those we loved the most.

So how could we "stop drill" in our lives? "We could meet up with an accountability partner," a friend suggested at the ladies' Bible study.

"Or we could exchange the permission with our husbands to ask each other the hard questions."

"What do you mean?"

"For instance, if we've entertained romantic thoughts about someone other than our spouse."

"And us married ones need to give our marriages a high priority. Life can get so busy that we don't take enough time for the relationship with our husband."

We had lots to think about. Nobody had ever talked to us about issues like these before. As Proverbs 27:17 suggested, we could sharpen each other's minds, conscience, and understanding of God's Word just as iron sharpens iron. One thing was clear: we had to keep our guard up at all times. We would all be tempted and only in a close relationship with Jesus and by His grace could we live pure lives.

We would also be more aware of red flags in each other's behavior. As we had seen, one sin wasn't isolated. If we noticed irregularities in someone's behavior, it was quite possible there were other underlying issues which had to be addressed. We needed integrity in each and every part of our lives. Accountability was a key factor in achieving this goal.

"I've heard the main temptations for guys are girls, gold, and glory," a friend said.

In general, for women, it was more about having emotional or even spiritual needs met than the outward appearance. Often it started with people spending time with each other at work or in ministry. We looked at several Bible verses which all stated one thing: our capability for self-deceit was limitless!

"We need to commit to Jesus to live pure lives and to guard our hearts."

"Exactly, taking captive every thought—and feeling for that matter—to make them obedient to Christ."

"Then there is the other side of the coin. Are we possibly causing others to have impure thoughts about us?"

"Good point. I think we need to be conscious about the way we dress and interact with people, especially in this culture."

Most summer clothes worn by people in our home countries would be grossly inappropriate in the Indonesian culture. Whether we liked it or not, if we dressed like the mainstream back home, we might be perceived as prostitutes here.

The damage had been done, and there was no way to undo it. But with God's help, we would give our best to learn from the situation and to help each other remain pure. Nothing should jeopardize our calling of reaching the last lost tribes with the good news of Jesus Christ—especially not ourselves!

Life and work went on, and I had learned a lot, but the joy and beauty seemed to have left my life since this issue of moral failure had emerged. Many of my missionary friends were struggling too. The recent events had stirred up various other issues and left many insecure even in their marital relationships.

How could we go on from here? It would be a long process.

"I'd like to read some verses to you," Jessica said at another ladies' Bible study meeting. "*'Finally, brethren, whatever things are true, whatever things are noble, whatever things are just, whatever things are pure, whatever things are lovely, whatever things are of good report, if there is any virtue and if there is anything praiseworthy—meditate on these things. The things which you learned and received and heard and saw in me, these do, and the God of peace will be with you.'* Philippians 4:8-9."

While these verses washed over me and penetrated into my heart, it felt like the pain, ugliness, heaviness, and despair crumbled away and hope, joy, and peace returned to my life. The occurrences couldn't be undone and would haunt me long after, but I didn't need to stay in that place of hopelessness and despair only looking at the mess. Instead, I could shift my focus back to Jesus. The key to overcoming all obstacles in our lives and ministry was to walk closely with Him and to read the truth of His word over and over. This way we would calibrate our minds and hearts out of which flowed our attitudes, words, and deeds.

A Matter of Perspective

June 2002

"Oh boy!"

I looked at the Yetni River's gray waters rushing downhill in its rocky bed. Hans and I were on our way to Polimo and still glad we got away from home despite Hans' not feeling well in the morning. Almost every time we planned to do something enjoyable or take a break, something happened. This was the second time we had planned to visit Kaethe in Polimo and to service the generator at the women's school and dormitory. The first time around, Hans had just dislocated his knee and hadn't been supposed to go hiking for several weeks.

The Yetni was the constant unknown on the way to Polimo. While we dreaded crossing the rushing gray waters, the local people crossed it swiftly and surefootedly with heavy loads on their heads and backs using thin, crooked logs tied together. Two men had mercy on us when they saw the scared looks on our faces. They helped us across by carrying our load and holding our hands. Most Papuan people in town seemed to look up to us because we had decent clean clothes and a motorbike and for some strange reason they seemed to think white people could do anything. (This went so far that a lady once asked Hans, who was next to his toolbox, to operate on her. She walked away deeply disappointed and angry when he referred her to the hospital, not understanding he wasn't a doctor and simply couldn't do it.) Here on the side of the Yetni, we were on the Papuan people's turf, admiring how surefooted and strong the men and women were while we were NOT.

"Where are you going?" the men asked after getting us to the other side despite our clumsiness.

"We're on the way to Polimo to visit Sister Kaethe. Thank you so much for your help," I replied and handed the men a little money.

"No, no. If you are friends with Sister Kaethe, we're glad to help."

This again was so different from life in Wamena where everything seemed to be done for money. So all we could do was to thank the men again and give them a big smile and a handshake before continuing on our way.

"*Wah, wah, wah—La-ohk!*"

I had been to Polimo several times but never had I seen the women in their gardens so excited. They waved at us and cheered. Then it dawned on me: Hans was the hero of the day, and if he had run for a political office, the ladies would have certainly voted for him. In their culture, the women carried the heavy loads and were rated and valued for their carrying capacity. The men usually walked in front with the hands on their backs and just an ax over their shoulders. Since Hans' knee was still recovering after being dislocated, I had planned on carrying our luggage and Hans was supposed to only carry his small toolbox. After feeling his knee was strong again, he took the backpack off me and was now carrying both bags. The Papuan ladies probably congratulated me for having made such a catch.

After a warm and cheerful welcome to her simple but cozy wooden mission house, Kaethe led us into her living and dining room.

"Wow, Kaethe, are you expecting the queen?" I asked. She had set the table with beautiful German china. "I've never seen anything like this out here before."

"Well, people have different opinions," Kaethe explained. "Some say all you need on a mission station is plastic camping dishes, but I think in a place where everything is simple, you need something nice for special occasions—something that reminds you of home and gives your life a festive touch."

She had a point there. When the weather was bad, and everything around looked dark and dreary, something like this could certainly brighten up your day. And there must have been many dark days in the over twenty-two years Kaethe had lived here.

Our room was just as welcoming. There were thick down quilts and pillows on the beds and flowers in tiny vases. Kaethe had outdone herself to make us feel welcome. Trijntje, her Dutch housemate of many years, had retired a few months earlier, and Kaethe still had several months to go until she was ready to retire herself.

"So, Kaethe, how is life by yourself now that Trijntje is gone?" I asked while sipping my coffee.

"Well, that's the strangest thing. I didn't think it would be a problem since I lived by myself for many years before but I must admit, it has been quite a change, and it gets lonely."

This remark made it easier for me to accept all this hospitality and generosity from a lady we came to serve. We enjoyed helping that problem for a weekend and got spoiled rotten in return.

My sentence, "Everything tastes better in Polimo," had become almost proverbial to me. The locally grown and freshly roasted coffee, prepared in a plastic jug and poured through a strainer tasted much better than any coffee out of a high-tech machine. The bread we had for another meal, coated in beaten eggs and fried on the woodstove was a delicacy to my taste buds.

While the oven heated our food, it also made hot water which we filled up in buckets and used for our dipper-showers in the simple bathroom. Who needed five-star hotels? The views from the windows were spectacular, the food tasted great, and there was always something curious to discover among Kaethe's treasures that had found their way into the house over the course of two decades. I looked around the room and then out the window. While the simple wooden house was a far cry from the solid and well-equipped houses in our home countries, it was probably the best one in the village.

"Kaethe, how have you come to terms with living in a house that's better than the ones of the local people and with having more stuff?" I struggled with this in my situation.

"I've actually asked the people what they think about that, and you know what they said?"

"What?"

"Sister Kaethe, if you'd live like any of our women, we wouldn't respect you and take your advice."

Now this made sense. In a culture where women were traditionally treated as a possession, single ladies wouldn't have had a chance to make a difference, teach, or give advice and medical help if they weren't different. However, Kaethe also believed the women had a lot of say in their society. They were the ones working in the gardens, and they would divide the sweet potatoes at night.

"If a man doesn't bring home enough firewood, he might not get a lot to eat."

We visited the girls' and women's boarding school which was the main part of the mission station.

"Hello, Okto! Here are the visitors I told you about," Kaethe introduced us to one school staff member.

"Selamat datang!" Okto welcomed us with a warm smile and a handshake. She was a friendly, corpulent, self-confident, educated lady from the area. Kaethe and Okto showed us around the premises and told us about the work that was done here at the women's ministry of the church. Girls and women from the highland villages came here for school in a safe environment.

This place had been created to avoid grave dangers. Going to a town like Wamena from an isolated subsistence farming community was a big shock for the girls. Many fell prey to people who wanted to exploit them. When they stayed in the boarding houses in town or with relatives, most fell victim to sexual abuse, resulting in unwanted pregnancy and disease. Here the girls had a safe environment for their studies. The curriculum included literacy, health, hygiene, and home economics. The girls learned to make crafts, cook, and sew while being prepared for the step into the information age. They were also taught to hold children's church and Christian women's groups and be village church fellowship helpers. The local Polimo women could also come to the school for reading and writing classes. This ministry had brought great improvements to the highland people and their overall health.

I was impressed. "Fantastic work you are doing for the people here."

"Well, not everybody seems to think so," Kaethe said.

"How so?"

"You would think it was easier to convince men to let their wives and daughters come here to learn about hygiene, to sew, and get an education," Kaethe explained.

"Why would that be a problem?"

"You see, while the women are here to study, they aren't working in their gardens and preparing the food and the men are afraid that when they learn to sew, they'll want clothes which they might be unable to afford. And also the men feel threatened if the women are more educated than them because they might lose power over them."

It hadn't crossed my mind that not everybody was happy about women getting an education. I had always taken it for granted to go to school and learn a profession. The mindset of the people here was so different from the one I had been brought up with.

"But the people are becoming more open to other ways of life," Kaethe continued. "Look at Okto here. She went to the coast to study land surveying and measuring. She stayed at the church's women's home similar to this one in Sentani. She then trained for the women's work instead so she could teach other girls and women from her area."

Some families were more open to breaking with the traditions and embracing progress and education. In Okto's case, this had been a success, but many young people felt lost in the towns, separated from their clan's traditional way of life. They were easily led into trouble, contracted diseases, and sadly, some never returned or came home in a coffin. There was no way to escape the encroaching civilization, but many people weren't ready for it. Places like this were invaluable for young women as a bridge between their way of life in the village and the wider world of the towns with all their opportunities, problems, and temptations.

Hans gave the generator a thorough service while Okto and I lent him a hand. The ladies were doing a good job taking care of the generator, but once in a while, a mechanic's work was appreciated.

Kaethe was a midwife. She had been sent to Papua in response to the high child mortality rate the missionaries had encountered all over the area.

"The shamans used to be the only ones who came to help if a woman had problems giving birth," Kaethe explained. "They'd work some magic, but wouldn't give any actual physical help. The people traditionally didn't help each other during childbirth."

"Why was that?"

"Well, if something would go wrong with the mother or child, the person who had helped would be held accountable. They would have to pay compensation to the family—usually pigs."

Kaethe's job was to give advice to expectant mothers. She'd also give them preventive check-ups during the pregnancy to determine if a problematic birth was to be expected and medical intervention needed. Otherwise, she encouraged the women to give birth the traditional way in their huts. In the case of unforeseen complications during the birth, she'd walk to the woman's village to assist. Besides caring for the mothers, Kaethe also treated sick children.

Since one midwife wasn't enough for such a large, mountainous area without road access, Kaethe trained local women in basic midwifery. An intelligent local woman named Paulina; a graduate of the government elementary school; had been trained as a midwife. The Indonesian government had then recognized her training.

"The people say there are a lot more children now," Kaethe concluded.

It was fantastic to see how the work of one woman, sharing her knowledge with others could have such a positive effect in such a large area.

Apart from the mother and child care, Kaethe was an advisor and mentor for local evangelists. Once a month they met at the mission station or in the Mugwi Valley to prepare sermons for the different evangelists' posts. They would read through Bible portions and talk about them and also discuss the problems these men faced at their stations. Life for new Christians was hard in communities which remained in their old animistic ways. Conflict arose, for instance, when a new garden was made by cutting trees, slashing, and burning. The old way was to sacrifice to the earth spirits which the Christians refused to do. If they no longer took part in the spirit cults, they were excluded from their clan. Kaethe was encouraged by these faithful men, and together with the Lord's help, they found solutions to their problems and more people from their clans found freedom in Christ. This mentoring role would have been a pastor's job, but over the years, the mission could not find a man who wanted to live in a place like Polimo for an extended period.

Single Heroes

The Yetni crossings on the way home from Polimo often cost me a lot of nerves and adrenaline. I wouldn't risk crossing the flooded Yetni on the way out to Polimo if I could avoid it, but sometimes I didn't have a choice on the way home. One day I watched in horror when parts of the steep bank upriver broke off and crashed into the gray mountain-stream-turned-rushing-torrent. A few minutes later, two strong, surefooted Papuan men held my hands on either side while I inched my way over the thin logs, trying not to get dizzy while looking at the fast flowing gray water washing over them. While I only had to cross the Yetni once in a while, it had been a necessity of life for Kaethe and Trijntje for many years. Unless aircraft picked them up (the grass airstrip hadn't been usable for their last few years before retiring), they had to cross the river each time they needed to get to the outside world.

One day Kaethe was in town running errands, and we talked her into having lunch with us. With this delay, she finished her tasks late.

"Why don't you stay the night, Kaethe? You can go back first thing in the morning," we tried to persuade her.

"No thank you, I really need to go."

"Well, if you must go, at least let us drive you to Sogokmo. You won't find an angkot at this hour."

"All right, I won't say no to that."

The weather was miserable, and daylight would run out soon. We got to the end of the road, parked the car, and walked with Kaethe. We knew we wouldn't be able to sleep unless we'd see her cross the

Yetni safely. Even after the river crossing, Kaethe would have to walk in the dark for another hour. We felt so bad for her. The wind was blowing the slight rain into our faces. We were still hoping Kaethe might come home with us and spend the night but she remained determined.

We were relieved to find the Yetni wasn't too high yet and there were even dry rocks Kaethe could tread on. Still, it was raining in the mountains so the river could flood in an instant. Hans stepped onto a rock to give Kaethe a hand and in the short moment he was standing there the water rose and covered the rock—it was high time. With thick clouds obscuring the fading daylight, it was getting darker by the minute, and in a matter of moments, it would be completely dark. Kaethe made it across the river safely. We waved good-bye and watched her disappear into the darkness.

Oh dear, it will be pitch black in a minute. I hope we'll find our way back to the car.

We walked through the rough terrain as fast as we could. To our relief, the faintest bit of light remained as there must have been a full moon behind the clouds. We eventually made it back to the car. I prayed for Kaethe, who still would have at least another half hour to walk in the dark by the time we'd reach Wamena. I couldn't help but admire her. She had lived here and dealt with these logistical problems—which were only the tip of the iceberg—for twenty-three years after previously working in a different part of Indonesia for another eleven years. She had a resolute, determined mind and a strong faith and trust in the God who had called and sustained her here for all that time.

Besides Kaethe and Trijntje, there were many other single female missionaries who served God here for many years. They too had taken upon themselves loneliness, hardship, and life in impossible places. They walked all over these mountains and through these jungles of which I had only gotten the slightest taste. Many of these ladies sacrificed dreams of having a happy family life in their home countries and instead made a huge difference to innumerable families in Papua. As nurses and midwives, they saved countless lives or worked in literacy and Bible translation, and brought God's Word and education to the Papuan people who loved them dearly for it.

Others worked in community development projects bringing clean water into villages or building bridges. Next to their work, these single ladies were faithful, godly, and praying friends to many people who needed sound advice or a cup of tea and some sympathy. I was thinking of my friends Sue, Jessie, Alinda, Annemieke, Anke, Alie, Aagje, and others.

Although sometimes there were people who took advantage of the single missionaries or were opposed to empowering the women in their tribes, it was apparent the people loved these foreign ladies. There were many rewards for their dedication such as seeing the communities transformed for the better and living a fulfilled life of serving their loving God.

Then there were the single teachers who gave years of their lives to teaching missionary children so those families could continue serving here. Many, like Robin, became wonderful friends to us.

Some of these single missionaries would marry later, but others remained single for the rest of their lives.

> *"'Sing, O barren, You who have not borne!*
> *Break forth into singing, and cry aloud,*
> *You who have not labored with child!*
> *For more are the children of the desolate*
> *Than the children of the married woman,' says the LORD"*
> *Isaiah 54:1*

What's in a Name?

July 2002

Jan was phoning from the coast.

"Hi Elke, we're on the way to the hospital. Have you and Hans come up with a name yet? Please tell me quickly, because there isn't much mobile phone coverage at the hospital."

Jan had married and his wife, Yessy, was expecting a baby. A little while ago, Jan, who had become like a brother to us, had asked us to choose a name for their first child. We were truly honored. However, this concept was foreign to us, and we were insecure. Which names sounded good to Indonesians? Imagine if somebody wanted to call your child Xantippe? There was no time for philosophical questions—Yessy was in labor right now!

At least we knew the baby would be a boy. My all-time favorite boy's name was David. The study by Beth Moore on King David's life at the ladies' Bible study had helped me through a difficult time. Sometimes, I had even shared what we learned with Jan and Hans while we were all down and discouraged. Besides, Jan was a fan of David Beckham, the soccer player, so David might be a safe suggestion.

"That's fine," Jan said on the other end "but is that all?"

"What do you mean?" I started to panic.

"Don't you have a middle name as well? Most people have a middle name."

"Right, let me think for a moment and talk to Hans."

"How about Michael, like your brother?" Hans suggested. Brilliant. Jan was also a fan of Michael Schumacher, the Formula 1 driver, so another safe guess.

"David Michael, that's great, thank you."

I was relieved Jan seemed pleased.

"Elke, can you talk to Yessy for a moment?" Jan continued. "She could use some support."

I came close to panicking again. I hadn't experienced childbirth, so what sort of support could I possibly give Yessy—and in my limited Indonesian? Well, they say all pain is forgotten as soon as you hold the baby in your arms. So I hope that whatever unhelpful things I might have said are forgotten too by now.

God answered our prayers and David Michael, the cutest little boy, was soon delivered, and mother and child were well. I prayed the Lord would make David a man after His own heart—like King David was—who would have the courage to take on a giant for his God, delight in God's Word and His ways, and have a humble and contrite spirit.

High and Dry

August 2002

"Whoa!"

I was riding my motorbike around a street corner and barely slammed down my helmet visor before a dust cloud hit me.

New Guinea was a lush, green island with frequent, heavy rainfall most nights and often also during the day. Mud was almost always present. However, every year there were several weeks when it rained less than normal in the highlands and the ground dried up quickly. During these times, the *angin Kurima*, a strong southeast wind setting in most afternoons, wouldn't only rattle our metal roofs, but would also blow dust around all corners of Wamena, into our louver windows and our eyes. Usually, this dry spell lasted about four to six weeks, and our rainwater tanks held enough water to last through that period. This time, the dry spell didn't seem to end.

As I did every day, I climbed the wooden ladder to the top of the large concrete tanks, opened the round sheet metal lid, and checked how much water was left. Each day the gaping vacuousness was getting more depressing. Soon, there would be a gurgling noise from the water pump, air would get into the pipes, and no water would come out of the tap. I needed to get water from somewhere.

During the dry season, we enjoyed the advantage of a beautiful mountain view, unobstructed by clouds. Each time I climbed on the tanks, I took a deep breath and enjoyed the gorgeous view of the rugged, tall, gray mountain behind Wamena. We had lived here for two years now, but I couldn't get enough of this beautiful sight. With a sigh, I climbed down the tanks and thought about ways to make do without tank water. I had another idea.

We should make the most of the opportunity and clean the tanks while they're empty. But how?

Over time, a sludge from algae and decomposing leaves accumulates on the bottom and sides of water tanks. Friends recommended a Papuan man who had experience in cleaning water tanks. He agreed to do it and to teach our night guard for next time. I went to the hardware store and bought brushes for the men to scrape down the walls, rags to mop the dirt, and also large plastic jerry cans which I could fill with water at the hangar and take home. While our roof was too small to collect much water during the weekly light rains, the enormous hangar roof collected a lot.

"Look at us two ladies at the hardware store again!"

I turned around, and there was Luana. I hadn't thought about it that way, but yes, in our home countries our husbands would probably be the ones going to the hardware store. Since they were working such long hours, we wives were the ones buying paint and thinner, motor oil, garden hoses, wire, brake pads, nails and screws, and the like without thinking twice about it. I tied the jerry cans together and put them on the back of my motorbike. It looked like a mule with a large load on its back. Luana laughed and took a photo.

Maybe I'll show that one to my friends at the council office in Germany. I chuckled when I imagined their facial expression.

The water in the jerry cans was used up quickly for cooking, drinking, and washing dishes, so we showered at the hangar.

"I'm so glad we put the shower in when we built the hangar," Hans told me.

"I know! Who'd have thought we'd use it for our daily clean-up?"

Flushing the toilet and washing laundry still used a lot of water. We had adopted the rule: "If it's yellow let it mellow; if it's brown flush it down" a while ago, but it wasn't enough. We had to come up with another solution.

The old 500-liter plastic tank was no longer used for fueling the helicopters but had been cleaned and recommissioned for water transport. I learned that outside Wamena, at Pikhe, there was a spring with clean water where people were allowed to fill containers. The tank just fit into the Daihatsu when the back seats were taken out. We loaded it up along with a long hose, a water pump, and a generator. I was glad that Kam, a hangar guard, was sent along to assist me. Fresh, clear, cool water emerged from under a beautiful, lush, green tree at the Pikhe spring.

Blessed is the man who walks not in the counsel of the ungodly... He shall be like a tree planted by the rivers of water.

During a drought, this comparison found in the first few verses of Psalm 1, became especially powerful.

Several basins had been built around the spring to make the water easily accessible. Since all the Wamena residents had the same problem, a number of people congregated at the spring. Some were filling bottles and jerry cans, while others were washing their clothes around the basins. Kam and I connected the hoses, started the generator, and filled water into the pump to prime it. While the tank filled up painfully slow, I looked around and chatted with the ladies washing their laundry. The people around us were as desperate for water as we were. However, they used buckets and jerry cans which they transported in angkots or on bicycle rickshaws while I used a car, technical equipment, and a 500-liter tank. I always hated standing out and needing so many more resources to live than the local people, but such was life. I had come to terms with the fact I would always stick out like a sore thumb.

After about forty-five minutes, the tank was full. We emptied the hose, rolled it up, and loaded it into the car along with the generator and water pump and drove back to town.

At home, I pulled out the hose again, rolled out a long cable, and squeezed myself between the car roof and the top of the tank to put in an electric pump. Next, I put the hose into the concrete water tanks, poured water into the hose to get the air out, and prayed it would work. About an hour and several problems later, the tank in the car was empty, and water covered the bottom of the concrete tank. We had already shut one of the two tanks off, but five hundred liters just didn't look like much. I returned the car and all the equipment to the hangar, took my motorbike back home, and washed the laundry. Afterward, I checked the water tank.

This is ridiculous. I just spent hours to haul water, and now it's almost gone!

I climbed down the ladder.

"Agustina, where is the best place to wash laundry around here?"

It definitely could not be the brown Baliem River, so I thought it would be best to make the most of Agustina's local knowledge.

"That's probably on the side of the Kali Oue a bit down from our place," Agustina replied. "We can go together, and I'll show you, sister."

A few days later we were on our way with the motorbike. A net bag full of dirty clothes was hanging from my shoulder and Agustina, was riding in the back, holding a bucket containing a dipper and detergent. She gave me instructions, and we reached a tributary next to the rushing waters of the Oue River. We had to walk through the premises of a school and down an embankment to the water.

What did I get myself into now? I wondered when I staggered down the slope, climbed over slippery rocks, and then inched myself over a steel beam used as a bridge. We found a nice, quiet spot with lots of watercress around. It seemed so wrong to my environmentally-minded conscience to put soap into a clean river, but there wasn't much else I could do. We washed the clothes, got back to the motorbike without breaking any bones, and returned home.

This drought was wearing me out. I hadn't been bored before the water problems, and now there were days when I was busy for five hours just getting water to run the household. When I rode through the streets, I noticed people walking around with jerry cans looking for water as well. The range of vegetables in the markets declined, and prices soared. (Thankfully, more airplanes were flying rice to Wamena and the supply crisis had ended.)

Lord, please send rain!

I looked at the clouds forming on the southeast end of the valley as they did every afternoon. But as it did every afternoon, the wind came and dispersed them all. If only this drought wouldn't get as bad as in 1997/98 when the El Niño caused a famine all over the highlands! The nights with beautiful starry skies were bitterly cold. The days were hotter than usual, and the dust was getting everywhere. I worried about the local people whose gardens and wells were drying up. All this extra work and worry were taking a toll on me.

I was thankful when an unexpected trip to Germany came up. My brother and sister-in-law had asked me to become their second child's godmother and even paid my way to Germany.

"I finally made it to Grebenstein," I told Hans over the phone after six flights and two hours on the road.

"Good for you. I'm still stuck in Sentani."

While I made it half way around the globe, it took Hans—who had accompanied me to the coast—four days to get back to Wamena while waiting for a functioning plane and suitable weather.

"Oh, this is wonderful," I said to my mother when I turned on the tap. "Clean water straight from the tap and I can use as much as I want! And no rats in the house!"

I hadn't realized how much I needed this break.

During dinner, I kept looking over to my dad. I hadn't seen him in his role as a grandfather yet. And I hadn't heard Daniel, my cute little nephew, talk before! How much we had missed from our family life and yet, what a gift it was to see my family, including baby Victoria, the new arrival! Although I missed Hans, I thoroughly enjoyed this time with my family and friends.

When the time came closer to head back to Papua, I shopped. I bought as many lightweight gifts as I could for our friends and co-workers. I also stocked up on herbal and fruit teas, nuts, and other ingredients for special Christmas baking and jelly powder to make jam. How I wished I could take more than twenty kilograms on the plane! There were so many things I would have loved to have in Wamena.

On my return trip, I looked out of the taxi taking me to my hotel in Bali, Indonesia. We decided a twelve-hour layover was too long to wait at the airport after fifteen hours in the air on two flights. I had never been to Bali before and was surprised by all the religious activity. People in festive attire were holding ceremonies at shrines. The smell of burnt incense filled the air, and I heard the sound of traditional metallophones and xylophones. It turned out I arrived in the middle of a Hindu festival. The little offerings placed on sidewalks, taxi dashboards, motorbikes, shops, and hotels, however, were a year-round occurrence. They were flat square baskets (about four by four inches) made of coconut leaves filled with flowers, rice, candy, cigarettes, or whatever else the people had. Stone statues were draped in checkered cloth and decorated with flowers.

After I rested at the hotel, stretched my legs, and showered them with hot and cold water (to reduce swelling from the long flights), I went back to the airport to catch my two a.m. flight.

I guess I don't need to worry about falling asleep and missing the flight. The raucous, fast, metallic sounding Hindu music made me uncomfortable and kept me awake.

I was amazed how different the Indonesian cultures were. On my way to Germany, I had enjoyed a few hours exploring the area around Makassar/South Sulawesi with its cargo sailing ships, rice fields, and a cave and waterfall in a national park. While most people in Sulawesi were Muslims, like the majority of the over two hundred twenty million Indonesians, most Balinese were Hindu. All the different islands and areas had their own cultures, languages, and customs.

I was on the last of the six flights to Wamena. My heart beat faster when the airplane made its way through the North Gap and entered my beloved Baliem Valley. I sighed when I saw how low the river was and how dry the land looked. The rains hadn't resumed yet.

The water tanks were still empty, but my batteries were recharged. I could deal with the situation with renewed strength—hauling water when the tanks ran dry and firing up the woodstove when the gas bottle was empty.

One day the clouds gathered, the sky turned dark and poured down the precious rain we had spent over six months praying for. I jumped up, put on my rain clothes and rubber boots, ran outside, and watched and listened to the water pouring into the tanks. I didn't care what our guest thought. Somebody who hasn't experienced a drought will never know the incredible joy and relief this rain brought.

Along Came Lady

September 2002

Brian and Luana were two of the most generous people we had ever met. They seemed determined to teach us all a biblical lesson on receiving like a child. The gift they brought back for us from a trip brought us more joy and comfort over the years than we could have imagined. (Well, there were hiccups on the way to comfort, but a living room with garbage spread all over the floor is a small price to pay!)

Lady looked as if she had jumped out of a calendar. She was a two-month-old Golden Retriever puppy which didn't seem to have legs, just huge paws. She was the cutest thing I had ever seen, and I couldn't believe she was ours!

Lady, the "calendar girl"

After the failed attempt to bring the Golden Retriever from Jakarta, we gave up on trying to add fresh blood to the rather degenerated dog population of Wamena. But then a rare holiday trip to a rabies-free island had presented a perfect opportunity for Brian and Luana to buy a German Shepherd puppy as a guard dog for themselves. Moving animals within Indonesia involved not quite as much paperwork as getting a visa for a foreigner, but it came close. It didn't take much more effort to take two sets of paperwork to the veterinary department than one. Remembering how crushed we were after Freckles was killed, Brian and Luana brought back Lady for us along with their German Shepherd puppy.

Lady was a typical Golden Retriever. She was sweet and friendly which helped her to become friends with Aldo instantly. People generally suspect Golden Retrievers would lick a thief's hands before helping him to carry out the valuables. Lady, however, learned to be a watchdog from Aldo. If Aldo barked at the gate, Lady would too. We kept Lady inside the house at night, even when she grew up. Her large dog's voice would echo through the house, and nobody ever dared to break in.

Lady loved people and swimming — but most of all, she loved food.

"Hi, Elke, when you come over tonight, bring Lady along to play with our dogs," Luana suggested. We enjoyed another fantastic meal and good fellowship at Brian and Luana's house and forgot all about the dogs playing outside.

"Uh-oh!" was all we could say when Lady came in after a while. She looked as happy as ever, but her tummy resembled a furry soccer ball.

"She must have wiped out our dogs' food bowl," Luana said while we closed our gaping mouths and stopped blinking. "We usually fill it up once a day for the three of them."

Lady showed no signs of feeling stuffed but checked out the cat's food bowl too. It was embarrassing. To our relief, Lady didn't suffer any negative effects from her gluttony.

People stopped in at our house more often than usual. Not to visit us, mind you, but to visit our dog. This had the advantage that finding a dog-sitter was never a problem.

The Flying Housewife

Early November 2002

Once more I had a toothache and needed help from my new best friend, Bob. The helicopter was flying to Sentani to do shuttle flights to a mission station from there. Since it was leaving from Wamena without cargo, I got a ride. What a nice change after all the flights in more or less trustworthy cargo airplanes. This time Tom was the pilot, and we had another passenger: Ashley, one of the missionary children from Moi.

I got into the helicopter's co-pilot seat with a big grin which got even bigger when I noticed the dual controls. We took off, crossed over the runway, and headed straight for the hills.

"Do you want to climb over this mountain?" I had hoped Tom would offer but had not expected it so soon and much less before even leaving the valley. My feelings fluctuated between anticipation and apprehension as I put my hands and feet on the controls. So far, I had only steered a helicopter straight and level for a few minutes on our way to the Moi. Because of the cloudy weather, it was over before I got used to it.

My heart pounded. We had already gained good forward speed, so it was not too hard to keep the helicopter from making any drastic moves (which was good for Ashley who probably wasn't in the mood for a sick bag). The helicopter was climbing, but it still didn't look as if we'd be able to clear the ridge. Tom seemed relaxed, so

I thought we must be doing all right. Soon we cleared the ridges without a problem.

Because of the heavy air traffic between Wamena and the coast, we had to reach and maintain an approved altitude to prevent a mid-air collision. This was easier said than done! We were constantly on the lookout for airplanes and listened to the air traffic advisories of the other aircraft on the radio.

A few minutes ago, I had worried about clearing the mountain tops, but now we had to dive back down to cruising altitude on the other side of the range. I pushed the stick forward to descend which resulted in more forward speed.

"Watch your airspeed there. We can't exceed the red line," Tom reminded me.

"Oh boy!"

Everything above one hundred thirty knots (240 km/h) was marked red on the airspeed indicator. I pulled the nose up slightly with the cyclic control stick. The indicator needle slid backward slowing down at about the same rate as my heartbeat. We were high in the cold mountain air but nonetheless, I was perspiring out of every pore of my skin while having so much fun.

Now I needed to hold the heading to Sentani for about one hundred nautical miles which meant I needed to keep an eye on the compass and the horizon. Another challenge was to keep the helicopter at the right attitude (this is not to imply it was opinionated or something of the sort). For this, I needed to monitor a gauge on the other side of the cockpit and to make sure the little ball stayed between the two lines showing the whirly bird was still aligned with our direction and not flying slightly sideways. When the ball went outside the two lines, I carefully used the foot pedals to control the tail rotor to fly the helicopter straight again.

I couldn't believe how hard it was to stay at the correct altitude. Going down, we gained speed each time while going up we slowed down. We had to avoid over-speeding because this could cause permanent structural failure. My eyes constantly went from the horizon to the compass, to the little ball, to the airspeed indicator, and the altimeter. I was busy.

"Is Ashley getting sick yet?" I asked Tom who looked over his shoulder to the back.

"She's still eating chips," Tom reported. That was a good sign. I felt bad for giving everybody a less than smooth ride. It felt like we were sitting in a ball hanging from a string swaying from side to side. Once again, I admired the pilots who not only could do all I was struggling with but even do it in bad weather and while maintaining radio communication. They also had to find their way through the clouds and valleys, keep an eye on the fuel gauge, and look out for possible spots for emergency landings should the one and only engine ever go out.

We made it out of the mountain pass. Dense jungle and swamps covered the lowland area as far as the eye could see. Underneath us, the mighty Memberamo River wound its long way to the coast. After flying for about an hour, we got closer to the Sentani airstrip. Tom pointed out where I needed to go, so we could prepare for landing and align with the runway.

"This is getting way too exciting for me," I told Tom. "Your controls!"

Wow, what an experience! I was pleased with my success in not making Ashley sick. This, however, was probably more to her credit than mine. Despite her young age, she was a frequent helicopter flyer and must have been through many turbulences before.

Rats!

Flame out!

It was better for this to happen on the gas stove in the kitchen than on the gas turbine engine in the helicopter but still, I was in the middle of cooking, and a meal was at stake. I called the hangar to ask for another propane gas bottle.

"We only have small ones left, but someone will drop one off shortly."

"Thanks, Jan, that will save our dinner."

It would have been next to impossible to get the woodstove heated sufficiently in time to save the meal.

It usually took several weeks for the empty propane gas tanks to be flown to the coast, refilled, and flown back to Wamena, but the small one would be enough to bridge the time. When it was delivered, we placed the small bottle into a compartment inside the oven instead of outside where we kept the large ones.

A few days later, while putting dishes away, I cringed. A long thin tail was sticking out behind a stack of crockery.

How did you get in here?

Then I realized we hadn't plugged the hole in the wall after pulling out the hose for the large gas bottle and now rats were using it to get into the house.

Oh no! How do we get rid of them again? And how many have come in anyway?

It was an unsettling thought that these critters were now walking all over our plates, pots, pans, and going through our pantry. Rats could spread diseases like typhoid fever, so we needed to do something about them quickly. We plugged up the hole, and I thought of ways to combat our uninvited guests. What was the first line of defense against rats? Cats! When I next saw the rat in my pantry cupboard, it was time to deploy M.G., Briana's black tomcat. I phoned Luana, and a few minutes later she delivered the feline. We opened the cupboard, put M.G. inside, closed the door, and listened. Nothing. We tapped on the wood to set things into motion. Still nothing. We cautiously opened the door to take a peak. A pair of big round eyes stared back at us. M. G. was scared stiff—just like the hiding rat, smelling a cat. My plan wasn't working. M. G. jumped out of the pantry and bolted behind the woodstove (maybe we should have given him a proper briefing beforehand).

"Get something to hit the rat with," Luana instructed me and pulled things out of the pantry. I raised an eyebrow and grabbed a broom. Nervously, I watched as foil, wrap, corn flakes, flour, sugar, noodle packages, etc. came off the shelves.

Zing!

We both screamed as we watched the rat fly from a top shelf and land on the floor. While the rodent was stunned from the impact, I pounded it with the broom—and hated myself for it. Oh, the poor little thing. It was still small but already had a long tail.

One down. How many to go? Where was the rest of the family?

As a child, I kept mice in a cage and loved to watch the cute little animals, but I put my sentiments aside. This was different because these rats were putting our health at risk and destroying our food. Why couldn't they open just one package and finish it? It seemed as though they wanted to try all the different flavors and textures. They chewed holes in the packages of oatmeal, milk powder, cocoa powder, and whatever else they would find that we didn't keep in tins or glass jars. They even chewed through my sturdy Tupperware containers.

On one of the following days, while I worked on the computer in the study, there was a rustling noise in the wastebasket. Next, I saw something small and brown speed from the desk to the guest bed.

What now? Cat failed—need a new strategy.

I closed the door to confine the rat in the study. I had to be quick before it got into the bag of rice we kept in the wardrobe in the study (to keep it safe from the rats in the storage shed—what irony). I firmly closed the built-in wardrobe. The next time I looked, I saw teeth marks inside the wardrobe door and concluded the rat had tried to gnaw its way out. With this abundant food supply in reach, that could mean only one thing: the rodent was thirsty. I got a bucket of water, put food scraps on its rim, and used an umbrella as a gangway. Then I left the room and shut the door. Less than an hour later, I peeked into the study.

"Gotcha!"

This was definitely "Dad" if not "Grandpa" swimming laps in the bucket. My delight turned into worry and pity. I phoned Hans.

"Can you please come quickly? I have a large rat swimming in a bucket. I can't just let it struggle and drown. Can you shoot it to put it out of its misery?"

Hans came home to execute the task—and the rat. The air pellet broke the bucket in the process. We would have to come up with another strategy next time.

Strange Encounters

It was getting late, and Hans hadn't come home for dinner yet. The phone rang.

"Mausi, I need to finish something before coming home."

"What's going on? Something wrong with the heli?"

"No, the strangest thing just happened. I was turning off the hallway lights and when I walked past that warrior statue I had something like a panic attack."

Short term mission travelers had received the one-meter-tall carved and painted wooden warrior statue as a gift during their visit to a lowland tribe, unaware of any cultural or spiritual complications. When they left Wamena, they hadn't fit the statue into their luggage. While we hadn't been keen on having it, it somehow ended up in the hallway. None of us felt good about the statue, but in our busyness, we had ignored it.

"Oh, that thing! That always gives me the creeps too."

"Yeah, I called Jan and told him about it, and all he said was: 'We've been wondering what you westerners are thinking, keeping such a thing at the hangar.'"

"Really? And they never said anything? What are you going to do now?"

"Jan is coming over, and we'll burn it."

A while later, I rode the motorbike to the hangar. The flames from the pyre were still as tall as a man. Hans and Jan collected wood, cardboard, hay, and empty cement bags—anything lying around the hangar that would fuel the fire. The men wanted to ensure the fire thoroughly consumed the softwood carving. They even poured kerosene over it.

"Ugh, that will still take a while, I think I better go back home," I said and left.

Hans and Jan waited for the flames to die down. Eventually, Hans came home.

"What took you so long?" I asked.

"You won't believe it! When the fire finally burned out, we checked on the statue."

"And?"

"We shined our flashlights into the ashes, and there he was. The statue didn't have a scratch; we could have put it in the living room!"

"No way!" The hair was standing on the back of my neck.

"Yeah, we were a bit perplexed too. Then we prayed the thing would burn in the name of Jesus and when we lit it again it burned right away."

"Wow! That makes you wonder about all the creepy stuff in the souvenir shops."

"I asked Jan what else we should steer clear of, and he said that in Sentani people sometimes use rabbit fur for magic. Apparently, it's different in each area."

Later on, I read in a travel guide ('IRIAN JAYA Indonesian New Guinea' by Kal Muller, Periplus Editions) that in many areas of Papua, especially in the Asmat region, carvings were inextricably connected with the spirit world, and many were being produced in a ritual context. I had heard before that many decorative souvenirs, some with pretty feathers, were actually fetishes—magical objects. This all made us aware that magic and fetishes weren't just games and decoration. There was real power to these things. While we, as followers of Jesus Christ, were protected from those powers, they still seemed to have discomforting effects on us if we willingly kept them in our possession. We decided not to keep any artifacts and not to visit temples for the sake of tourism. Our God should not become jealous because of our actions, and we would not give Satan room to attack and scare us through entering known risks.

I remembered a night in the first house we stayed at. We had come home in the dark, and I had gone straight inside. Hans had taken a while to close the garden gate.

"I just saw the strangest thing," Hans reported when he eventually came in. "There was a guy in a pulled up hood standing in the yard, so I watched him. When the guy walked toward the gate to leave, he stopped and flashed his torch at the closed gate and then—as if he couldn't be bothered figuring out how to open it—he walked right through the closed gate."

We also heard reports in town of thieves throwing magical objects over people's roofs before breaking into a house. The inhabitants were then rendered motionless in their beds, even when they were awake, while the thieves took what they wanted.

Spiritual powers were very real to the vast majority of Indonesians, including Papuans. This was apparent in most aspects of their lives. While according to surveys, people in Europe mostly feared for their retirement fund and health, in Indonesia the fear of vampires and ghosts prevailed. Spirituality, rituals, and magic were commonplace. Even to fix a dent in the car there was the choice between the conventional panel beater and the "Ketok Magic." The latter would require the car to stay for the night and remove the dent through magic. Someone declaring to be an atheist was considered out of touch, as it was obvious there were higher powers at work in this world. Atheists had trouble filling in their immigration forms since ticking a box for the religious affiliation was a requirement.

Some westerners vehemently denied the presence of spiritual beings and magical powers and claimed that during stays in the tribes they never came across or heard anything about it from the local people. We asked Papuan friends about this.

"Well, if the foreigners dismiss the existence of spirits and say they only exist in our imagination, of course, we stop talking about such things," they replied.

Spirituality was a real experience for them, whether this was from animism or Christianity. Some villagers would get aggressive and feel threatened when tourists wanted to go to spiritual places, sometimes ignorantly.

Since Jesus Christ has overcome the evil forces, we should not be intimated by them, but we should also not discount their existence or experiment with them. As unpleasant as encounters with such magic powers may have been, people with strong links to magic and witchcraft seemed to be much more intimidated by our presence and actively avoided us. There is definitely more power in the name of Jesus, and He gives us peace in our hearts. As said before, we do not play with darkness.

At the Neighbors

December 6, 2002

I breathed in the clear air and enjoyed the sound of the Oue River rushing past and the feel of the pebbles under my feet. Hans and I had taken the dogs for a walk, and it was amusing to see how Aldo tried to keep his feet dry at all cost while Lady, who had multiplied in size by now, couldn't get enough of playing in the water.

"Hello, good afternoon! Stop in at our house!" our Indonesian neighbors called to us when we returned from the river. This was interesting. Hans was always friendly and greeted them on the way to work but had never gotten much response. Hans had noticed the Indonesian neighbors, who were Muslims, didn't give him many friendly looks—especially after the USA and allied forces started airstrikes in Afghanistan. Most people here seemed to put all westerners into the same category no matter where they came from. I sometimes talked to the neighbors and bought things at their kiosk, but we had never gone beyond small talk. I almost dreaded going there because small talk in Indonesia would go to some areas that in Germany were reserved for the closest of friends. ("Are you pregnant yet? No? There is medicine, you know.")

We were especially surprised by this invitation since we had the dogs with us which were considered unclean animals in their religion.

"*Terima kasih*! (Thank you) We'll get changed and come right over."

We washed our hands—only once, not seven times as the Koran would have demanded after touching dogs—put on nice clean, dry clothes, and walked across the street.

The occasion for the invitation was the end of Ramadan, the Muslim month of fasting. This festival was called *Idul Fitri* in Indonesia or *Lebaran*. As with Christmas in many parts of the world or for Thanksgiving in the USA, people traveled all over the country to spend this special time with their families. During breakfast, we had already observed people walking home from the mosque in festive apparel, the men wearing caps and sending up puffs of smoke while enjoying their first day-time cigarettes in a month.

"*Silakan masuk!*" (Please come in!) Our neighbors, Pak Komaruddin and Ibu Jumiati, welcomed us into the living room of their wooden house where a few other people were already sitting and eating sweet treats. We were ushered through to the simple kitchen with a bare concrete floor, a kerosene stove, a few chairs, and sitting mats on the floor. A wooden table was loaded with food. Plates were neatly stacked with folded paper napkins and cutlery between them. They obviously expected hordes of people to come to eat.

"Silakan makan," (please eat) Ibu Jumiati invited us, handing us plates and cutlery. We started out with gray unappetizing-looking soup which turned out to taste delicious. We were given long banana leaf packages filled with sticky rice which had been cooked with coconut milk for a full day and was now ready to be eaten as sticks or cut up and put into the soup. Next, we tried all the different beef and chicken dishes prepared after recipes from South Sulawesi where the family originated.

"*Tambah!*" (have more) Ibu Jumiati prompted us when she returned to the kitchen and noticed we were slowing down with eating. While she was petite and pretty in appearance, she was also energetic and assertive.

"Thank you, the food is delicious!"

We loaded our plates again and continued eating. I savored every one of these delicious foreign-tasting spicy dishes.

After enjoying the main meal in the kitchen by ourselves, we were invited to sit in the comfortable living room chairs. We were given sodas and offered an array of tasty homemade cookies which left a slight aftertaste of cooking kerosene. Ibu Jumiati must have baked countless batches in her little oven over the last few weeks to end up with such large quantities. We still didn't know Indonesian brilliantly but had a nice, relaxed conversation with our gracious hosts. Thankfully, this time we weren't instructed in detail what might help us to have children (as would happen when I was by myself). My limited Indonesian never failed to get me into trouble when we got onto that subject.

"Well, Hans is so stressed and comes home so late at night," I launched into an explanation why we weren't so keen on having children yet while the base was understaffed and we were overworked. We had enough sleepless nights as it was and a crying baby would have probably been more than we could have handled. At the time, not having children wasn't a problem for us. Now what our neighbor perceived and vocally shared with everybody in the greater round sounded slightly different.

"Hans is always so tired when he comes home that he falls asleep immediately."

"Actually ..." I started out, but my Indonesian soon left me, so I had to let it go.

The thought someone would choose not to have children or wait for a convenient time in their lives as is often the case in western cultures these days was inconceivable to our neighbors. In their culture, the most important thing in a marriage was to have children, especially sons. Failing to produce offspring brought much grief and heartache to countless families in Indonesia, often ending in divorce. Children were the future and hope of every person. They would give their parents financial security and care for them in old age. Having just one or two children was not a good option in a country where many children and young people died of sicknesses or accidents. People would get anxious if a woman didn't fall pregnant within the first few months of the marriage. It was normal to have several generations living in the same house and putting elderly parents into aged care would have been considered cruel and was out of the question.

The couple had been blessed with a son so far which they were proud of and thankful for. After a nice time of eating, drinking, and fellowship, we excused ourselves and were sent home with extra food and sweets and the invitation to come back anytime. On that day, another long-term friendship was formed, and besides other occasions, we would visit each other for Muslim holidays and Christmas meals in the years to come.

Worn and Broke

Around the time of 1985, most mission organizations had decided to discontinue paying their overseas staff. Instead, the expectation was everyone working abroad would be supported by personal donors who would hopefully also commit to praying. Helimission also used this approach. This meant we didn't have a regular income and never knew in advance, how much money we'd receive each month. At times, we were running low, and other times we would get a large one-time gift, keeping the momentum going. As a result, we adjusted our spending to the income and learned to pray for our daily bread.

It was the end of the fasting month of Ramadan which resulted in the banks—in fact almost the whole country—shutting down for the best of two weeks. By now, Christmas was getting closer, and we needed to pay our house helper's salary too. Donations had been slow lately, and the (not yet online) overseas money transfer was even slower due to the festivities. My heart was pounding when I approached the ATM. I took a deep breath, put in the card, punched in the PIN, closed my eyes, and prayed: "Lord, please let the money have come through."

I opened my eyes and looked at the display: Rupiah 17,000 (approximately US $1.50). My heart sank.

I went to a little shop to get a few things. I picked up a small package of pasta but put it back a minute later. *I can't afford to buy this!*

I knew that for many of the people walking the streets of Wamena this was an everyday reality, but I had never been in this position before. It turned out to be a Christmas without gifts and instead we ended up borrowing money. This was especially hard for Hans to swallow and he was disappointed not to be in a position to provide better.

A fun Christmas party with the whole Helimission team, including spouses and children, cheered us up. We had become a sizable cross-cultural team. It was great to meet our team's family members. We also wanted everybody to know that no matter how insignificant their work may look in the great scheme of things, it mattered!

An unlikely donor made it possible for Hans and me to have our single friends over for a Christmas Eve dinner, despite our lack of finances. The wife of the friendly butcher I had met on my first day in Wamena, gave us a large pot of soup and rice sticks in banana leaves to go with it. Who would have thought a Muslim family would make such a lovely contribution to our Christmas celebration?

We also enjoyed a nice Christmas Day with our team colleagues and later joined our single friends on a beautiful trip to Lake Habbema. We had a special festive season after all. There was nothing like the natural beauty of Papua and the fresh, cool, clean mountain air to make me forget my troubles for a little while.

However, the long hours of hard work under several pressures, the tight financial situation, and the grief about the upheaval in the mission community earlier on took a toll.

"Either we are going on a really long holiday or we need to go on home assignment soon," Hans told me one day. He was tired and exhausted. By now he only weighed fifty-nine kilos and had dark rings under his eyes. Hans phoned headquarters to discuss the options. Thankfully, it was decided we should go on home assignment soon. The knowledge that change was coming gave us a new boost which kept us going for the remaining two months.

Closing a Chapter

End of February 2003

I rode the motorbike through the streets of Wamena and looked up to the mountains. The smoke of countless fires left a light haze over the Baliem Valley. Afternoon sun rays broke through holes in the clouds, creating streaks in the misty air and making spots in the foothills glow in vibrant green shades below the gray mountain tops. I caught a whiff of smoke and corn. People on the street corner were roasting corn cobs to sell. Bicycle taxis tried to find the last customers before it got dark.

I felt torn. I was in the middle of packing up and preparing for our first furlough. While I couldn't wait to see my friends and family again, it was hard to leave this beautiful place, our work, our friends, and our dogs behind. However, I desperately hoped Hans would get the rest he needed during our time in Europe. It was also time to report to our faithful prayer supporters what the Lord had done, using us and their prayers.

"Hello Mister, I loff you!" a boy shouted at me from across the street.

I won't miss that!

What an incredible first term this had been. It was as if we had landed in a situation we were totally unprepared for—apart from Hans' professional training—but the Lord and our teammates had not only helped us to survive but to thrive. I had seen God at work in seemingly impossible circumstances—like providing a pilot/

mechanic who could do a root canal on my aching tooth and letting a hangar building go up despite riots, evacuation, earthquakes, and supply shortages. My faith and trust in Him had grown by leaps and bounds. Hans' words when he had preached at the missionary fellowship were still echoing in my mind: "It is a privilege to work here in Papua and to use the best hours of the day to serve God."

This was so true. For some people, it always seemed to be a sacrifice to live in uncomfortable circumstances in Papua, far away from their friends and loved ones, while for others it was a privilege, a joy, and a gain. I had long found out being happy here was rather a matter of attitude than of circumstances, training, or suitability.

I had fallen in love with the Papuan highlands and could only bear the thought of leaving because we were planning to come back. I felt so blessed we had played a part in all that had been accomplished here over the last three years. The hangar had been built and become operational. A mission station had started from scratch in the middle of the jungle, using our helicopters. We had assisted in search and rescue operations and medevac flights and shown the *JESUS* film. During all this, we had been sick and recovered many times. We had been hard-pressed but not crushed, stretched to our limits, but not torn. We had met some of the finest people who walked this earth and made friendships for life. We had seen God at work in every situation and realized He would get us through anything, as long as we did our part—trusting and obeying Him.

I had put my foot into my mouth countless times and unintentionally offended people left and right, but still, I found wonderful and loyal friends who loved me anyway. No, it hadn't been pleasant to always attract attention and get stared at, sift weevils out of the flour, haul water, fight cockroaches and rats, and worry about getting a visa renewed, but you never get light without shadow or mountains without valleys.

My first term on the mission field had been everything I had hoped for and so much more.

Would I have come here if I had known everything that would happen? No way!

Would I have wanted to miss it? Not for anything in the world!

The Race Against Time

I was walking home from the missionary fellowship Sunday afternoon. The words of Stephen, our friend working in the Moi tribe, were still going through my mind as I walked between the bicycle taxis, people, and motorbikes. He had reported about his work in the Moi tribe and then shared the testimony of Piyagui (a tribesman I met during my stay there) in his name.

"I am Piyagui. I didn't really know my father well because he fell out of favor with other men in the tribe. They lured him into a trap and killed him. I didn't like him very much anyway, so I didn't mind. My sister got abused. Fair enough, I've also abused girls. My first wife kept running away from me, so I beat her. She still kept running away, so I killed her with arrows. She never liked me anyway."

We had all been hanging onto Stephen's words waiting for what he would tell next. But he stopped.

"That's Piyagui's testimony," Stephen said. "That's all there is. Since we started a few years ago, the people wonder what we actually want and why we've come to them. So far we've been putting them off, telling them that soon we'd bring them the message of the Creator.

In a hamlet a few ridges over, the chief has said his heart would burst if he couldn't hear that message soon. We still don't know the language well enough yet, so we continue to live in the tribe, learn the language and culture and hopefully in a few years, we'll be able to share the Gospel with Piyagui and the other people for the first time in their history."

I was deep in thought when I turned right into another street continuing my way home. My heart ached for the Moi people I had met like Grandma, Weiwa, and her son.

How much longer would it take until our courageous, hardworking friends would be able to tell them the gospel and bring them hope for today and eternity? How many more people would be killed through revenge killings and warfare? How many more would bleed to death due to getting slashed after suffering a centipede bite? How many more would be raped and abused?

Would Grandma even be alive by then? Would Weiwa's kids be amongst the four children out of five who didn't live to the age of five?

How many more tribes were out there who hadn't yet been discovered? Beautiful people, whom God loved so dearly but whose names had never been heard outside their tribe?

As I entered the house, I knew our work had made a difference, but so much more needed to be done. We were in this for the long run. And we were in for a race—a race against time.

To be continued ...

"And Jesus came and spoke to them, saying, 'All authority has been given to Me in heaven and on earth. Go therefore and make disciples of all the nations, baptizing them in the name of the Father and of the Son and of the Holy Spirit, teaching them to observe all things that I have commanded you; and lo, I am with you always, even to the end of the age.' Amen."
Matthew 28:18-20

"And this gospel of the kingdom will be preached in all the world as a witness to all the nations, and then the end will come."
Matthew 24:14

To God be the glory!

Glossary

Angkot:	abbreviation of Angkutan Kota—Public transport vehicle in Indonesia, usually a minivan traveling a specific route, picking up and dropping off passengers as requested along the way.
Bakar Batu:	(Indonesian: roasted/burnt rock) a traditional feast cooked in a pit with rocks (previously heated in a fire), leaves, vegetables, and meat.
Becak:	Bycicle taxi
Cabe:	Indonesian for chili; pepper
Cicak:	(pronounce: chee-chuck) Indonesian for lizard or gecko
El Niño:	(detailed articles about this can be found online—see: El Niño Southern Oscillation) In short: El Niño is a weather phenomenon. While ocean currents warm the sea surface along the South American coast annually, once in several years the ocean surface becomes warmer than average. This causes weather changes in other parts of the world, often leading to droughts in Indonesia and Australia and increased rainfall over the tropical Pacific Ocean.
Expat:	abbreviation of expatriate—a person living abroad
Gudang:	Indonesian for storage room, shed, or warehouse
Honai:	Papuan windowless hut made of wooden boards and a roof of grass, bark or leaves. There are different shapes and sizes.

Irian Jaya: Irian Jaya was renamed Papua in January 2000. It was previously known as Dutch or Netherlands New Guinea and West Irian. It is often politically incorrectly referred to as "West Papua" today. From 2000 – 2003, Papua covered the entire western half of the island of New Guinea, which has been a province of the Republic of Indonesia since 1969. In 2003, the area was further broken up into two provinces: Papua and West Papua.
Ibu: Indonesian for mother—also Mrs.
Jalan: Indonesian for street
***JESUS* Film:** The film *JESUS* (often referred to as the *JESUS* film) is a dramatized version of the life of Jesus Christ. It is based on the gospel of Luke and was produced in 1979.
Koteka: (also penis gourd or horim)—a penis sheath made of a dried-out gourd traditionally worn by Papuan men and boys of several tribes, mainly in the highlands of New Guinea
Mausi: (pronounce: mouzy, mowsy) German term of endearment
Noken: extremely versatile bags of different styles, shapes and colors, traditionally handmade by Papuan women from plant fibers. Now, they're also produced with artificial and more colorful fibers. The baggier net bag styles are used to carry firewood, plants, babies, food, piglets, and other things that elsewhere would be hauled around in tote bags, prams, backpacks, purses, baskets, or pickup-trucks. In some tribes, nokens are part of the women's clothing and cover their backs. More recently, they're also used to cover the women's chests in parades and festivals in towns.
Pak: short for Bapak—Indonesian for father or Mr.
Polyclinic: a clinic providing examinations and treatments to outpatients
Pondok: Indonesian for hut, cabin, or shack, but in this case describing a Papuan-style gazebo with a traditional thatched roof

Glossary

Rupiah: abbreviated: Rp. = Currency of the Republic of Indonesia
SAR: Search and Rescue

Transmigrant: In 1969 the Suharto government started a transmigration project to move families from overpopulated Java to less populated and developed Indonesian islands. People who took part in the project and settled in areas like Papua or the Malukus are referred to as transmigrants or "pendatangs".

Helimission Helicopters in Wamena in the timeframe of this book:
PK-HME – Bell 206L4 LongRanger (seven seats)
PK-HMF – Agusta-Bell 206B3 JetRanger (five seats)

In aviation, the International Radiotelephony Spelling Alphabet, also referred to as ICAO phonetic alphabet or NATO alphabet is used, e. g. for the call sings which indicate in which country an aircraft is registered (PK for Indonesia) and the individual designation following. The helicopters used by Helimission in Papua were pronounced

Papa Kilo - Hotel Mike Echo and
Papa Kilo - Hotel Mike Foxtrot.
In short: Mike Echo and Mike Fox.

Recommendations for Further Reading:

More than an Adventure by Hedi Tanner

Lords of the Earth by Don Richardson

Torches of Joy by John Dekker/Lois Neely

To learn more about Helimission go to https://www.helimission.org/en/

CPSIA information can be obtained
at www.ICGtesting.com
Printed in the USA
FFOW02n1019100518
46554370-48571FF